Laura Corn's

101 Nights of Grrreat Romance

How to
Make Love
with Your
Clothes On.

Published By:
Park Avenue Publishers, Inc.

Printed in United States of America

ISBN 1-56865-495-2

DISCLAIMER
PLEASE READ BEFORE PROCEEDING

This book is sold with the understanding that is intended solely for the use of informed, consenting, and hopefully monogamous adults who want to rejuvenate, enliven and sustain a romantic relationship. The author is not a medical doctor or therapist. She has, however, studied relationships for the past eight years and is the author of two best-selling books in this genre.

The reader is reminded and cautioned that following the suggestions and scenarios contained herein is strictly voluntary and is at the readers sole risk and discretion. The seductions and products mentioned in the book are generally safe and satisfying for most adults. Every individual is unique and you should not employ any product or recipe which is not suitable to your limitations or circumstances.

Neither the author, publisher or distributor endorses any specific product or assumes any product liability for any product mentioned in this book. The decision to act and the responsibility from any consequences which may result from the use of any product or following any suggestions or scenarios herein belong to the reader.

The author and Park Avenue Publishers, Inc. shall have neither liability nor responsibility to any person or entity with regard to any losses or damage caused or alleged to be caused, either directly or indirectly, by the information contained in this book.

If you do not wish to be bound by the above understanding, you may return the book intact to Park Avenue Publisher, Inc., 903 South Hohokam Drive, Tempe, AZ 85281 for a full refund of the purchase price of the book.

Cover Photography by Michele Clement
Book Design by Vigon/Ellis

Acknowledgements

I am deeply indebted to a host of wonderful friends, mentors, associates and "cheerleaders" who made this book possible. To each of you I extend my heartfelt gratitude for your encouragement, support and contributions.

Most of all I am indebted to all the radio personalities across this grrreat nation, *some of the most dedicated and talented people in show business*. I am so thankful that you have welcomed me to your unique fraternity and have so generously provided the venue and audience which made it possible to accumulate the background necessary for my work.

Especially to Bill Wright, my best friend and business partner. I'm so lucky to have you in my life. *I don't know what I would do without you.* Your hard work, dedication and support continue to amaze me. God has blessed me with your love.

To Marty Bishop; World Class writer and DJ extraordinaire. Your unparalleled and indispensable wit and wisdom has kept this project sizzling. Marty's remarkable talent and wonderful imagination permeates this book.

To my friend and associate, Meg Gallagher. Megala, you are the best! Your talent and zest for life makes everything so easy and possible. I treasure our friendship.

To Gregory Godek, Romantic Genius, author of six best selling books, including the classic "1001 Ways To Be Romantic" a *must* for anyone with a smidgen of romance in their soul. For your inspiration to me and the world you should be awarded the Nobel Prize for Romance.

To the ebullient Kimberly Bennet. You have no idea how much your sincere *"How's the book coming?"* and eager *"Let's go over titles"* helped in putting this book together.

To Barry Young author of the very cool * Free Stuff for Science Buffs*. Your advice and editorial skills were immeasurably helpful.

To Larry Paregis, thank you for always being there with an attentive and receptive ear and for your creative input.

To everyone at the incredible Vigon/Ellis Design Studio; Larry, Brian, Sam, Mark, David and Heather. You are all so grrreat to work with and every page is a work of art! Many, many thanks!

To Paul Joannides, author of the *you-should-go-out-and-buy-it-right-now-book* * "The Guide To Getting It On", Multiple thanks for your invaluable contribution.

To Hutch, thank you so much for your encouragement, patience and support. You are so wonderful!

And To Jeff, my sexy romantic sweetie. Thank you for all the love and monster support you've given me. The closeness and surprises we share keeps my heart dancing and my creative juices flowing. *Without you, this book would never have been written.*

To all the people who have written and called with your comments and testimony to the influence of my books, you have been the biggest reward of all.

And last, but not least, I am grateful to Morning Mouth, Bit Board, Radio Star, Don Anthony and Allison, Bob Earle, Ellen Kreidman, John Gray, Ellen and Michael Albertson, Tracy and Donald Sonek, Tomina Edmark, Derek Povah, Gil Rozzo, Eric Seidell, and Kathleen Conway.

Finally, a personal tribute to the aforementioned radio personalities. Gals and guys, I love you sooo much and wish I could personally repeat my thanks to each of you for your invaluable contribution. Your numbers are legion and, again I apologize for inadvertent omissions and misspellings. If I have goofed, please let me know so I can get it right next time. Thank you so much.

Jeff 'n Jer and Tommy, Kidd Kraddick, Brother Wease, Cindy & Charlie, Mancow, Johnathon Brandmeier, Buz, Carol Harmon, Tim & Mark & Mike, Mark & Brian & Frank Murphy, Don & Mike & Rob, Jim & Scott & Bob & Chris & Pepper, Connie Powell, Scott & Todd & Naomi, Lamont & Tonelli, Bob & Tom & Dean, Ron & Ron & Denise, Steve & D.C. & Courtney, Eddie Fingers, Bob Berri & Jimmy the Weasel, Jeff, Mark, & Cat, Charlie & Ty, Shelly, Dana, Kim Petersen & Mike Rose, Troy & Rocky & Danger Boy, Kent & Allen & Leonard & Renee, Jennifer, Mike & Tyler, Chris & Beth & Kevin, Bobby & Footy, Peter Tilden & Tracy, Matt & Dave & Kathy & Merlin, Lewis & Floorwax, Rob Johnson, Lex & Teri, Dave Ryan & Pat Ebert, Kent & Allen, Paul Barsky, Grego & Moe, Donna, Brother Jake, Jeff Chambers, Jeff & Flash, Manson & Sheehan, Kevin Baker, Sheri & Bob, Tommy & Rumble, Nicki Reed, Future Bob, Opie and Anthony, G.G.Young, Max & Tanna, Moffit, Scott & Erica, Jason, Lanigan, Webster & Malone, Bob Rivers, Spike, & Downtown Joe, Rick & Leah, J.D. B.J. & Jeff, Mike & John, Eric Seidell, Johnny and Corey, Jerry Williams, Steve, Bill & The Coach, Christopher & Kerrigan, Joe & Stan, McGee & Beck, The Freakin Brothers, Kerry & Bill, T.J. & Jer, Mark Shannon & Ron Spensor, Dirk & Tom, Darla, Rick, & Scott, Andy & Scott, John Patrick & Cat Thomas, Chris & Steve, Don Kelly, Allen & Karen, Pete & Dave, Mike Pentek, Eddie & Jobo, Robin & Bob, Lee Rogers, Stevens & Pruett, Brian Shannon, Danny and Rhoda Douglas, Carol Arnold, Paul & Phil, Fred, John & Richard, Gary & Erin, Susie, Dom Testa, Coach & T.K. Skywalker, Gary Burbank & Mike McConnel, Joe Elliott, Dave Otto, Dave Sposito & Ken, Mike Thomas & Steve Rouse, Samantha & Hollywood Hamilton, Jim Murphy, Tyler, Guy & Julie, Marc Anthony, Bo & Bamma, John McCormick, Tim Spencer, Bev Hart, Dan Weber, Terri Evans, Pat McMurry, John & Scott, Bucky Barker, Coffy & the Jammer, Matty in the Morning, Andy Barber, Pete McMurry, Barry Beck, Rick Moffit, Dr. Drex, Terry DiMonte, Jack Diamond & Burt, Jim Kerr, Skip & Ben, Bob Boz Bell, Jeff Walker, Willie Rich, Ben Baldwin, Larry & Willie, Paul & Phil, Greg And Bill, Susie Waud & Mark The Shark, Spike & Bryon, John Lyle & Steve Hahn, Chris & Fred, Jeff Styles, Dave & The Fatman, Chris & Woody, Bob And Steve, Those Guys In The Morning, Joe Nugent, Kevin & Pete, M.C. Mitch & Rob, Ted & Marla, Phil Tower, Ted & Tom, Gina Miles, Daniels & Webster, Bax & O'Brien, Rex & Tim Parker, John & Dan & Clide, Kerry & Bill, Tommy Tucker, Ben Smith, Max Stewert, Phil & Brent, Keith & the Bearman, Billy, Super Dave, & Jack, Jeff & Phil, Sam Giles, Rob Reinhart, Fanny Koeffer, Dana, Rick & Suds, Beth & Bill, Ross, Pete DeGraff, Franky C, Howie & Fizz, Jeff Slater, Ross Brittan, Dave Kirby, Dave Abbott, Lee Fowler, Buck & Peg, Greg Holt & Muddman, Mike Miller, Doug & Mike, Rick Tower, Myrna Lamb, Gary Thompson, Picozzi & The Horn, Ed, Lisa & Dr. Drai, Art Sears, Rick Moffat, & Ben & Jim & Baxter, MoJo & Buckethead, Big Dave, Bill Carroll & Mike Cartalano, Chris & Rebecca, The Duke & Beth, Jerry Hart, Byrd, Mark & Lopez, Bruce Bond, John Swanson & Kathy Hart, T.C. & Dave, Much Music - Bill Welychka & Natalie Richard, Carolyn Von Vlaardingen, Art Sears, Carol & Paul Mott, Cindi Henderson, Frank Foley, Larry Norton, Darien Mckee & Colleen, Danny & the Barber, Gary Stone, Nancy Shock, Marc Razz, Ethan Carey, Larry & Lou, Steve Hansel, Johnny Danger, Lisa Butts & Mike, Ric Walker & Brad Kopeland, Gator, Josie Vogel, Dean, Roger & Joey, Mary Marlow, Scott Taylor, Larry & Willie, Nasty Man, Clay & Janice, Dave Welsh, Steve & Johnny, Katherine John, Tony Nesbitt, Sue McGarvin, Mark Benson, Randy Miller, Kimberly, Rick Lawerence, & Brad & Jim Bone, John Boy & Billy, Tim & Darren, Stew Williams, Joe Mattison, Jennifer Sexton, Kevin & The Blade, Phil & Billy, Steve Ryan, Bob & Madison, Kato & Tom, Tim & Darreen, Mel & Frank, Billy Kidd & Phil, Larry & Lou, Billy & Jack, Paul Turner, Dirk Rowley, Bill & Norman, Ben Davis, Mike Spears, Steve Downs, Susan & Scott, Chris & Rebecca, Simon Will, and Thanks Again !

Table of Contents

71. HANDY MAN
His Eyes Only

72. HONEYMOON AFTERNOON
His Eyes Only

73. TOUCH OF CLASS
His Eyes Only

74. KING OF HEARTS
His Eyes Only

75. AN ENCHANTED EVENING
Her Eyes Only

76. SOMETHING'S COOKIN'
Her Eyes Only

77. BUILDING A FIRE
His Eyes Only

78. BETWEEN VENUS AND MARS
Her Eyes Only

79. RHAPSODY IN GOLD
Her Eyes Only

80. NEWLYWED GAME
His Eyes Only

81. ONCE IN A LIFETIME
His Eyes Only

82. SUNRISE DREAMER
His Eyes Only

83. WHAT MONEY CAN'T BUY
His Eyes Only

84. JUST BECAUSE
His Eyes Only

85. TOKENS OF AFFECTION
Her Eyes Only

86. SAVE IT FOR A RAINY DAY
His Eyes Only

87. LOVE IN A SECRET PLACE
His Eyes Only

88. SPECIAL DELIVERY
Her Eyes Only

Introduction to Grrreat Romance

To be Read Together

Ahh, *romance!* It just might be the greatest thing in the whole universe.

What else makes you feel as good as being head over heels in love. Romance puts a twinkle in your eye, and a spring in your step. It boosts your confidence It turns the routine of everyday life into a thrilling adventure. It reduces cholesterol and increases your chances of winning the lottery.

Hah! Just kidding about that last part. But no doubt about it, romance is really important. After all, it's the thrill of the chase that makes the capture so sweet. It's the foreplay *before* the foreplay. Here's the best definition I've ever heard:

Romance is how we make love with our clothes on.

(And, needless to say, it's usually what determines whether we get them *off!*)

Most of us, though, don't have nearly as much romance in our lives as we'd like. Oh, sure, we all get a taste of it when we first fall in love. But after a while, ordinary *things* can get in the way. Jobs and kids and bills and problems all compete for our attention. Slowly, so slowly that we hardly even notice it, the romance that used to fill the air around us starts to . . .

Fade.

But it doesn't have to be that way. Because, romance — *grrreat* romance — is really simple. Even, easy! All it takes is a willingness to make it a priority in your life.

That, plus a little help from this book!

With just these two things, you have all you need to reignite the sparks that flew when you first fell for each other. Better yet, as you go through one exciting seduction after another, you'll learn how to *create* that same magic anywhere, anytime. In short — if you follow the suggestions in this book, you're going to be treated to a romantic date or event or surprise every single week, twice each week, *for one full year!*

And if that doesn't fit your schedule, well, stretch it out — do it once a week for two years. (If you also have my other books, *101 Nights of Grrreat Sex* and *101 Grrreat Quickies*, hey — you may be set for the rest of your lives!)

101 Nights of Grrreat Romance eliminates the single biggest reason romance slips away: *most couples simply fail to make time for it.* From now on, you and your partner have a standing date to get together once each week and flip through this book. Check out the titles. Talk about the ones that catch your eye. Think of it as going window-shopping for love!

Once each of you picks out a page, *tear it from the book.* That one simple act represents a major promise. Your partner has just made a pledge that, sometime during the next seven days, *no matter what,* you are going to be romanced in a fresh, exciting, and original manner. For at least one night — or day! — *your pleasure* will be the only thing that matters. You, of course, have just made the same promise in return.

On every page you'll find four ways to romance your lover. *There's the Kiss Of The Week*, the Passion Coupon, the Conversation Piece, and, of course, the Romantic Seduction itself. Here's how they work:

1. The Seduction

Each of these special recipes contains one complete romantic seduction, spelled out step-by-delicious-step. I hope you're inspired to customize them, to make each one uniquely your own. *But you don't have to.* All the important elements are already right here. If you do nothing more than follow the plans just as they're written, you'll both have a blast. (I know, because I've personally tested most of them myself. And in case you were wondering, yes, I just *love* my job!!)

Some of these romantic scenarios are sweet and simple — exactly the sort of tender gestures couples say they miss most in a relationship. (And just the sort of thing I hope you'll be inspired to do every day!) Others are more like traditional dates, but with some fun, romantic twists thrown in. And there are a few that are just *off the charts* — spectacular, once-in-a-lifetime, fall-in-love-all-over-again events, the kinds of things you'll talk about for years to come. These might require some real planning, but the results, I promise, will be absolutely unforgettable.

All of them, however, have this in common — they require you to *demonstrate your affection.* Sure, you *know* your mate loves you . . . but isn't it so much more fun when you see that love in action? In almost every chapter you're both asked to write love notes, or offer small gifts, or decorate the house in some way. These little acts are *essential* to romance. They're signs of respect. They say, "I think you're worth going to a little trouble for." So please — *don't skip the small stuff!*

2. 101 New Kisses

How many ways do you know how to kiss your lover? Well, you'll find 101 new kisses in here, described in detail. The kisses marked with an asterisk (*) come from a neat little book called *365 Ways To Kiss Your Love*, by Tomima Edmark. Tomima also invented the topsy tail. She is one talented lady!

Just wait 'til you try The Emergency Kiss, or The Suck-The Mango Kiss. There's The Tush Kiss, and The Blindfold Kiss, and my personal favorite — *The Weak-At-The-Knees Kiss!*

Every week you surprise your mate with a different kiss. Practice makes perfect, though, so don't hesitate to try out your new kiss as many times and as often as you wish!

3. Passion Coupons

Every seduction also has a Passion Coupon, redeemable for, *passion.* I'm talking about love in it's most physical form. (Hey, what good is a romance book if it doesn't help you generate a little *heat*??) Now, a lot of these are *anything goes* and *fill-in-the-blank coupons*, so you'll be able to ask for precisely what you want. (But remember — these are *passion* coupons, not I-want-you-to-do-all-my-chores-this-week coupons! Think of them as perfect opportunities to fulfill your wildest fantasies.) Remember, the bearer is always the one who tears out the coupon and hands it over. The recipient follows the bearers wishes.

Like the seduction, the Passion Coupon stays a secret until you hand it over to your mate — and at that moment, he or she has to *drop whatever they're doing and give you exactly what the coupon says.*

Yes, you read that right. Instant affection. Instant *hanky panky.* Really fast, totally hot, and *right now.*

4. Conversation Piece

The second page of each seduction is one that *isn't* a surprise for your lover. In fact, just as soon as you've both read your instructions, **you should read this part out loud to each other.** It's what I call a *Conversation Piece* -an excerpt from one of over forty best-selling books. John Gray is quoted in here, along with Barbara DeAngelis, Greg Godek, Deepak Chopra . . . even humorist Dave Barry, whose view on the unromantic nature of Guys is just flat-out *hysterical!* You'll get to read some of the most important ideas from *Real Moments For Lovers, Hot Monogamy, The Seven Habits Of Highly Effective People,* and lots more. Look at it this way — you're getting the best parts of an *entire library* right in this one book. What a deal!

These Conversation Starters are *not* like a class or a lecture; in fact, they're usually just a paragraph or two. Some are powerful and insightful; some are funny. Some are there just to remind you why romance is so important — and others will spark hours worth of discussions. And that's their second major benefit. Since you read these quotes out loud to your partner *they get you both to talk.* Even better, they get you both to listen. All the experts agree that couples should spend time away from all distractions every week just to talk about the relationship. And the result? Improved communication. A deeper intimacy. A chance to get to know each other again.

Put it all together, and here's what happens

All these elements combine to create a new **romantic ritual** in your lives, designed to do several things —

- *It makes your relationship a priority.* Love, after all, *is* a verb. It requires action. Unfortunately, most people simply forget to put it on their list of things to do . . . and then they wonder why the passion they once felt has slipped away.

- *It creates a commitment to romance.* Remember, your mate *sees* you tear out the page — there's no turning back after that! You'll want to follow through.

- *It creates private, intimate time together,* just like the experts suggest. You'll come to cherish these special, quiet moments when you look through the book together, and pick out your seduction — especially if your lives are jam-packed with activity. A lot of people tell me Sunday nights work best for them. No kids, no phones, and they go work the next morning *with romance on the brain.*

- *It renews your sense of romantic excitement.* *Surprise* is what keeps a relationship from getting dull. In these scenarios you don't know *when* your mate is going to pop up with a Kiss, or a Passion Coupon, or a Seduction . . . but you know *some* romantic surprise is going to come your way each week! Most of these recipes also ask you to do something to *tease your lover* before the actual seduction arrives. That feeling of anticpation is what makes the final event so sweet!

Now, for one reason or another you might find that you have to modify one of these seductions. After all, there's no way I could come up with 101 scenarios that are perfect for everybody. So change the ingredients, or add some of your own. Customize the recipe! But please, whatever you do — keep those dual elements of *surprise* and *anticipation.* They're really the heart and soul of this book.

- *It allows you to take all the credit!* Your lover will never be certain if some outrageously romantic idea came from the book, or from your own inspired imagination.

Ultimately, though, the answer will be *both.* That's because you'll be mastering the *fine art of seduction* with every passing week. Soon you'll not only know how to create supremely romantic moments, you'll find yourself doing it automatically, every day, in big ways and small. When you discover how well these simple ideas work — and how happy they make your partner! — you'll naturally start to make them a part of your everyday life. In short, you'll *learn by doing.* (And doing, and doing, and doing, and doing... 101 times in a row! *Wheee!*)

To make these plans as easy to follow as possible, I've added a list of ingredients to each page. These tell you all the things you'll need in order to pull off your assignment. Some don't require anything more than a smile! On the other hand, several of them suggest you buy some specific items. For those that are not commonly available, I include phone numbers and mail-order addresses.

Here's How It Works

Fifty of these seductions are written for *His Eyes Only,* and are designed with only one goal in mind — making *her* feel cherished, adored, and special. Another fifty are written for *Her Eyes Only,* and everything in them is aimed at making *him* feel like a winner at the game of love.

Now, you may have noticed that *fifty for her* and *fifty for him* only adds up to one hundred seductions. What about Number 101? I'm glad you asked — *it's the only one here that you <u>both</u> get to read together.* Think of it as a kind of graduation ceremony! And save that one for last.

So there you have them — the four keys to *Grrreat Romance*. A little smooching, a lot of snuggling, some deep conversation, and at least one spectacular romance every week. After an entire year or two of this, you'll both be experts — Masters of the Art of Romance. And by then you should be able to conjure romance in your *sleep*.

(But I bet you'll be doing a lot more in bed than just sleeping!!

*   *   *

Some final notes before you start your big adventure —

Kids. Got 'em? Then time and privacy are probably in short supply around your house. But please — don't let that stop you. *Create* the time for each other. Find someone you trust to watch your kids once a week, if you have to. (Remember — when it's your turn to pull off a seduction, it's also your responsibility to arrange for a babysitter.)

And guess what? Your children might be the best reason to make time for these recipes. Don't they learn from your example? Well, then, set a good one. If they see Mom and Dad snuggling and kissing, writing love notes and buying gifts, chasing each other around the house and generally acting like loving, caring people — then that's *just the kind of adults they'll grow to be.* And I for one think the world will be a better place for it.

Besides, the closeness that comes with true romance is a force that heals us and sustains us. It gets us through the tough times together. It gives us the strength to deal with things like, well, *kids*.

Hygiene. It's critical! I can't tell you how many men and women have told me they've lost interest in their partner because of some personal grooming flaws. Think of it this way — as you go through this book, your love is going to kiss and nibble various parts of you *every single week*. Sometimes without any warning! You're going to do the same. Neither of you wants any unpleasant surprises, right? And you *sure* don't want to give your mate a reason to avoid intimate contact in the future.

So check yourself out! Fresh breath, clean teeth, shampooed hair, scrubbed skin — it's part of the official Romance Uniform. Put it on and wear it proudly.

Money. A lot of these seductions are free. But for those that aren't, I've included little icons on the title pages to give you an idea of what to expect. (By the way, when you see a seduction that's rated over sixty dollars, you'll almost always find a *budget tip* that can cut the cost dramatically.)

No $ means it's free, or under ten dollars.

$ means 10 to 25 dollars.

$$ means 25 to 60 dollars.

$$$ means 60 to 100 dollars.

⭐   means over a hundred dollars.

Trust me, there are only a handful that fall into that last category! But a few of them do, and if your budget permits, then heck, the sky's the limit on those. *Just don't skip the big ones.* Once in a while, you *should* pull out all the stops, even if you have to save up for it. Think of those occasions as *investments*. Anniversaries, birthdays, Valentine's Day . . . what you're buying are memories that will last a lifetime.

The Other Icons:

🚗 The car means you're going somewhere.

☀ The sun means you should try to plan your seduction during the summer.

🍃 The leaf means you should try to plan your seduction during the fall.

❄ The snow flake means you need *cold* weather.

✿ The flower means you should try to plan your seduction during the spring.

🍴 The fork-and-spoon indicate food is involved.

♥ The heart is a special one for ***men only***. Guys, you'll learn about it in your secret introduction.

🌙 The moon means you should check the calendar and *try* to plan your seduction for a full moon. . . *The full moon is a lover's moon.* It makes us just a little bit **lunier** and is the perfect romantic backdrop for some of the *zanier* seductions.

*(**Here's a hint:** The more icons you see, the more preparation is usually required. When you see the car icon, you'll probably need a babysitter. If there is more than one sesasonal icon, you can choose any of those seasons to do it in.)*

Props. Lots of these scenarios involve the use of special items to dress up the event. *Please don't ignore these suggestions!* It's those extra touches that help convince your sweetheart you mean business. If you can't find what I recommend, then use your imagination. Substitute To make it easier, I've included a list of mail-order suppliers in the ingredients.

Pictures. When I ask my radio audiences to name the *four essential items* every romantic couple should keep in the bedroom, almost nobody ever guesses *pictures*. But displaying pictures of each other — alone and snuggled together — is a perfect way to constantly remind yourselves of the importance of your relationship. Have a special location in the house which features pictures of the two of you (the fridge works great) and change these pictures frequently. This constant change is a symbol of the continual renewal of your commitment and your determination to keep it fresh by building *new romantic memories,* (By the way, can you guess what the other *three* essential bedroom items are? You'll find out in this book!)

Special Secrets. There are a few little things I want to tell each of you . . . but not together! You'll find two different introductions, one for *His Eyes Only,* and one for *Her Eyes Only,* following these pages. Read them right away. In private, please!

Getting Seduced. You know, it may take a lot of nerve for your love to try some of these techniques, especially at the beginning. So play along! Be encouraging. You will *not* regret it.

Laura Corn, I just CAN'T do that! *Yes, you can.* Sooner or later you may come across a seduction that seems too wild or too extravagant or simply too much for you. I say — just do it! *Do it do it do it!* Your partner will be totally thrilled. You might learn to love something totally new!

No, Laura, I mean I can't do it <u>right now</u>! Yes, it's true, several of these do require some advance work. You might have to buy tickets for a show that's weeks away, or make some arrangements for your kids. And you might even find one that just isn't your cup of tea.

Well, if you really can't follow the recipe *this* week, don't give up on your promise to your mate. Pull out another seduction. Make up one of your own. **The only truly important thing is to *keep your commitment to make your partner feel special* at least once a week.**

So please — *destroy this book.* Tear it apart, one wonderful page at a time! Go on, start ripping and reading. Start with any page you like. Right now! In a year or two, you'll be left with one tattered, empty book cover....

And a lot of *grrreat* memories.

Wishing you love, grrreat romance, grrreat sex, a lifetime of surprises, and all the laughter in the world!

Laura Corn

FOR HIS EYES ONLY.

Finally, two words of advice about *Grrreat* Sex, which is what you'll get when you practice *Grrreat* Romance.

Be safe. (And buy my other book!)

ISN'T THAT ROMANTIC
by Joseph Lipari and Leonard Jobin

Flowers and Their Meanings

Sending flowers is a beautiful gesture all by itself, but to add a little extra meaning, choose flowers whose traditional meanings coincide with the message or feeling you want to convey. The list below indicates the meaning of some popular flowers.

Flower	Traditional Meaning
Aster	Talisman of love
Begonia	A fanciful nature
Bellflower, white	Gratitude
Carnation, pink	Emblem of Mother's Day
Carnation, red	Admiration
Carnation, white	Pure and ardent love
Chrysanthemum, red	I love you
Chrysanthemum, white	Truth
Cockscomb	Affection
Daffodil	Regard
Daisy	Innocence, gentleness
Forget-me-not	True Love
Globe Amaranth	Unfading love
Heliotrope	Devotion
Hibiscus	Delicate beauty
Honesty	Honesty
Jasmine, white	Amiability
Jasmine, yellow	Modesty
Larkspur	An open heart
Lily of the valley	Purity and humility
Pansy	Thoughtful recollection
Peony	Healing
Phlox	Sweet Dreams
Primrose	Young love
Rose, pink	Perfect happiness
Rose, white	Charm and Innocence
Rose, white & red	Unity
Rosebud	Beauty and youth
Sunflower	Homage and devotion
Sweet alyssum	Worth beyond beauty
Tuberose	Dangerous pleasures
Tulip	You are the perfect lover
Verbena	May you get your wish
Violet	Modesty and simplicity

A Word to the Wise, Guys

A Special Secret Message Just For Men

Women *need* romance, guys. We need it like air and sleep. John Gray really hits the nail on the head in his excellent book *Men Are From Mars, Women Are From Venus*, and the follow up, *Venus And Mars In The Bedroom*. (And if you're serious about making your sweetie happy, those books belong on your shelf!) He says that women these days fill completely different roles than their grandmothers did — and he's so right. A working woman has to spend a lot of time in a "man's world," competing with men and often having to think like one.

Romance lets her come back to her female side. Every time you chase her and seduce her, you remind her that she's a highly desirable woman. You make her feel cherished. That's a feeling she just can't get from her job, or any other source, and that's what the seductions written *For His Eyes Only* are all about. Along with all the flowers and gifts and phone calls and kisses and romantic surprises, these pages give your mate what she really, *really* wants . . . .

A chance to be a woman again.

So what do you have to do?

Well, everything in the book. By that I mean that you *must not skip the small details!!* You might have to modify one of the recipes I've designed, or even create a new one to suit your circumstances. But drop the flowers, and you've dropped the ball. Skip the love notes and you're out of the game. *All those sweet extras* are what the woman wants! They make her feel special. And in return, she'll make *you* feel special.

There's more to Grrreat Romance than just, well, romance.

You get *101 different kisses* to play around with. (And please don't skip over these!! Kissing is grrreat foreplay.) And then there are 101 *Passion Coupons*. **Quickies!!** Yesiree, Laura Corn's lookin' out for you, guys. Just tear 'em out, hand 'em over, and *get some serious skin-time* as a result. Romance and *sex*—(the *chase* and the *capture*)- it doesn't get any better than that! (Remember, the more attention you pay to romance the more likely she is to redeem her coupons and deliver on yours.)

Now — three special instructions.

First, you have a *secret icon* to watch out for. It's the **"heart"** symbol at the bottom of some of the title pages. You're the only one who gets to know what it means, and it means *you have to buy flowers* for that week's seduction. It happens a lot in this book, and for a good reason — women love them!! Sometimes it's just a single rose, sometimes a bouquet — so pay attention to the money icon, too. Together, they'll help you plan your flower budget and spread out your purchases.

Cool tip: the *way* you hand over a gift is as important as the gift itself. So in this book, every bouquet or flower arrangement is presented in an surprising, unique manner. You're going to look like a brilliantly creative and terribly romantic guy. All year long.

Second, there may be times when you can't pull off the seduction I've suggested. You might be asked to do something that can't happen before the week's out . . . . or maybe you'll find one that's just not your cup of tea or not in your budget. *So change it.* Dream up a new one. Just be sure to do *something* before the end of the week! Remember — for your sweetheart, ninety percent of romance is just seeing you make an effort.

Third — *Hide this introduction!!!* Sheesh, you don't want to give away all your secrets, do you?

FOR HER EYES *W* ONLY.

book, "Light His Fire", if you don't have an affair with your partner, someone else will! That leads me to the final key to Grrreat Romance: *you have to put it on your schedule.*

That's one of the reasons this book works so well. It sits there on your dresser or nightstand, reminding you that every week . . . or twice a month, or whatever suits you . . . *you have a commitment* to bring romance into your relationship. And fulfilling that commitment is as easy as sitting down with your mate and tearing out a page. It's as simple as following the recipes.

Sure, you can change them! Cut out parts you don't care for, shorten the seductions if you must, add in elements that appeal to you!

But do it. *Do it! Do it!* Show your lover that he's a priority in your life. Show him how much he means to you by following through with these seductions *no matter what.*

Every month, every week . . . eventually, I'll bet, every day . . . he's going to show you the same.

And *that's* how you turn a relationship into a really *Grrreat Romance.*

IN THE MOOD
Doreen Virtue

When I began surveying men about romance, I expected to read many answers that connected sex to love and romance. I was pleasantly surprised to find that the men's answers were much more removed from the act of intercourse than I expected.

Here's a list of the actions most often cited by men as turn-ons leading to a romantic mood, listed in order from most to least frequent:

1.   Being with a woman who looks good or dresses seductively
2.   A home-cooked dinner
3.   Non-sexual touching, such as hugging, massaging, or caressing
4.   Eye contact or a special way of looking at each other
5.   Low lights or candlelight
6.   Having a partner who makes a special effort to make a romantic evening
7.   *Having a partner who is spontaneous or who surprises me*
8.   Kissing
9.   Soft music
10.   Wine or champagne
11.   A woman who smells great
12.   A quiet atmosphere

All these turn-ons strike me as gentle, tender expressions of male and female bonding. A romantic setting is very important to a man —- he enjoys dimmed lights, soft music and a quiet atmosphere. His romantic mood is aroused when his female partner puts a special effort into making him feel like a king.

Girl Talk

So how do you turn your relationship into a *Grrreat* Romance?

The first thing you need, of course, is the simple *desire to do it.* You have to want to bring Grrreat Romance into your relationship.

And believe me, men respond to that. If your lover senses that you're going through these pages because you cherish him and truly want to make him happy, he'll light up. He'll instinctively want to turn around and do the same for *you.* So approach each of these fifty seductions with a smile — or, more to the point, with a mischievous seductive grin!

And of course, you should show that same positive attitude when he pops his secret surprises on you. Now, some of them will be small. In his part of the book, I drive home the importance of those sweet considerate gestures women never get enough of.) Several of his seductions involve *huge* surprises for you! But big or small, they should all be greeted with an enthusiastic thank you. Thank you, thank you, *thank you!* Your appreciation is so important. It's just human nature at work — if he feels your gratitude, he'll keep it up. If he senses disappointment or criticism, he's not likely to stage a repeat performance.

Speaking of human nature — *Grrreat Romance* requires you to respect the differences between you. And one of those differences is sex.

Guess what? *Sex probably doesn't mean the same to him as it does to you.* It's tough to generalize about something so profoundly personal, but I've interviewed thousands of couples over the years, and learned this —

Women enjoy sexual relations the most when their emotional needs are being met. And men are much more open to the emotional side of a relationship when their physical needs are being met.

In other words, your mate wants to express some of his romantic feelings through sexual intimacy. *And you should let him.* About ten percent of your seductions in this book are sexual, and when you carry them out, you're sending a very powerful message to your mate. Other scenarios will tell him he's funny and charming and that you love him dearly — but a few of these say, *"I want you. I crave you! You turn me on."*

That's something every man needs to hear. Heck, it's something we all need to hear . . . and trust me, *you'll* get to hear it, too! Besides the heat generated by a few of his secret seductions, there are 101 Passion Coupons in this book. *101 chances to get physical!* Approach these with as much humor as heat. Think of them as playground games for grownups!

They work like the romantic seductions, with this exception: When it's your turn to spring one on your partner, you're doing it for your pleasure, *not his.* Remember, you are the bearer, even after you hand it over, and it is your game, your rules. . *He has to do everything for you!* And vice versa. Believe me, there's nothing that adds spice to a relationship like occasionally turning your total attention to the needs of your mate. Some of these coupons are "quickies." In fact, quickies are so important to men, that John Gray devotes an entire chapter to them in one of his books! I hope you redeem all your Passion Coupons. I have a feeling he'll be a lot more romantic!! These Passion Coupons are hot, fun, and *now* — perfect for busy couples trying to juggle romance along with jobs, chores, friends, and kids.

Uh-oh. Kids. If you've got 'em, you know how they can put a damper on romance. It's so hard to find time and energy to devote to your relationship. But as Ellen Kreidman points out in her terrific

1 | *She'll Like It, She'll Love It, She'll Want More of It!*

FOR HIS EYES ONLY. *M*

CONVERSATION PIECE

CHICKEN SOUP FOR THE SOUL
Jack Canfield and Mark Victor Hansen

For Me To Be More Creative, I Am Waiting For . . .

1. Someone to change

2. An absence of risk

3. More time

4. A significant relationship to: a) improve; (b) terminate; (c) happen

5. A clearly written set of instructions

6. My love to rekindle

7. The rest of the rules

8. Inspiration

9. Spring

10. My turn

11. The right person

12. The kids to leave home

13. The things that I do not understand to go away

14. A more favorable horoscope

15. My youth to return

16. Tomorrow

17. A better circle of friends

18. The stakes to be higher

19. Permission

20. Someone to discover me

21. Logic to prevail

22. Someone to smooth the way

23. The alimony payments to stop

24. Better birth control

25. My ego to improve

26. Various aches and pains to subside

27. My new credit card

28. This meeting to be over

29. My receivables to clear

30. A signal from Heaven

31. The next time around

She'll Like It, She'll Love It, She'll Want More of It

This is one sweet seduction.

Literally, that is! It takes two of mankind's, uh, I mean, womankind's greatest pleasures and puts them together in one romantic evening. Who can resist kissing — and cookies!

These are not ordinary cookies, of course. Oh, on the outside they may look like regular Chinese fortune cookies. But inside, they're as unique and special as your sweetheart. That's because *you* get to write the fortunes!

Invite your soulmate out for Chinese food. (Or really, any restaurant will do. The surprise comes *after* the meal.) When dinner's over, your waiter — who's already in on the joke — brings the check and a handful of fortune cookies. Wait 'til she opens the first one!

Becky — tonight you will be kissed by a tall blond man named Doug. (Uh, you *do* realize you have to change that to match your own description and names, right? I knew you knew that.)

Wow! That is some accurate fortune! Try another. *You are about to win the lottery. Buy Doug a car.* Huh?? What?! *Are you wearing your black lace panties tonight? Can I see them?*

She may not be able to figure out how you got these things printed and stuffed in the cookies, but she'll be *thrilled* as she breaks each one open. *Good for one free 30-minute footrub . . . Becky, you're more beautiful tonight than the day we met . . . Confucius say: navy blue suit with short skirt make you look hot . . . Can I wash your hair this weekend? . . . Quick, show me where you want to be kissed . . . Doug loves Becky . . .*

Each one of these cookies is a romantic treasure chest begging to be opened, and best of all — *they aren't expensive!* Let her read several in the restaurant, but then hide more of them around the house — in her lingerie drawer, the bathroom, all over the kitchen. Anytime, day or night, she might stumble across one and be reminded of your passion for her. And who knows what that could lead to?

Well, the ancient Chinese knew. *Confucius say: Smart good. Lucky better. Fortune cookie good. Nookie-cookie better!*

INGREDIENTS

Ask you favorite chinese restuarant for the name of their baker. Some can furnish cookies without the fortunes.

Or call one of the numbers below. I've worked out a special deal with these companies for all you terrific guys!

Type your own fortunes, (the more the better) cut into strips, fold over and then slip them into the clever little

gap designed for this purpose. I know it's a little extra trouble but believe me, her response will be worth it!

Wing Hing Noodle Co., Will ship you 50 fortuneless cookies for only $19.95 postage paid!

(213) 231-1127 - 1642 E 23 st. Los Angeles, Ca 90011

Amay's Bakery & Noodle Co., Will ship you 450 cookies for $16.00 plus postage. You, your sweetie and a whole

bunch of friends can be in fortune cookie nirvana for months to come!!

(213) 626-2713 - 837 Commercial St. Los Angeles, CA 90012

2 | *Make Him Tremble*

FOR HER EYES ONLY.

CONVERSATION PIECE

THE LOVERS' BEDSIDE COMPANION
Gregory J.P. Godek

To be loving is to be creative. To be creative is to express love.

A relationship is an act of creativity. You either re-create your relationship each and every day, or you're stuck with something old, inadequate, boring, and ultimately, unsatisfying.

MEN ARE FROM MARS, WOMEN ARE FROM VENUS
John Gray, Ph.D.

Love Motivates Martians

Most men are not only hungry to give love but are starving for it. Their biggest problem is that they do not know what they are missing. They rarely saw their fathers succeed in fulfilling their mothers through giving. As a result they do not know that a major source of fulfillment for a man can come through giving. When his relationships fail he finds himself depressed and stuck in his cave. He stops caring and doesn't know why he is so depressed.

At such times he withdraws from relationships or intimacy and remains stuck in his cave. He asks himself what it is all for, and why he should bother. He doesn't know that he has stopped caring because he doesn't feel needed. He does not realize that by finding someone who needs him, he can shake off his depression and be motivated again.

When a man doesn't feel he is making a positive difference in someone else's life, it is hard for him to continue caring about his life and relationships. It is difficult to be motivated when he is not needed. To become motivated again he needs to feel appreciated, trusted, and accepted.

Not To Be Needed Is A Slow Death For A Man.

Make Him Tremble

When was the last time you saw a television commercial that totally grabbed your attention and inspired you to rush out and try something new?

It's easy to ignore most ads — we get flooded with them every day. But I saw one recently that just knocked me out. *This*, I thought, is some *Grrreat Romance!*

It was a commercial for Polaroid, and it featured a busy executive surrounded by people in an important meeting. Someone hands him the phone, and a sultry voice at the other end says, "I want you to come home early." The man starts to explain how much work he has to do, but the woman on the phone simply replies, *"Look in your briefcase."* He fumbles around and finds an instant picture. Now, we never get to see what's in that shot — but every man and woman on the planet would recognize this guy's reaction to it! Surprise, intrigue, and desire spread across his face all at once. Clearly, this guy's day just took a dramatic turn for the better.

The commercial made me smile. It made me think that romance is one of the few forces in the world that can turn your life upside down in a heartbeat. *It made me run right out and do the very same thing!*

And that's just what you're going to do this week. First, of course, you've got to get a camera, and an instant camera is ideal for this job. Second, you've got to take an enticing picture — and that's half the fun right there! You can do it alone by using the camera's self-timer, of course, but you'll have a blast if you get a close friend to help. (Be prepared to loan her the camera when you're done, though. She'll want to pull the same stunt on her sweetie!)

And third, you have to hide the picture where your lover won't find it until you want him to. Your guy doesn't use a briefcase? Well, be creative. Does he carry lunch to work? Could you slip it into his jacket? If nothing else, you can always stick it in the glove compartment in his car.

And now, The Phone Call. What an incredible tease! Believe me, you'll know the very instant he actually lays eyes on your picture! It can reveal as little — or as much — as you wish, but there's no mistaking it's message: You want him. You want him at home. You want him *now!*

I'll bet he's home in, well, an instant. *Smile!*

INGREDIENTS

1 instant camera • 1 provocative pose • 1 sexy outfit (or not!) • 1 busy sweetheart

*(EXTRA COOL TIP: Is there a hotel near his office? Bonus points if you call him from **there**!)*

FOR HIS EYES *M* ONLY.

CONVERSATION PIECE

HOW TO ROMANCE THE WOMAN YOU LOVE THE WAY
SHE WANTS YOU TO!
Lucy Sanna with Kathy Miller

Our survey made this very clear. In answer to the question "Why isn't he more romantic?" survey respondents told us, "He doesn't know what I want."

But isn't this her fault? After all, if she wants something, why doesn't she just say so? Because it's not romantic, that's why.

Romance is a pretty little drama played out with suspense, intrigue, and surprise. Romance involves working behind the scenes.

Besides, women have been taught that asking for something is rude. If a man cares enough, they say, he'll find out what she wants. In any case, it's much more romantic if it was his idea. Well, that's the way many women think.

BORN FOR LOVE
Leo Buscaglia

Love is Enriched by Play

Too often we relegate playing to childhood. Adult games are usually structured, have defined rules and are played to win. Children play just for the joy of it.

Lovers who play together know the value of fun, laughter and surprise. When they indulge in make-believe, they find it opens areas of imagination that are often lost in the routine that most relationships fall into. Creative play can help us relate to people and things in new ways. Play encourages lighthearted cooperation and gets us away from the competitiveness of our society. There is no striving to win when we are playing for fun.

The sole purpose of play is to have fun, to be diverted and amused, to frolic meaninglessly and gleefully for a while, outside the realm of the intellect. When we do this, we discover a positive side of ourselves that celebrates life without analysis, one of the basic components of love.

The House is Rockin'

What is it that makes a relationship? What is it, ultimately, that makes us the people we are?

Memories. Shared memories, in the case of couples. Every time the two of you pull through a crisis together, or celebrate terrific news, or laugh yourselves silly over a dumb joke, what you're doing is cementing the bond between you. You're building a future by bracing your past.

And it doesn't happen all by itself. It's like maintaining any complex piece of equipment — you have to work at it, or it all eventually just falls to pieces. For example, you put fresh oil in your car from time to time, right? Such a simple task, and yet so necessary. Well, put fresh memories into your relationship! Do sweet things for your sweetheart — like this:

One day she comes home to find a basket filled with small rocks on the dining table. *"That's, uh, interesting, dear...."* Well, it is interesting, once you show her that these are special love-stones each with a message written in Magic Marker on one side.

MS loves SR! . . Sally is the most beautiful woman on earth . . . I will love you forever . . . Take one of the stones and put it somewhere just outside your house. Your garden is a good choice, or right behind your air conditioner. Pick a place that's out of the way, but one you'll both remember. Do the same thing with a second rock.

And then this weekend, take the rocks with you in the car as you run your errands. Visit your favorite spots in town — a park, or the beach, or a lake — and leave your solid-state lovenotes hidden in special places. Put one high in the crook of a tree, another at the bottom of a duck pond. Bury one in sand. Toss one onto the roof of a building. Talk about *Romancing The Stone* — Every time you throw one of your Love Rocks, you're expressing your commitment to your mate. Some guys carve initials into a tree. Imagine how you'll knock her socks off when you express your love in a way that could very well outlast any living thing.

Twenty years from now, people may still be discovering your declarations of love. They'll wonder about the two crazy lovers who put their passion on display for all the world to see. From time to time you can check up on the visible ones to see if they're still there. Each time you do you'll stir the memories of the great weekend you had planting your words of devotion around town.

So go — get your rocks. (And when you're ready to get them <u>off</u>, check out my other book. *101 Nights Of Grrreat Sex!*)

INGREDIENTS

Several rocks • 1 felt-tip permanent marker

4 | Satins and See Throughs

FOR HIS EYES ONLY.

$$

CONVERSATION PIECE

1001 WAYS TO BE ROMANTIC (NEW & EXPANDED)
Gregory J.P. Godek

Surprise!

It was Valentine's Day, 1989. My boyfriend had invited me to his place for breakfast. I arrived to find the kitchen table in the living room, in front of the fireplace. It was set with flowers, candles, a delicious breakfast and champagne glasses filled with ginger ale. Although this was a wonderfully romantic setting, I began to sense that my boyfriend was somehow uncomfortable. I waited a while, and finally asked him if anything was wrong. He looked at me kind of funny. Then he stood up and told me he had something for me. He reached down, unzipped his pants, and revealed . . . a heart-shaped note with "I love You" written in orange crayon! The note was tied to his *you-know-what* with a *burlap* string. No *wonder* he'd looked uncomfortable! He'd had it tied there all morning. To this day I have that heart tied-with the burlap string-to the trunk of a stuffed elephant he gave me.

-A.L., British Columbia, Canada

HOW TO ROMANCE THE WOMAN YOU LOVE THE WAY *SHE* WANTS YOU TO!
Lucy Sanna with Kathy Miller

Paying attention to how your partner looks has its own rewards. In fact, it's the best way you can let her know that you desire her. And if she knows you desire her physically, it helps her feel more relaxed with you and less inhibited. So tell her now. Even if she's a brilliant Nobel Prize winner and she knows that you're attracted to her for her intelligence, don't forget that she's also a woman. And tell her what it is about her physically that turns you on. Be specific. Tell her again and again.

There is nothing more romantic than a man who loves women — loves the way their bodies look, the way they smell, the way the move.

Satins and See Throughs

Most of this book is about the gentle, thoughtful side of love. After all, that's the easiest part to overlook when you've been together awhile.

But it's also surprisingly easy to forget the *other* crucial part of a relationship — and no, I don't mean sex! I've never met a guy who forgets about *that!* It's actually something kind of like sex, but a lot more powerful. More interesting. And very important....

Seduction.

That's all the flirting and teasing and touching and talking that lead to the act itself. Skip all that and intercourse gets... well, okay, it never gets *boring!* But it sure isn't as exciting as it can be. There's still only one tried-and-true, guaranteed way to raise a woman's temperature in bed, and here it is — *convince her that she's one hot babe.* Make her believe that she's a strong, supremely sensual lover with the power to make you crazy with lust. In other words, seduce her.

And believe it or not, you'll be assisted in your efforts by a uniformed representative of the U. S. Government!

Yep — every single month, the mailman will bring a brand new and sexy pair of panties right to your door after you join the Panty-Of-The-Month Club. You can include a card with each gift.... *"I've been dreaming about what these will look like on your fabulous body. I can't wait to see if I'm right."* Give her a shot of self-confidence — never pass up an opportunity to tell her how good she looks, or how much she turns you on when she dresses up. (Or down!) Once she sees how wild you get when she models her lingerie, she'll look forward to each delivery.

But remember, she'll want to warm up before the evening's main act. So every month, ask her to wear her new panties out on a date. And every so often, in a dark corner, or an empty elevator, or at a red light... *try to sneak a peek at them.* She'll get a huge kick out of watching you squirm when she "accidentally" flashes them at you during dinner. (And, trust me on this, she'll be getting as aroused as you are by her little private-in-public show!)

There's only one thing that turns a man on more than a woman with a strong sense of sexual confidence. And that's a beautiful girl in her underwear. Lucky you. Thanks to the Panty Of The Month Club and the Post Office... *you've got both!*

INGREDIENTS

1 membership to the Panty-Of-The-Month Club / 1-515-469-6800

(Budget Tip: buy them and mail them yourself!)

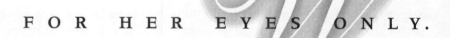

FOR HER EYES ONLY.

CONVERSATION PIECE

THE ROAD LESS TRAVELED
M. Scott Peck, M.D.

True listening, total concentration on the other, is always a manifestation of love. An essential part of true listening is the discipline of bracketing, the temporary giving up or setting aside of one's own prejudices, frames of reference and desires so as to experience as far as possible the speaker's world from the inside, stepping inside his or her shoes. This unification of speaker and listener is actually an extension and enlargement of ourself, and new knowledge is always gained from this. Moreover, since true listening involves bracketing, a setting aside of the self, it also temporarily involves a total acceptance of the other. Sensing this acceptance, the speaker will feel less and less vulnerable and more and more inclined to open up the inner recesses of his or her mind to the listener. As this happens, speaker and listener begin to appreciate each other more and more, and the duet dance of love is again begun. The energy required for the discipline of bracketing and the focusing of total attention is so great that it can be accomplished only by love, by the will to extend oneself for mutual growth.

Dale Carnegie

You can make more friends in two months by becoming interested in other people than you can in two years of trying to get people interested in you.

The Laura Corn Challenge

"But Laura, which romantic recipe is *your* favorite?"

You can't write a book like this one without getting asked that question *a lot* — and here's the answer. This is the special evening I dreamed up seven years ago when I was invited to be a guest on The Love Connection, and it was such a big hit with the audience (and my date!) that it inspired me to make a career out of spreading the gospel of Grrreat Romance.

You start by calling him up one day and asking your sweetie some very specific questions. *What is the color of passion? What aromas and fragrances seduce you? What foods put you in the mood for romance? What's your favorite music to kiss by?*

Now you've got him guessing!! And you've got all the information you need to create a singular, remarkable date custom-tailored just for him. It starts when you lead him to a tent set up in the most beautiful spot you know. There's nothing rustic about this campground, though. Inside the tent, he'll find blankets and pillows spread all around, along with a picnic basket and portable stereo. The food, the music, the colors and fragrances are all exactly what he suggested. The tent should be the kind with a skylight so you can watch the stars wheel by.

He'll be stunned. He'll be grinning from ear to ear! And once he's recovered from your spectacular surprise — focus all your attention on him. You're going to spend the entire evening getting him to open up. *You're going to make love to his mind.* And you'll do it by asking questions.

What makes a woman unforgettable? If you could be famous for one thing you don't do now, what would it be? What movie character is most like you? If you could have any book instantly memorized—cover to cover—which book would you choose? If you were an entry in the dictionary, under which word would people find you? When does a woman's face look the most beautiful to you?

Every time you ask him a question, you're seducing him. Listening, after all, is the highest compliment you can pay to *anyone*. You'll be amazed at what a man will tell you when he feels that you truly want to hear his thoughts, without judgement, and with a totally open and loving heart. For him, an entire evening of devoted attention to his innermost thoughts will be a powerful and moving experience. For you, it's a chance to discover a whole new side to the man you love. By the end of the night, you'll share a deeper level of intimacy than you ever dreamed possible.

When I pulled this off at the beach, I had a close friend help set it up and make sure the music was playing and candles were lit just before my date and I arrived! Believe me, *it's a night he'll never forget.* The idea may have started with Love Connection, but he'll feel like he's dropped into the middle of another old TV show . . . .

Fantasy Island!

INGREDIENTS

1 tent with skylight or windows, borrowed or rented (only $12 to 18$!)

Blankets and pillows • music • picnic basket • And maybe just a little help from a friend

Books of questions — I recommend: The Book Of Love And Sex Questions, by Gregory Stock, 237 Intimate Questions Every Woman Should Ask A Man, by (surprise!) Laura Corn, or The Conversation Piece, by Bret Nicholaus and Paul Lowrie

6 | *Moonlight and Roses*

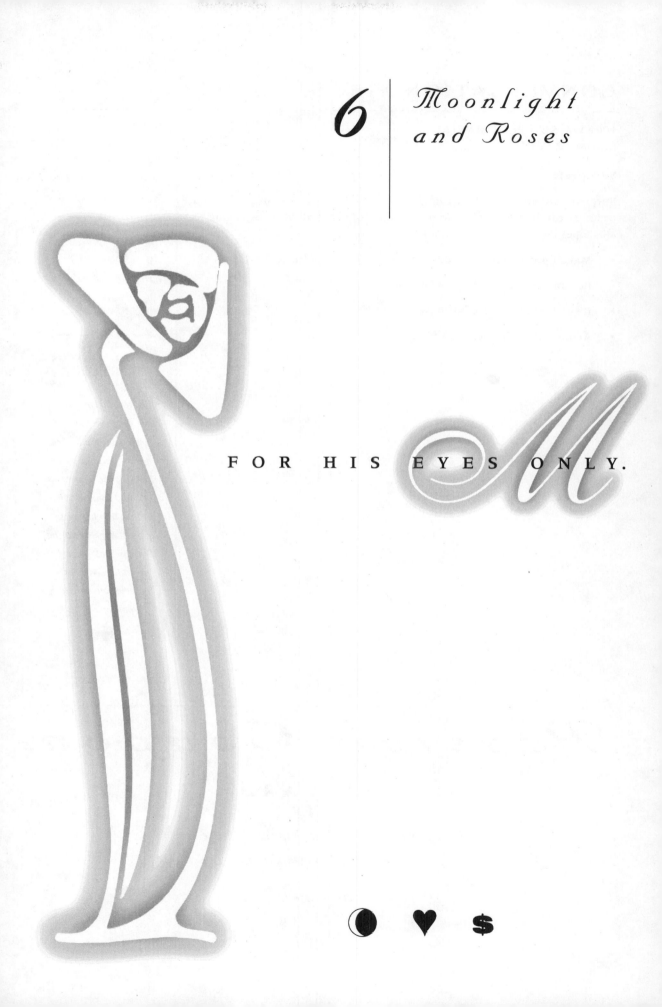

FOR HIS EYES ONLY.

CONVERSATION PIECE

1001 WAYS TO BE ROMANTIC
Gregory J.P. Godek

Surprise!

Surprises are an integral part of the romantic lifestyle. The everyday and ordinary can be made into the unexpected and special. Surprises come in all shapes and sizes . . . and in all budget ranges.

- Make up your mind to add surprises to your repertoire.

- Become an artist of your relationship.

- It's not what you do, but how you do it.

- Actions speak louder than words.

101 NIGHTS OF GRRREAT ROMANCE

Kiss of the Week

FULL MOON KISS

Next full moon, take your lover to a spot where you are bathed in it's glorious, silver light. Wrap your arms around your sweetie, look into her eyes, and tell her three things you really love about her. After each, give your love a passionate kiss.

Passion Coupon

WILD CARD

Bearer is entitled to a 20 minute massage on the body parts of his choice.

Starting now!

Moonlight and Roses

Through the ages, women have often complained that the men in their lives just weren't romantic enough.

I'm not sure that I agree. My own suspicion is that men are, in fact, very romantic . . . they just have this testosterone-driven idea that, as with cars and toys and rude noises, *bigger* is always better. And a man who is not quite sure he's ready to play Major-League Romance often won't even suit up for the game. After all, most men think, it only *really* counts if you can hit one out of the park, right? Does this describe your attitude toward love?

Well, get rid of that silly idea right now! Expensive gifts and grand gestures are lovely things, but it's most often the simple, small, thoughtful surprises — the base hits, if you will — that move a woman the most. This one starts with a note left on the fridge:

May I have the pleasure of your company for a moonlight stroll this evening after dinner?

Wow! A high fly to center field and already you're on second base! What woman wouldn't melt over an invitation like this? It's elegant, sweet, and so romantic. Naturally, you'll continue to be the perfect gentleman as you step outside. Is it chilly? Put a sweater over her shoulders. Hold her hand, or slip your arm around her waist. Pay attention to her, and listen to what she says, all while subtly steering her to your prearranged spot — some bushes or trees where you suddenly stare off and say *hmm, this is interesting . . . there's something here you should see . . . .*

And *voila!* You'll pull out two beautiful long stem red roses — which, of course, you had carefully hidden before your walk! Do you live in an urban area? Don't have a safe place to hide a little gift like this? Then ask the clerk of a nearby store to keep the flowers behind the counter — but be sure to take them right outside to admire them. There's something beautiful, and deeply romantic, about roses in the moonlight.

The surprises, and the seduction, continue when you get home. As she gets ready for bed she'll be thrilled to discover another gift waiting for her on the pillow. It's a book of poems . . . love poems, naturally, with a book marker leading her to a specially marked passage. Now she's in romance heaven, and at this moment you couldn't buy her for all the money Cal Ripkin makes.

(And I'll bet Cal would love to be as certain of getting a home run as *you* are tonight! Batter up!)

INGREDIENTS

1 moonlit evening • 2 roses (or as many as you can hide)

1 book of poetry (or one of my favorites — Gregory Godek's The Lovers' Bedside Companion. Not poetry,

exactly, but you gotta love a book that has to be read in bed!)

7 | *Double Dare You!!*

FOR HER EYES ONLY.

CONVERSATION PIECE

SECRETS ABOUT MEN EVERY WOMAN SHOULD KNOW
Barbara De Angelis, Ph.D.

TURN-OFF - Women Who Wear Ugly Underwear

"My biggest turn-off of all is when women wear those underpants like my mother wears-the cotton ones that come up to their waist with thick leg parts on the sides. UGH! I see a pair of those, and I have no interest in what's underneath."

"When I undress a woman, and notice that she is wearing ugly underwear, it makes me feel three things: One, that she must not care that much about herself if she can actually wear that stuff; two, that she must not care that much about me to let me see her wearing that stuff; and three, that she must not care that much about sex, because she couldn't possibly feel sexy wearing that stuff!"

1001 MORE WAYS TO BE ROMANTIC
Gregory J.P. Godek

Satin and Lace

Ladies: If you remember only one thing from this book, remember this: Men love lingerie. Hundreds of men in the Romance Class have confided or complained that having their ladies wear more lingerie is the one thing they want intensely that their women tend to hold back on. (Scan through a Playboy or Penthouse magazine. You'll discover that there are very few naked women in them. They're almost always wearing stockings, garter belts, or lacy/frilly little things.) Take note. Take action.

Passion Coupon

S O M E T H I N G   W I L D

*Bearer is entitled to 1
Fear of Getting Caught Quickie!*

Starting now!

Double Dare You!!

"Know what comes between me and my Calvin's? Nothing."
BROOKE SHEILDS

That advertising campaign may have sold a lot of jeans for Calvin Klein, but it sure didn't make a dent in underwear sales. He and the pantiless Miss Sheilds overlooked a basic tenet of human nature — *men love underwear.* They spend the better part of their lives just trying to see what ours looks like. They actually sneak glances at the Sears foundation sale ads! The things we put on just to keep the breeze from tickling, men fantasize about.

And so you're going to give your man an eyeful of exactly what he wants this week! Your friends and colleagues might assume you are as straight and stuffy as a minister's wife, but your love will know the truth — *underneath your street clothes is a slightly wild and extremely sensuous woman.*

Start your tease by leaving a Victoria's Secret catalog on his pillow. *"Circle some of your favorites,"* the attached note says. *"And get ready for a fashion show this Thursday!"* Let him think about it for a day or two, then — take him shopping!

It doesn't have to be Victoria's Secret, of course. Most towns have boutiques that specialize in lingerie, from the thoroughly tacky to the divine. (I suggest sticking with the divine, but hey, *you* know what he likes) Let him help pick out some items, *then bring him into the dressing room.*

What an incredible turn-on this will be for your sweetheart. First, there's the thrill of being in that private space for your very private show. And second, *you're going to look like a million bucks.* The nicer shops have elegant changing areas with soft, subtle lights. Retailers know that the better they make us look, the more likely we are to buy — so they've learned how to make us look *grrreat.*

And I double dare you to bring a camera! Every man on earth has dreamed about being a Playboy photographer — and now you can make his dream come true. Flirt and tease and pose and *show off* for your guy. You can spend as much as you want, but the only thing you really have to buy at the end of the show is a pair of sheer, elegant stockings and a garter to hold them up. That'll be the feature at the *next* show that evening —

A movie. Which may not be a truly relaxing experience for the poor guy (but what fun for *you!*), since the centerfold sitting next to him will be fidgeting and showing just a bit of bare thigh from time to time. Hmm. Pictures on the screen... or sexy girl flashing her panties. Which do you think *he'll* be concentrating on?

INGREDIENTS

1 lingerie shop • 1 catalog • 1 camera • 1 movie • 1 full moon (A grrreat excuse to go a little wild!)

8 | *Get Wet!*

W

F O R   H E R   E Y E S   O N L Y .

CONVERSATION PIECE

BORN FOR LOVE
Leo Buscaglia

When Love Loses it Zest

Over time we have a way of taking each other for granted, falling into predictable routines and making what were once provocative actions into conventional ones. It's naturally our fault, it's just that love seems most susceptible to this.

After years of two people being close, it's not uncommon to find that novelty is replaced with predictability. Spontaneity gives way to habit and routine. Where once being with that special person was always intriguing and adventurous, now it seems mechanical and monotonous. Fortunately love is easily rekindled with a little freshness and surprise.

I have a friend who is seen by many as being rather eccentric, but has found many special ways to keep her husband alert and interested. She is forever dreaming up crazy things that add spice to their lives, from suddenly greeting him at the door with an enticing negligee, to presenting him with inexpensive non refundable tickets on a cruise to exotica. His initial response is always one of annoyance, but he is soon won over by the sheer joy of it all. Their relationship continues to flourish. For them, the magic is never gone, they're still creating it.

HOT MONOGAMY
Dr. Patricia Love and Jo Robinson

Once you start letting go of unrealistic standards of beauty, you can begin to appreciate what really makes people sexually attractive. The media drill the message into our heads that sexy people are young, slim, firm, and classically beautiful; we labor under the illusion that we have to look that way to be sexy. But that' s not what I heard from the majority of people I interviewed for this book. I heard over and over that it is responsiveness, not attractiveness, that makes a person a memorable lover.

✂ *You fill in the blanks. He follows your wishes.*

Passion Coupon

ANYTHING GOES!

*Sometime between now and midnight, recipient must leave
the bearer smiling from ear to ear by surprising her with*

_____

_____ .

Get Wet!

What turns a man on more than anything else in the universe?

A woman who's turned on by him! That's because, way down deep inside, a man only wants two things. The first is the *knowledge that he makes you happy.* He wants to know you appreciate him. The second, and this will come as no surprise to anyone who's ever been in T.G.I Friday's at Happy Hour, is, of course, sex.

This week, you're going to combine those two concepts, and put your guy in seventh heaven. All you have to do is demonstrate that you're *happiest* when you're *physically intimate* with him. Remind him that he's a desirable man who completely satisfies you. It's good for his ego, and great for your relationship. It also happens to be a *lot* of fun!!

Start with a little tease early in the week. Buy a small water pistol and leave it dangling by a string from his rearview mirror. The attached note says, *"Bring this to the bedroom Saturday night at six. Loaded and ready for action. The gun, I mean!"*

I'll bet that toy doesn't leave his sight the rest of the week! The mystery deepens Saturday morning when he finds a small package on his dresser. It's a Polaroid camera and film, plus another note. "You'll need this to judge the Contest tonight!" Contest? With *pictures*??! This is getting better all the time!

Finally, on Saturday evening, invite him to bring the gun and the camera into the bathroom, where you'll give him a big smooch and announce that he's been selected to judge this year's *Wet T-Shirt Competition!* Stand back, pose seductively, and let him fire away. You'll both share a lot of laughs as he soaks your top, but watch his eyes. You'll see him getting highly aroused, by your *look* and by your extremely suggestive *attitude.* Now, invite him to take a snapshot of you... and then change into a new T-shirt for round two! After three changes and a whole pack of film, dry off, clean up, and take him out to dinner.

Once you're out in public, you'll no doubt start acting like a lady again. But he'll know better... and you'll remind him of your naughty side when you pull out those photos for him to judge, right there at your dinner table! He'll love them all, but only one can win, and that one goes into a small frame for him to keep. (*In a very private place, of course!*) Naturally, he'll be pretty hot after your show. Imagine his reaction when you lean over and whisper, *"That was just so... erotic today! All that wet fun was great.... And thinking about it is making some of my other underthings a little... wet, as well...."*

Ohhhh, yes. Time to go home for a little fun with his squirtgun. (And his waterpistol, too!)

INGREDIENTS

1 water pistol • 1 Polaroid camera (Borrowed, if necessary)

FOR HIS EYES ONLY.

CONVERSATION PIECE

ROMANCE 101 LESSONS IN LOVE
Gregory J.P. Godek

Shopping

True Story: He wanted to get her a nice outfit for her birthday. She balked, pointing out with four kids-two in college-money was tight. He had to think of a clever way to get past her logic. He invited her out to dinner, and asked her if she would trust him to select her outfit. She agreed. He set-out on the bed: Her raincoat and a pair of shoes! She, being a good sport, went along. He took her to a mall, saying that she had to be dressed *decently* if he was to take her out to dinner. She giggled throughout the whole evening. He loved every minute of it. She tried on several outfits, giggling and confounding salespeople throughout the mall. He bought her an outfit, cut off the tags and she walked out of the store fully dressed. Years later, it's one of their favorite memories.

✂ *You're the bearer. She's the recipient.*

Passion Coupon

WILD CARD

*For the next ten minutes, recipient must
join the bearer — bare! — in his favorite chair.*

Got You By the Malls!

"All I'm asking for is a little respect . . ."
ARETHA FRANKLIN

What do women want?

The great Sigmund Freud himself spent a lot of years pondering that question. My guess is that he didn't get a lot of dates.

Because *it's not that hard to figure out.* Women want surprises. They want gifts. They want to be loved. They want to be seduced. They want a man who really, *really* wants them right back. And if they can get all that while working in a little shopping, well, all the better!

This week, you're going to spring a seduction that combines all these elements. It's a supremely romantic gesture in what might, at first glance, be the least romantic place of all. You're going to the mall!

You'll need an hour or two to prepare your treat. Sneak out Saturday morning and head to the nicest mall in town. Find the managers of a some special stores and let them in on your plan — they'll love to help. When you've made a few strategic purchases and had them gift-wrapped, it's time to return home, get your sweetheart . . . *and head right back to the mall.* Act nonchalant; you want her to think this is just another lazy Saturday afternoon. But as you stroll along, arm in arm, steer your baby to the fragrance counter in one of the department stores. Use your prearranged signal — to let the clerk know it's time to put on the show.

"Well, as a matter of fact, Ma'am, one of these items has already been selected for you. It's a gift from an admirer . . . "

Her jaw will drop when she sees that you've bought her a new perfume . . . and that you obviously planned it a while ago! And if she's thrilled at the thoughtfulness of your gesture, wait until she steps up to the counter at the bookstore — *and finds yet another present waiting for her!* This time it's a book by her favorite author, and again it's clear that you spent quite some time plotting your surprise. This trip to the mall has suddenly become an exciting treasure hunt! She'll be bouncing from store to store, wondering what else you might have cooked up for her.

She won't be disappointed. Because before you leave the center, you have to make a stop at the lingerie store, where another package is waiting to delight her. Something refined and elegant? Or wild and totally hot? Hey, you know what she likes.

(Of course, she also knows what you like. And after a day like this, boy, are you gonna *get it!*)

INGREDIENTS

1 mall • 1 book • 1 bottle of perfume • 1 sexy teddy

(BUDGET TIP: Consider a new CD, bath oil, scented candles, a thoughtful card)

10 | *You Have The Right To Remain Silent*

FOR HER EYES ONLY.

CONVERSATION PIECE

MARS AND VENUS IN THE BEDROOM
John Gray, Ph.D.

Try to get away at least one night once a month. If you can't visit a vacation spot or a neighboring town, go to a local hotel. Sometimes just getting into a different bed can do the trick.

Women particularly often need a change of environment to be aroused. This change frees a woman from feeling responsible for the family and the home. When the environment is beautiful, it awakens her to her inner beauty.

What Men Need

A man is empowered and nurtured most when he feels appreciated, accepted, and trusted. When a woman is aroused, she is actually giving a man megadoses of what he needs most.

When a woman is longing to have sex with a man, she is most open and trusting. In a very dramatic way, she is willing to surrender her defenses and not only reveal her nakedness, but bring him into her body and being as well. By desiring a man in this way, she makes him feel very accepted. Then, when his every touch creates a pleasurable response, he feels greatly appreciated. In the most tangible and physical way possible, he feels and experiences that he is making a difference.

✂ *You're the bearer. She's the recipient.*

You Have the Right to Remain Silent

Like Ben & Jerry's ice cream, or a Mozart symphony, there's nothing quite as beautiful as a simple, classic idea that's perfectly executed. This recipe might be based on the world's oldest seduction technique, but it's still one of the best. (And it involves the second most popular male fantasy, according to my surveys — a woman taking charge. Men go wild over this!)

This week, you're going to kidnap your lover. *But I don't think he's going to press charges!*

Now, the trick to a quick romantic escape like this is to tie up as many loose ends as you can . . . and *forget about the ones you can't*. Children? Arrange for someone to watch them. Household chores? C'mon — are they really more important than grrreat romance with the love of your life? Put 'em off.

Work? Well, here's my solution. *Handcuffs!*

Uh-huh. Handcuffs. Sometimes that's what it takes to drag a man away from his job. Late Friday afternoon, stroll into your mate's office with a set of manacles . . . and a sly grin. (Sneak them in, if you want. But believe me — even in the stuffiest workplace, his reputation will only be improved when his friends see him hauled away by a beautiful woman! These guys may start *cheering*.) They're toy cuffs, of course, backed up by a toy pistol.

"Mister, you're charged with working too hard, and if you know what's good for you, you'll come along peacefully . . . ."

March your smiling prisoner out to the waiting car. *But, honey, I need to straighten my desk . . . .* No you don't! *But what about the kids?* Gone! *Weren't we planning dinner with your folks . . .?* Handled. *B-b-but . . . .* Shut up and kiss me! And get in the car!

Your destination doesn't have to be far, or even fancy. (Check around; most hotels, especially those that cater to business travellers, have deeply discounted weekend packages available.) The magic of this seduction lies in two powerful concepts — *plan for romance*, and *change the scenery*. Together, those ideas can completely free your lover from his troubles. For one special night, all he has to do is relax and become reacquainted with you. You've arranged for everything else — drinks, dinner, maybe even room service. You packed all his necessary gear. You've made everything so easy.

Well, not exactly *easy*. I'll bet you can find *something* that's hard. (Especially after you unpack that new satin teddy!)

INGREDIENTS

Toy handcuffs and gun • 1 hotel room • 2 suitcases • 1 teddy • no excuses!

(BUDGET TIP: Pack your own dinner picnic!)

FOR HER EYES ONLY.

CONVERSATION PIECE

LIGHT HIS FIRE
Ellen Kreidman

When I asked Dee if her husband had ever come home to find a candlelight dinner and his wife waiting in a seductive outfit, she laughed derisively. "Are you kidding? I have four children under the age of twelve and a full-time job!" My reply to her was, "how would you like to have four children under the age of twelve, a full-time job, and NO HUSBAND? Because that's what you'll have if things continue in this way."

With some difficulty, I persuaded Dee to approach some of her neighbors and ask if they would watch her children for one night, if she would do the same for them. They all jumped at the chance, and Dee proceeded to plan a special night for herself and her husband, Ned, without telling him about it.

When he came home on that special night, he almost passed out from shock. Was he in the right house? Who was that gorgeous woman? What was that wonderful aroma? Where was that beautiful music coming from? He was absolutely stunned by the magical evening Dee had planned. They made beautiful love all night long, and Ned, whom Dee had never seen cry, wept in her arms as he told her how much he had missed her being his lover.

Take time to stop and smell the roses. Take time to do something unpredictable. Take time to do something out of the ordinary. Take a baby step toward a giant change in your boring life!

STOP !! Do Not Read The Menu Below To Your Sweetie!!

- Melt 6 ounces semi-sweet chocolate chips together with 1/2 cup heavy cream and 3 tablespoons honey over low heat. Let cool, stirring occasionally. Whip 1 cup heavy cream until soft peaks form gently fold into the cooled chocolate mixture. Pour into 4 dessert cups and chill for at least 2 hours.

- Rinse and dry a pound of uncooked, unpeeled jumbo shrimp. Toss the shrimp with 1 teaspoon freshly ground black pepper and 1 teaspoon minced garlic. Place in a baking dish. Slice 1/2 stick of butter into small pieces and distribute over the shrimp. Bake at 350° F until cooked through, about 15 - 20 minutes.

- Toss 2 cups washed and dried baby greens together with 1 tablespoon chopped thyme and 1 tablespoon extra virgin olive oil. Sprinkle with lemon juice and salt & pepper. Steam the asparagus tips until tender. Serve the shrimp with French bread for dipping.

101 NIGHTS OF GRRREAT ROMANCE

Kiss of the Week

BALLOON KISSES

Cut out small red tissue lips and place them inside an opaque balloon filled with helium (any party goods store could do this for you). Tie the balloon to your love's chair at dinner. Dessert is a shower of kisses delivered by a sharp pin. *

✂ -

Passion Coupon

BITE ME, IT'S A FULL MOON

The bearer of this coupon wishes to be ravished. And to that end, she is wearing a very special outfit. The moment you finish reading this coupon, you must grab your lover and kiss her hard. Fondle her, squeeze her, slide your fingers beneath her skirt. Lay her across your bed and tear the buttons off her blouse. That's right. Rip it open. You do not need to remove it — but don't be afraid to make a mess of it. Now, take her the way they do in romance novels — forcefully, and with passion. And then . . . Go buy her a new outfit!!

Bite Me!

There's a powerful connection between great romance and great food. Preparing it, touching it, smelling it, watching it — these things all stimulate the appetite, which in turn stimulates, well, the rest of us. In fact, in survey after survey, men put a *delicious home-cooked meal* and a *beautiful, seductively-dressed* woman at the top of their lists of things that turn them on.

This week you'll be practicing the ultimate seduction when you offer your mate *both*. On the night of the full moon evoke the powers of Aphrodite, ancient goddess of love, with a five course meal, and an outfit, guaranteed to turn your lover's libido to boil.

Now don't panic! Preparing a spectacular and sensuous dinner is not as hard as you might think, especially when you have a little help from the experts. For advice, I turned to The Cooking Couple, Ellen and Michael Albertson, who suggested a combination of classic aphrodisiacs to set the night *and the two of you! — on fire*. It's one of their favorite recipes, and I've included it on the next page. (But please — you owe it to yourself to get a copy of their wonderful cookbook, *Food As Foreplay*.)

Early in the week, write out a dinner invitation — and then pin it to a pair of your best panties, and hang them from his rear-view mirror. *"Special treat Friday. Starts at seven; don't be late. P.S. — the kids will not be here."*

When he walks in the door Friday night, the stage has already been set. Lights are low; candles are glowing. A glass of wine is waiting for him, along with a tray of brie and stone-ground wheat crackers. And then there's *you*, looking like several of his fantasies rolled into one.

There's no mistaking the message of your outfit. You are *sexy* tonight. Stockings and heels. A little black number reveals occasional flashes of smooth satin underneath. He's salivating, and it's not just because of the incredible aroma in the house.

Ask him to lend a hand after he freshens up. Nothing complicated — he's only there so you can brush up against him as you move about the kitchen. Soon his libido will be rising faster than the steam off the stove. Finally, it's dinner time...

Start by slowly and suggestively nibbling the tip of his . . . Steamed asparagus. (And watch his eyes as he watches you!) The Tossed Baby Greens are sprinkled with Thyme, reputed to make you extra kissable. The sizzling sautéed shrimp is an aphrodisiac dating back to the Romans, who believed it called forth the powers of Aphrodite, born from the ocean's thundering surf.

No erotic dinner is complete without chocolate, of course. Modern science has confirmed it's reputation — it actually contains some of the same chemicals your own body makes when you're falling in love. This particular dessert, Chocolate Honey Mousse, is perfect for applying to lips and other lickable places.

With every dish, serve up a kiss; with every course, open another button. By the time this feast is over, your man's hunger will be quite satisfied. His hunger for food, that is.

His appetite for the *cook* is only getting bigger.

(Time to turn in your Bite Me. It's a Full Moon Coupon!)

INGREDIENTS

1 seductive Aphrodite • 1 aphrodisiac dinner (recipes next page)

1 Passion Coupon • 1 lucky man • 1 full moon

FOR HER EYES ONLY.

CONVERSATION PIECE

MARS AND VENUS IN THE BEDROOM
John Gray, Ph.D.

In the Middle of the Night

A combination of great sex and the quickie is doing it in the middle of the night. It is a wonderful feeling for a man to have his wife wake him up in the middle of the night pressing her warm and wet vagina against his leg as she presses her bare breasts against his chest.

A woman who is feeling in the mood might want to take twenty to thirty minutes touching herself and masturbating herself until she is almost about to have an orgasm, then move over to his side of the bed and climb onto him. He'll find this a particularly wonderful way to wake up.

HOT MONOGAMY
Dr. Patricia Love and Jo Robinson

It is quite common for one person in a love relationship to be more focused on sex and the other person to be more focused on intimacy. All too often the person with the high sex drive resists intimacy, and the person with the ability to be emotionally intimate resists sexuality. Clearly this arrangement doesn't work. It's one of those instances when two halves don't make a whole. In order to experience passion, both individuals have to transcend their limitations. The person with the high sex drive has to become more emotionally available, and the person with the intimacy skills has to become more sexually charged.

✂

Passion Coupon

WILD CARD

(For the next 10 minutes, anything goes!)

Sleepless in the Saddle

We've all heard some women complain that men aren't romantic. You might have felt that way yourself sometime. *But it's not true!*

Men just have a different picture of romance. Different *priorities*, really. Women, for example, usually find that they're more interested in the physical side of a relationship when their emotional needs are being met — but for most men, that order is reversed. When a man feels physically connected to his partner, he is much more open to the romantic and emotional side of a relationship. *A man shows his loving feelings through physical intimacy.* (And if a woman rejects that intimacy, he feels like she's really saying no to his love.)

When a couple really understands that idea, and puts it into practice — *Wow!!* Each of you will get exactly what you want by *giving what your partner wants*. And that's a recipe for a lifetime of romance.

This week's seduction is a perfect example. Without any warning, you're going to overwhelm your lover with desire. You're going to prove to him, in the most obvious and direct way possible, that you find him *totally hot*.

You're going to wake him in the middle of the night and make passionate love to him.

Get up around three in the morning. Quietly slip out of bed, freshen up, and light a candle or two. Put on something really slinky, something daring. *Something that says you mean business.* He'll awaken to the most erotic sight on the planet — a half-dressed woman with passion burning in her eyes. "Hi, sweetie. I couldn't sleep. All night I kept thinking about you. So I wondered if you might be, uh, interested . . ."

Slip back into bed. Slide on top; let him feel the slick fabric barely covering your skin. *"Ooh! I think I have my answer!* Even men are startled by the strength of their response in the middle of the night. *Your* guy will be seventeen again. You have the power to make him feel young, strong, and highly desirable — simply be letting him *see himself through your eyes*.

Now, if you can figure out how to use that power to make him bring you breakfast in bed — *and then do the dishes afterward!* — give me a call. I think we'll have a whole new book on our hands.

INGREDIENTS

1 outfit of sexy lingerie • 2 candles • 1 pre-dawn fantasy

FOR HER EYES *W* ONLY.

CONVERSATION PIECE

LOVE NOTES FOR LOVERS
Larry James

LoveNote. . . Love is something you do. Love is as love does. Never be content with only telling your love partner you love them; promise to show it in expressions of affection. Plan to be spontaneously affectionate.

LoveNote. . .When relationships are fun they are easier to be appreciated. It takes steady work and a specific intention to have them be that way. It takes commitment, open communications and much love for one another. We must plan to have fun together. Playing and having fun together isn't so much what we do. It's how we feel about who we are with *and* what we do.

Passion Coupon

SOMETHING WET AND WILD

*Recipient is to go to the hardware store and purchase a hand-held shower head,
with adjustable pulsating jets. Immediately after installation, both plumber and
plumbee will explore it's various pleasures, at point-blank range.*

Waxing His Hood

"Well I'm not braggin', babe, so don't put me down, but I've got the fastest set of wheels in town...."
THE BEACH BOYS, *Little Deuce Coupe*

What is this thing between men and their cars? If we could get them to lavish as much attention on *us* as they do on their vehicles, there wouldn't be any need for this book! Or much call for divorce lawyers, either.

But let's be honest. That is never going to happen. The bond between man and machine is too great for even the mystical powers of *Grrreat Romance* to break. Psychologists like to say it's because — stay with me here —— a car represents *an extension of his manhood.* Uh huh. Yeah.

Well, whatever it is, don't fight it. *Use it to your advantage.* Make love to his car! And do it just the way he does — get up early Saturday morning, before your sweetie has stirred, and make that baby shine. I always recommend the old-fashioned Laura Corn method — a bucket of suds and a garden hose. This means a lot of effort, but leaves you with an excellent opportunity to engage him in a water-fight. (Whee! Now *that* could be the start of a whole different kind of seduction!) The easier route is to take it to a professional car wash, and get the full luxury treatment. Either way, it should absolutely *sparkle* when it's finished.

Now set the scene for your sweetie. He hears the radio blasting out in the driveway, and comes to investigate. He sees his pride and joy, glistening like new, with a great big red bow stuck to the grille. And lying back on the hood, catching some sun and looking hotter than any model- in the auto magazines, is the woman of his dreams. (I'm talking about you, of course! Oh, and here's a fashion tip: My surveys for *237 Intimate Questions Every Woman Should Ask A Man* turned up a surprising fact:— most men think *snug jeans or cut off's and a t-shirt* is one of the sexiest outfits a woman can wear.)

Hand him a camera; ask him to take some shots. Imagine what he must be thinking — right in front of him are the *two things that turn him on more than any other.* They both look beautiful. And he gets to take pictures of them! The poor guy might be so aroused he'll want to have you right there in the driveway. Which is not a very good idea, of course, what with the neighbors and all. So —— take him for a ride!

(I meant to *breakfast,* silly. Why, what were *you* thinking??)

INGREDIENTS

1 spotless car • 1 sexy, casual outfit • 1 camera • 1 big bow

FOR HIS EYES ONLY.

CONVERSATION PIECE

1001 MORE WAYS TO BE ROMANTIC
Gregory J.P. Godek

Want to keep your marriage (or long-term relationship) fresh and vital? Live as lovers. Remember that that's how you started your relationship. You can recapture the glow, the passion and the excitement. It's largely a mindset, followed by a few active gestures. Live as lovers. Not just as husband and wife, mother and father, worker and housekeeper. First and foremost you are lovers.

In the Romance Class I've observed that in general, young people and others starting new relationships start out as lovers; and, many older couples have rediscovered that they are lovers. It's those intervening years that trip-up so many of us. Live as lovers. Write it down; repeat it to yourself; remind each other; leave messages on each other's answering machines.

HOW TO ROMANCE THE WOMAN YOU LOVE THE WAY *SHE* WANTS YOU TO!
Lucy Sanna with Kathy Miller

Sweet Talk Her

Unless your partner is unusual, she probably will not become sexually aroused from conversations about sports, your job, her job, the children, the pets, the neighbors, your bad back, the things that need repair, the dirty dishes in the sink, the dust under the stairs, the relatives...

Instead, use "sweet talk."

Sweet-talk subjects include anything sensual: music, art, literature, (especially erotic or sensual literature), food and wine, nature, colors, fabrics, sex. Most importantly, sweet talk is about your partner.

Use a soft, low voice. Use passionate words that tell her that you want her. Keep the focus on her. Tell her wonderful things about her body– the way it looks, the way it smells, the way it reacts to your touch. Tell her how you want to make love to her.

Whisper words that make her feel that you are enjoying every moment with her.

Passion Coupon

SOMETHING TASTY

This coupon entitles bearer to _be_ breakfast in bed.

X Marks the Spot

Need to pull off a really cool date on a tight budget? Here's one that's loaded with drama, high expectations, fun and romance, and best of all— it costs practically nothing!

The anticipation begins when your sweetheart goes out to the car one morning and finds a large envelope taped to the steering wheel. The inscription reads, *"Study this. Geography quiz tonight at six."* In it is a map of your city, with intriguing marks all over. Dozens of places are circled, but the only clues to what they might be are the street addresses written out next to them.

Hmm... a puzzle! Well, one of the addresses is obvious— it's your house. And over here, that one has to be your favorite movie theater... and this one is the pizza parlor you go to all the time....

Why, it's a map of your relationship! She'll have a ball figuring out all the places where you two have shared your favorite moments... the park where you walk the dog, the restaurant where they know you by name, the comedy club where you laughed yourselves silly. (If you've ever made whoopee anywhere in town besides your home, be sure to draw a great big star around the location, in bright red ink!)

As evening approaches, ask her if she's ready for her test. Each spot she identifies on the map is another opportunity to reminisce about your best times together. With one fond memory following another like this, the Romance Quotient will definitely be on the rise! She might miss a few— and that's your chance to remind her about some of your history together.

But there's *one* spot on the map she just won't be able to figure out at all. Save this one for last, and when she finally admits that she hasn't got a clue...

"Well, I guess we'll just have to go look at it! C'mon, get your shoes on; I'll meet you in the car...."

Here's where your imagination gets put to the test. You have to come up with a romantic place in your town you've *never been before*. It could be free — a coffeehouse reading by a favorite author, or a concert in the park. Whatever it is, it'll certainly be the focus of your *newest* romantic memory. And also the site of your toughest challenge of the night -

Re-folding the map!

INGREDIENTS

1 map • 1 envelope • 1 marker • 1 new adventure

*(COOL TIP FOR SINGLE GUYS: If you're in a new relationship, there won't be many places you've been together. So present a map of all the really cool places you're **going** to take her in the future! Hey, how many guys show that much commitment and thought to a new girlfriend? She'll be totally blown away.)*

FOR HER EYES ONLY.

CONVERSATION PIECE

BORN FOR LOVE
Leo Buscaglia

Love Can Only Be Understood in Action

It never occurred to my Mama to define love. She would have laughed at the idea. Everything she did was a kind of loving act. She gave love in our home a tangible feeling. Her love for her children and husband was plainly evident. She was forever looking at us fondly, hugging us (over our false protestations), or sharing in our laughter or tears. She never saw my Papa as a saint, but she treated him as a very likely candidate. You could feel her high level of spiritual love; her every act, thought and deed was an affirmation of the presence God.

Love, for Mama, was not something she thought or talked about. It was something she lived in action. She showed us, as Mother Teresa has, that love is found in sweeping a floor, cleaning a sink, caring for someone ill, or offering a comforting embrace.

Mama, without trying, taught us the greatest, most enduring lesson of our lives; that love is far more than a feeling. It is something to be lived and acted upon, day in and day out.

✂   *You fill in the blank. He follows your wishes.*

Passion Coupon

SOMETHING HOT AND SWEET

Entitles bearer to 10 minutes of nonstop

_____

_____

followed by ten minutes of creative cuddling.

A Little Jingle in His Bells

"I saw Mommy kissing Santa Clause, Underneath the Mistletoe last night...."

"So... have you been a good little boy, or a bad little boy? Santa says bad boys get lumps of coal in their stockings. And good boys? They get bad girls in stockings!"

Now there's an intriguing note to hide in your sweetie's shirt pocket during the holidays! And it's a perfect example of the *essence of romance*— small gestures meant to be constant reminders of your affection. Ignore these sweet touches, and you'll find it easy to take your relationship for granted.

But practice them— show consideration, perform kind acts, *flirt* regularly with the love of your life— and you'll discover that, no matter how close you are now, *it is possible to build an even deeper bond.* True intimacy doesn't come without trust, or time.

Also, kisses. LOTS of kisses, and that's why December is my favorite month. There's mistletoe everywhere! Or there will be after you finish this week's seduction. You'll want to buy a bunch of it, because you and your lover will be acting out an old Corn family tradition— the Twelve Kisses of Christmas.

It's not complicated. The only rule is the one you already know— every time you find your love underneath mistletoe, you kiss him! The advantage to doing it my way is that you'll pick twelve places to hang the mistletoe, and that means twelve opportunities every single day to plant one on your baby's lips. Stick some of it in obvious places, like right over the front door so you can smooch as soon as he walks in. Tape a sprig to the ceiling above the refrigerator— that oughta be a prime target!

His favorite chair in front of the TV . . . in front of the bathroom mirror . . . his workbench out in the garage . . . Get creative! And plan some ambushes— the hall closet, where you'll grab him and pull him in . . . a tree along the route of your evening stroll . . . Your shower!

And in the spirit of the season, it's only appropriate to offer him a present. You don't have to make him hold out until Christmas, though. There's just too much fun waiting inside! His special love-gift contains yet another sprig of mistletoe— pinned to the front of a silky new pair of boxers.

(Now *that* oughta put a little jingle in his bells! *And to all a gooooooood night....*)

INGREDIENTS

12 sprigs of mistletoe • 1 pair of sexy shorts

16 | *A Senseless Act of Beauty*

FOR HIS EYES ONLY.

CONVERSATION PIECE

CHICKEN SOUP FOR THE SOUL
Jack Canfield and Mark v. Hansen

"PRACTICE RANDOM KINDNESS and SENSELESS ACTS OF BEAUTY", It's an underground slogan that's spreading across the nation.

It's a crisp winter day in San Francisco. A woman in a red Honda, Christmas presents piled high in the back, drives up to the Bay Bridge toll booth. "I'm paying for myself, and for the six cars behind me," she says with a smile, handing over seven commuter tickets. One after another, the next six drivers arrive at the toll booth, dollars in hand, only to be told, "Some lady up ahead already paid your fare. Have a nice day."

The woman in the Honda, it turned out, had read something on an index card taped to a friend's refrigerator: "Practice random kindness and senseless acts of beauty." The phrase seemed to leap out at her, and she copied it down.

They say you can't smile without cheering yourself up a little — likewise, you can't commit a random kindness without feeling as if your own troubles have been lightened if only because the world has become a slightly better place.

And you can't be a recipient without feeling a shock, a pleasant jolt. If you were one of those rush hour drivers who found your bridge fare paid, who knows what you might have been inspired to do for someone else later? Wave someone on in the intersection? Smile at a tired clerk? Or something larger, greater? Like all revolutions, guerrilla goodness begins slowly, with a single act. Let it be yours.

THE GIFT

Bennet Cerf relates this touching story about a bus that was bumping along a back road in the South.

In one seat a wispy old man sat holding a bunch of fresh flowers. Across the aisle was a young girl whose eyes came back again and again to the man's flowers. The time came for the old man to get off. Impulsively he thrust the flowers into the girl's lap. "I can see you love the flowers," he explained, "and I think my wife would like for you to have them. I'll tell her I gave them to you." The girl accepted the flowers, then watched the old man get off the bus and walk through the gate of a small cemetery.

✄ *You fill in the blank. He follows your wishes.*

Passion Coupon

SWEET AND SENSUOUS

Recipient will spend ten minutes simply holding the bearer,

and then ten more minutes of

_____

_____

A Senseless Act of Beauty

"Practice random acts of kindness and senseless acts of beauty."

Wow. What a powerful sentiment. I first saw it, believe it or not, on a *bumper sticker*. Now I don't usually pay much attention to stickers, but this little gem jumped out at me. Right away I realized that this is one of the essential elements of great romance. It's the perfect antidote to boredom in a relationship. And done on a regular basis, it just makes everything a little *better* — your love, your life, even your neighborhood.

Of course, a great idea doesn't do any good unless you *use* it! So this week you're going to brighten some lives, enlighten your mate, and learn an incredible lesson in long-term love.

And all it takes is flowers.

Start by taking your sweetie out to go people-watching. You know what I mean — just plop yourself down on a bench at a mall or park and talk about the bodies passing by. Have some fun with it! Pick out the couples who look alike; try to decide who's happy, and why. Me, I can't think of a better way to get you both thinking about your relationship than by observing *other* people's relationships.

Now grab your sweetie by the hand. *"Come on; there's something I want to do. It's a secret! You'll see . . . ."* Run to a flower shop for a dozen roses, and keep the mystery going until you pull up in front of a retirement home. Try to get there just before the dinner hour, when a lot of these folks will be relaxing in the game rooms. Just walk up and say hello — and then hand over a rose.

They'll be so *happy* to see you. You know, most of these senior citizens don't get much company — and that's a real travesty. There's so much history and experience there. Each resident holds a lifetime of wisdom, and most are *thrilled* to share it.

So talk to them. Remember, these were once young people just like you. And a lot of them have relationships that've lasted the better part of a century. So ask — *"My sweetie and I would really like to make this romance last forever. Can you give us any advice?"* Boy, were we startled by some of the answers! We got some wonderful insights about how to keep passion alive. *And it was such a rewarding experience.* Soul-stirring. As we moved around the room, handing over flower after flower, we got a real sense of ourselves, maturing and growing together. There was so much love and warmth in the room that I found myself getting goosebumps and misty-eyed. You, too, will have a hard time leaving. What started as a senseless act of beauty took on a deeper, more profound meaning after all.

Later, treat yourselves to dinner. After a special day like this, you'll have plenty to talk about! And even though the dinner table might have looked a little prettier if you had kept a few of the roses, I think you'll both enjoy their *absence* even more.

After all, no flowers in the world are going to be more appreciated . . . than the ones you just gave away.

INGREDIENTS

1 dozen roses • 1 retirement home • 1 happy crowd

(Cool Budget Tip: Balloons are a great alternative!)

FOR HER EYES ONLY.

CONVERSATION PIECE

LIGHT HIS FIRE
Ellen Kreidman

Planning a surprise for your mate is one very direct way to show that you really care and to create a memory at the same time. The one receiving the surprise only gets to enjoy it while it lasts or as a memory, but you'll have the added pleasure of planning and executing the entire event. I always tell women to plan an "Oh, no, I couldn't. That's not me " kind of surprise because when you do something that is completely out of character, your heart beats faster and your adrenaline flows. Do something unpredictable, spontaneous, and different. Don't worry that you're "not the type"-everyone has the ability to be creative and exciting. It just takes time, energy, and the willingness to try something different.

WARNING! STOP!
The quote below is for your eyes only. Please don't read out loud-you'll give away the surprise. Tease him instead!

1001 WAYS TO BE ROMANTIC
Gregory J.P. Godek

Many men would consider this the *Ultimate Gift: A "Fantasy Photo"* of you. You can get a sensual, provocative and stunning "Fantasy Portrait" made of yourself by contacting a photographer who specializes in the growing art form often called "Boudoir Photographer." Many of these photographers are women with a talent for making their subjects feel comfortable, and then bringing out the subtle, sexy side of your personality, and capturing it on film. "Lingerie" portraits seem to be the most popular, followed by "Fantasy Outfit" shots and nude photography.

✂ *You fill in the blanks. He follows your wishes. You both get to play.*

Passion Coupon

ANYTHING GOES!

Bearer should be left with rosy cheeks and a racing heartbeat after recipient surprises her with

The Best Kept Secret

When does a woman look her *very sexiest?*

This isn't a question about clothes, or makeup, or hair. I'm talking about her face, her eyes, her total look. Under what circumstances would a man, in a single glance, immediately know that he's looking at one hot, sensual, highly sexual woman? I'll save the answer for later, but leave you with a promise — this week, you're going to achieve that look and capture it on film for your lover to admire forever.

The best way to get this extraordinary image, naturally, is to use the services of a professional, someone who specializes in *boudoir photography.* This business is booming in America, and it's no surprise, really — women are often startled to see just how incredibly attractive they can be when a skilled photographer is behind the lens. Other women who've had tasteful boudoir shots tell me the same thing I felt when I did it — *it empowers you.* It gives you a whole new feeling about yourself. It can help to erase years of insecurities! Seeing yourself looking *that good* can deliver a tremendous boost of self-confidence.

The real power of these images, though, is in the effect they have on men. Your guy already *knows* that you're sensual and beautiful, probably even better than you do. But actually seeing the proof of it, on glossy paper and in living color, can absolutely *short-circuit* his little one-track mind!

There's a catch to this plan, however. *You won't be able to pull it off this week.* Don't let your mate down, of course; you'll have to come up with another seduction. In the meantime, you'll need to find a suitable studio — lots of them, by the way, are run by women with a real talent for making their subjects completely comfortable — and make an appointment. But be sure to make it for a weekend. Here's why:

You're going to make love to your mate before your photo session. And in case you hadn't guessed it already, that's the answer to the question at the top of the page. A woman always looks phenomenal — relaxed yet energized, completely calm and completely fulfilled, after a heart-pounding intimate encounter. Her face and body are flush, but her mind is serene; she's got that Mona Lisa smile, like she's hiding the world's biggest secret. Every man in the world can recognize it. It's called an *afterglow* . . . and that's what you're going to preserve in your portrait.

The week of your shoot, tape a note to the bathroom mirror for your sweetie: *"Special treat Saturday morning! Prepare to sleep late."* I'll leave the details up to your own steamy imagination! (Hint: This might be a good opportunity to hand over your Anything Goes Coupon!) Later in the day, your photographer will help you with clothing and makeup and the rest, but believe me — *nothing* can make you look sexier than the memory of your morning passion! It takes an army of artists and airbrushers to help those top-dollar models achieve a look that on you just, ahem, *comes.* Naturally.

And speaking of looks — just wait until you see the expression on your lover's face when you unveil your creation over a romantic dinner . . . and then explain exactly when the picture was taken! Now, every single time he gazes at your portrait, he'll relive that erotic memory.

And, no doubt, ask to *re-create it!!*

INGREDIENTS

1 extra seduction for this week • 1 suggestive photo session

*(NOTE: Please please PLEASE, do not put this off until you lose 10 pounds. **No excuses!** Your man loves you just the way you are. And no matter how you think you look now, you will look positively **awesome** if you follow this recipe.)*

FOR HIS EYES ONLY.

♥

CONVERSATION PIECE

LOVE NOTES FOR LOVERS
Larry James

A kiss has been described as the height of voluptuousness. It has a lovely, luscious and lusty legacy. Kissing is an act of quiet intimacy and often borders on the erotic. It can be brief and cool or lengthy and hot. It can be highly romantic, building to succulent crescendo of emotion and passion or passed off as something that is expected and therefore no big deal. Two pairs of lips are for kissing. It is an essential element for communicating love and affection in your relationship.

1001 WAYS TO BE ROMANTIC
Gregory J.P. Godek

5 minutes devoted to romance = 1 day of harmony

Think of all the times that your failure to do some little thing — like calling to tell her you'll be home late from work, or mailing her birthday card on time — has caused a full day of unhappiness. Consistent attention to your lover will keep your relationship balanced and happy. It doesn't take much! Little gestures go a long way.

✂ *You fill in the blank. She follows your wishes.*

Passion Coupon

ANYTHING GOES!

*The bearer of this coupon is about to stretch out
on the couch, where the recipient will*

_____

for twenty minutes.

Ding Dong Do Me

One essential ingredient in every romance is the *ability to have fun*. A lot of people who complain that their partner "just isn't romantic anymore," actually mean that their mate has forgotten how to relax and have a good time. That's why so many romances fade under the pressures of jobs and kids. That's why so many joyous, loving young couples slowly turn onto stiff, silent, distant housemates. Love-*fossils* instead of lovebirds.

And that's also why I wrote this book! By the time you get through all 101 seductions, you'll have developed a bunch of really good habits that are guaranteed to keep your lover smiling. One of them is to always *make a game out of romance*— a game where everybody wins, and no one has a bad time. Another is to find the romance in games! And that's just what you'll be doing this week.

Ever play "Ring And Run" as a kid? Kind of a silly game, but always good for a laugh, right? And it's always sure to get your victim hot under the collar. Well, here's a little variation on that old game. One that's going to get your target hot— *for you!*

Early one evening, when your sweetheart is busy with something in the house, grab your supplies and slip outside. Right by your front door, lay out a few dozen Hershey's Kisses in the shape of a large heart— but be quiet, and fast! You don't want her to come peeking just yet! In the center of your chocolate heart, place a single red rose, and under it, a note:

Want more kisses? The kind that have zero calories? First you have to find me....

Now use your remaining Hershey's Kisses to mark a trail that leads around a corner, or behind some nearby bushes. Ring the doorbell... and run to your hiding place! You don't think she'll be touched by your effort when she comes to the door? You don't think her heart will flutter when she reads your note? Then you don't understand the importance women attach to romance.

Or chocolate!!!

When she tracks you down, and you shower her with kisses of your own, she— just like those little foil-wrapped treats— will simply melt against your lips.

INGREDIENTS

1 bag of Hershey's Kisses • 1 red rose • 1 elegant note card

19 | *Total Indulgence*

FOR HIS EYES ONLY.

CONVERSATION PIECE

MARS AND VENUS IN THE BEDROOM
John Gray, P.h.D.

Going to Cultural to Events

Grant still remembers when he first recognized the importance of cultural events for creating romance. It was before he started taking charge of these matters. After hinting around for a while about going to the symphony, Theresa went ahead and bought tickets for them to go.

It was a great concert, and afterward when they were driving home, she greatly surprised him. He knew she had liked it, but he didn't realize how much.

She said, "Thanks so much for taking me. It was so good." Then, after a pause, she said, "I'm feeling really wet."

He said, "Wet?"

She nodded. "Yeah."

He got so excited that when they got home and into their own garage, they took off their clothes and did it in the car.

Needless to say, the next morning Grant got up early and called to get season tickets to the symphony.

Why Romance Works

When a man plans a date, handles the tickets, drives the car, and takes care of all the small details, that is romance. When a man takes responsibility to take care of things, it allows a woman to relax and enjoy feeling taken care of. It is like a mini vacation that assists her to come back to her female side.

- -

Passion Coupon

SOMETHING SENSUOUS

*Bearer is entitled to 15 minutes of creative kissing
on the body parts of his choice.*

Starting now!

Total Indulgence

You have forty-nine other incredibly romantic scenarios waiting for you in this book. This week, you might need one of them!

That's because you might not be able to make this *particular* seduction happen right away. You may just have to wing it. Borrow a suggestion from another chapter, or make up a spectacular date of your own. Just remember — *you're not off the hook!* After all, your sweetheart saw you tear this page out, and so she's expecting you to pitch some serious woo.

But while you make some other plan come to life, get to work at your real job. You're going to locate tickets for a major concert or event you know your sweetheart is going to *love*. And not just any old tickets — whatever it takes, you should get the best seats in the house. Front row, if you can; you should be close enough to see the performers sweat. There's something really awe-inspiring about the sights and sounds of a live show, isn't there? That something doesn't always make it to the back of the hall.

Like all great romantic moments, this one starts with a tease. A couple of weeks before the big event, make up a sign that says *"Watch this Space for Exciting News,"* and tape it to the refrigerator door. With a week to go, replace the sign with a great big enlarged photocopy of your tickets . . . but with all the important information blacked out!

Finally, with a few days left before showtime, present your mate with the real tickets, neatly tucked into a pretty card. Let her know that you've taken care of everything — dinner, a babysitter, whatever. Not just because you're a nice guy, and not just because it's terribly romantic. It's because, every so often, she *needs* the royal treatment. She's got a demanding life, too; these days a woman might also have to be a mom, chauffeur, housekeeper, employee, boss, decision-maker, worker.

But when you surprise her with a treat like this, when you take control and plan the entire date, when you *sweep her off her feet* . . . you give her a chance to relax. For one night, she gets to simply be a woman again, cherished and adored by her man.

(And for some *other* night, you've bought yourself a ticket to a whole lot more than a concert! Rock on . . .)

INGREDIENTS

2 primo tickets • 1 backup plan, if there's no show this week

FOR HER EYES ONLY.

$

CONVERSATION PIECE

IN THE MOOD
Doreen Virtue, Ph.D.

"There's something about her making me a dessert that puts me in such a great mood. I guessed it's the combination of all the trouble she went through and eating something that tastes so good. But, I'll tell you, if you give me dessert I turn into an instant pussycat!"

-29-year-old married man.

The link between chocolate and romance dates to the days of courtship, when a lovelorn gentleman caller would offer his intended a heart-shaped box of chocolates. Together, they'd sit in the parlor, gaze into each other's eyes, and feed each other one mouth-watering confection after another.

This scenario is no accident, however, because more research is revealing the powerful aphrodisiac qualities inherent in chocolate. Most people have heard by now that chocolate contains the same chemical that the brain creates when we are feeling the delicious emotions of romantic love and infatuation.

Remember feeling lightheaded, excited, and tingly all over when you first fell in love? Remember how high you felt, how right with the world? (Maybe you're lucky enough to be feeling that way right now!) Those physical sensations we call "Falling in love" have a lot to do with phenylethylamine (pronounced "fen-el-eth-el-a-meen") the chemical your brain secretes when you're deeply, romantically attracted to someone.

Chocolate contains phenylethylamine in the same form as the brain produces. Therefore, when you eat chocolate, you're apt to feel an enveloping sensation of warmth, tingles, and excitement similar to being in love.

✂

Passion Coupon

SOMETHING DELICIOUS

*Bearer is entitled to be the buffet table on which the recipient
will arrange, and then nibble, a small, sensuous feast.*

Starting Now!

Dip It in Chocolate

"If your rendezvous was a picnic on the bed, what foods would be in the basket?"
LAURA CORN, *237 Intimate Questions Every Woman Should Ask a Man*

Boy, did I get some grrreat answers to that question! In preparation for *237 Intimate Questions*, I interviewed thousands of men and women across the country, and in every case their faces lit up when I asked about the picnic in bed.

Clearly, it wasn't just because they were all hungry! Well, some of these guys would've gotten aroused talking about Big Macs, I think, but for most people, this question brought into focus humankind's two most powerful and basic needs.

I'm talking, of course, about strawberries and chocolate. *Ha!* Just kidding there, although those two items showed up on almost everybody's list, including mine. No, if you're looking for serious romance, you can't do better than by combining *food* and *clean sheets*. And that's at the heart of this week's seduction —

Begin with a tease that doesn't give away too much. Early in the week visit a gourmet sweet shop and pick up a couple of chocolate-covered strawberries (or make them yourself!). Put them on a pretty plate and leave them on his dresser with a note underneath — *I have more. Interested? Meet me Saturday afternoon at two. In the bedroom.*

Well, now, there's something that'll keep him occupied the rest of the week! And when the appointed hour rolls around, don't let him in the bedroom until you have the whole scene prepared: One big tray perched on your bed, loaded with bowls of sliced fruit. Try one cup of sweet, sticky, melted milk chocolate, and another that's decadently rich, creamy and dark. Whipped cream, of course, piled high and sprinkled with brown sugar. (Half the fun is thinking about the ingredients!) And then there's the pièce de rèsistance. It's you, wearing the one outfit that's always guaranteed to make men melt — *a great big oversized white dress shirt.* One of his, of course. *And that's all.* Well, not exactly all; as you move about, it becomes clear that there are some very interesting and extremely brief bits of satin and lace under there. But he'll have to wait to see more.

Right now it's time to crack open the bubbly, catch up on all the gossip of the week, and indulge in a little *chocolate foreplay.* And enjoy the first picnic of your life where there are no ants.

(Unless you count the ones in his pants!!) Bon appètit!

INGREDIENTS

2 chocolate-covered strawberries • 1 big spread • 1 big bed

21 | *Light My Candle*

FOR HIS EYES ONLY.

FOR HER EYES ONLY.

CONVERSATION PIECE

IN THE MOOD
Doreen Virtue, Ph.D.

Very few of the women interviewed for this book mentioned mere flowers as a romantic symbol. And no one, male or female, told me that presents put them in a romantic mood.

Many people told me that they liked to be surprised, and that they enjoyed it when their partners put effort and initiative into planning a romantic interlude. The *what* of the romantic evening wasn't that important; it was the *how* that mattered. The romantic setting could be at a restaurant, a five-star hotel, a drive-in theater-or at home. What matters is that some one cared enough to think up an original plan.

Here are some romantic moments that remained in the memories of men and women with whom I spoke:

* He picked me up for our date, held open the car door for me, and there was a single red rose sitting on the passenger seat for me.
* She arrived to pick me up at the airport, wearing nothing but a long coat and a G-string bikini.
* He made dinner reservations at the restaurant where we'd had our first date
* She surprised me with two tickets to the ball game. Then, when we went to the game, she was as much into the game as I was.
* He introduced me to his friends as, "The love of my life."
* She asked me what my favorite meal was, and then the very next night, she prepared it for me.
* She had this great great-smelling oil that she rubbed all over my body. She gave me an all-over body massage that left me feeling relaxed all evening and into the next day.

Some of these romantic gestures cost money, but most are inexpensive or free. The common thread in all these "gifts" of course, is that they convey expressions of love. The gift givers took the time to figure out what would make the other person happy. Then they orchestrated the romantic gesture into a surprise.

Passion Coupon

WILD CARD

(For the next 20 minutes, anything goes!)

Desktop Romance

Lunch with your beau is always nice. A surprise visit is nice, too. Put them together . . .

And you still won't have half as much romance as this sweet seduction will generate! That's because you're throwing in the *one extra element* that elevates love from mundane to sublime, one that I hope you will always try to incorporate into your relationship. It's a sense of *anticipation* — and it's one of the things couples tell me they miss most when it fades.

No wonder. Without surprises, partners start taking each other for granted. So toss a cup of tease into your lunchtime recipe, and you'll have your mate begging for more!

Here, honey, don't forget your lunchbox! Huh?? You've just handed him an ordinary kid's lunchpail, the inexpensive kind you can get at Wal-Mart. Tell him not to open it until *exactly* eleven o'clock. Don't explain; just give him a wink and a kiss and shoo him out the door.

Curiosity turns to wicked delight when he opens the box and finds a slinky teddy and a pair of stockings! Taped inside the lid is a note — *Hang on to these. I'll need them back tonight. Your real lunch will be there in thirty minutes.*

Now, I know it may not be easy to make all this happen. But believe me, even if you have to take a little time off and drive clear across town, it'll be worth it. Picture this — you look incredible when you stroll in at eleven thirty, dressed in your foxy best. Your picnic basket includes everything for an elegant meal . . . nice glasses, china plates and silverware, a tablecloth. Set it up right at his desk. He'll enjoy the meal, of course, and he'll love your sensuous surprise, but his biggest thrill is the chance to *show you off to his colleagues at work.*

I'll bet none of them has ever had a treat like this! Suddenly there's a bit more respect in their eyes, and with that comes a tremendous boost in self-confidence. This little show of yours could have a huge impact on his standing in the office, and when a guy feels good at work . . . he feels *great* at home!

Your big surprise even has one more little surprise waiting to be sprung. It's in the dessert — a piece of cake, but one you've sliced through the middle and then stuck back together with frosting. And hidden in the center, thoroughly wrapped in plastic, is a pair of tickets to a movie or ball game for tonight.

Remember what I said about the power of anticipation? Well, after a spectacular day like this, I think there's something you can anticipate. Dinner.

And the main course is *you!*

INGREDIENTS

1 lunch box • 1 dressy picnic • 2 tickets • lingerie

CONVERSATION PIECE

ROMANCE 101 LESSONS IN LOVE
Gregory J. P. Godek

There is a challenge and an opportunity in every intimate relationship. The challenge is to maintain sexual passion in the face of daily responsibilities and routines that promote boredom. The opportunity is that the security created by your commitment to one another opens the door to deeper intimacy and a new level of self-disclosure that combine to stimulate sexual passion.

THE GUIDE TO GETTING IT ON
Paul Joannides

Sex After Marriage

Studies show that within a year of saying "I do," most couples start saying "I don't want to." A recent study by Call, Sprecher & Schwartz investigated factors that influence levels of sexual activity in marriage. Contrary to what they expected to find, the authors state: . . . Couples who want to make time for sex do, even with the obstacles of schedules, fatigue, and work related emotional complications. The DINS dilemma (double income, no sex) may be a myth.

The authors of this well-designed study about sex in marriage suggest that one reason why sex declines within a year after the wedding is because marriage makes sex legitimate. This might cause it to lose some of its erotic edge.

THE LOVING TOUCH
Dr. Andrew Stanway

There are many advantages to quickie sex. It shows how much you fancy one another on a purely physical basis. Romancing and subtle foreplay are all very well, but there are times when one or both partners need to be shown that they are wanted urgently.

✂ *You're the bearer. She's the recipient. You both get to play.*

Passion Coupon

SOMETHING HOT AND WILD

*Recipient must immediately jump into the shower —
and then immediately jump the bearer!*

Hot Lunch

All of the romances in this book are designed with one objective in mind — *to remind your sweetheart that she's special.* Some focus on her beauty, others make her feel cherished. Many are just sweet acts of love and kindness. And a few are extravagant productions whose only purpose is to give you some *grrreat* memories to share and some outrageous tales to tell. But this one?

This one is pure, erotic, elemental pleasure. *Sex.*

It's the deepest form of intimacy, after all. It's also the most fun two people can have! So this week, you're going to blow her mind with one incredibly intense climax. You're going to make her, quite literally, *hotter than she's ever been in her life.*

Your date starts innocently enough. Early in the week, present your mate with a small wrapped gift, and ask her if she can get away for a long lunch on, say, Thursday. Yes? Good — but she can't open the present until she's at work Thursday morning, *and she must remember to bring it to lunch!*

She'll be bouncing with curiosity, of course, but if she's a good girl she won't open her package until the appointed day. And when she does she'll discover . . . *a bottle of sunscreen??!* Uh-huh! Now, don't give her a clue about it. Just show up at her office — you'll be a smash hit with all the women she works with when you walk in with a bouquet of flowers! — and whisk her off to lunch. But not a word about the sunscreen! She'll be ready to explode by dessert. (Which you'll pass up, by the way. *"Oh, I'll have dessert, but I'm getting mine on the way back . . . ."*)

Your return trip takes an unusual turn when you make an unexpected stop — at a tanning salon. *"Oh, I have a little surprise for you. Come on in!"* Rent a booth and lead her back. Once the door's locked, give her a big kiss and ask for the lotion. Help her out of her clothes and into the tanning bed.

The bed itself is a sensuous experience. She nude, but nearly helpless — the sun goggles are almost as good as a blindfold. The warmth relaxes her body, but she feels a risqué rush from the knowledge that there are other people just outside the door. She's stretched out bare before the man she loves, but it seems so much *naughtier* in a semi-public place, in the middle of a work day. She's slick from the lotion, she's glistening from the heat, and suddenly *ohmigod there's your face between her thighs, and your tongue tracing her most sensitive parts!!*

This is strictly for her, this oral treat. Let her set the pace, pressing against your lips and gliding along your tongue, as the heat from the bed and the heat from your mouth combine to lift her to a fast, intense, one-of-a-kind and completely mind blowing orgasm.

And let *her* try to explain how she came back from lunch with such a healthy glow!!

INGREDIENTS

1 tanning salon • 1 bouquet • 1 bottle of sunscreen

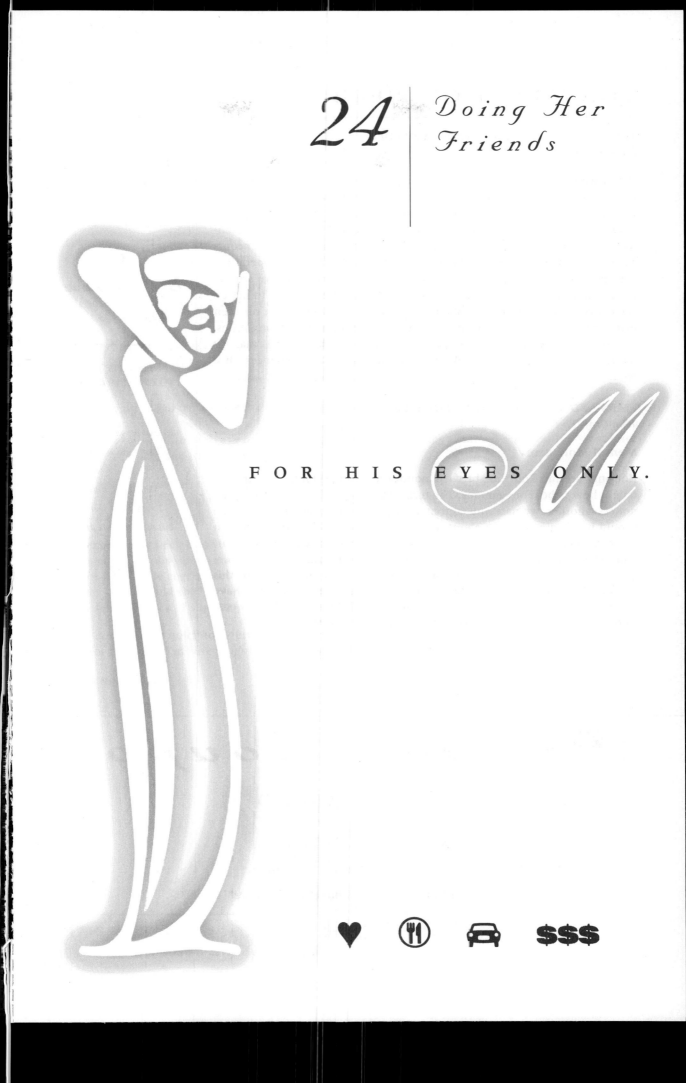

FOR HIS EYES ONLY.

FOR HIS EYES ONLY.

CONVERSATION PIECE

CREATING LOVE
John Bradshaw

Spirituality celebrates life and is in awe of higher powers. Some call the Higher Power God. Whatever we call the Higher Power, we believe that there is something or someone greater than ourselves. We are thankful for our life and feel like praising the Higher Power.

Spirituality leads us to service and solitude. We care for our fellows and take action to show it. We have a love for ourselves. We care for our own life. We love others as an expansion of our own life. We understand that by giving we receive. We grasp that by lighting others' candles, we do not lose our own light. The more candles one lights, the more enlightened the world becomes.

Soulfulness leads us to the realization that spirituality is our human destiny. To be fully human is to be fully spiritual. We are spiritual by nature. We are not material beings trying to become spiritual. We are spiritual beings on a human journey. Soul sees the depth of spirituality in everything and in everyone.

1001 WAYS TO BE ROMANTIC (NEW & EXPANDED)
Gregory J.P. Godek

Great relationships need to be both **deep** *and* **wide. Deep** qualities include intimacy, security and trust. **Wide** qualities include variety, spontaneity and flexibility. {Which do *you* need to work on?}

101 NIGHTS
OF GRRREAT
ROMANCE

*Kiss
of the
Week*

THE
NECKLACE
KISS

*Deposit sweet kisses
that circle your
love's neck.
Hint 1: Concentrate
your kisses along the
back of the neck.
Hint 2: If the first
necklace went well,
try a second.*

Passion Coupon

WILD CARD

*Bearer is entitled to 1 Get Away Quickie,
to take place anywhere except inside the house!*

Somewhere In Time

"When you wish upon a star, makes no difference who you are, Anything you heart desires will come to you..."
PERPETUALLY CHEERFUL CARTOON BUG JIMINY CRICKET

Love is in the stars this week!

There's a reason poets and lovers throughout the centuries have rhapsodized about the magic of the night sky. Those eternal, majestic lights seem to have a special hold over us. All by themselves, stars are just flat-out *romantic*. They hypnotize us. They inspire us. Chicks dig 'em.

But ever since the first light bulb gave our great-grandparents the ability to stay up past sunset, it seems we've been convinced we have to be doing something productive in the evening. So blame Thomas Edison if we don't do enough old-fashioned star-gazing these days. A genius, maybe, but a romantic he was not! (It took somebody else — somebody with seduction in mind, I think! — in order to come up with the light bulb *dimmer*.)

You, on the other hand, are the current King of Romance, with an experts appreciation of the classics. Start this week's seduction with a special phone call to your sweetie — *I see stars when I look into your eyes. I'd like to share the experience this Friday, after dinner . . . .*

That's all! Let her wonder what mysteries you've got planned. When Friday rolls around (and you've helped her clean up the dishes!), ask her to take a stroll with you. (Live in a big, well-lit city? You may need to take a ride out to the country, but the view and her smile will be worth every minute and every mile.) Pick a spot where you can throw out a blanket, lie back, and stare at the heavens overhead. If you can find it, make a wish on Venus, named for the Goddess of Love. Point out the North Star — it's always there, timeless and unchanging, and pretty good inspiration for lovers! A good star map will help you make sense of the riot of twinkling lights (and also prepare you for your big finale!)

Chilly? Be sure to bring along a comforter, or an extra blanket. And I'm sure I don't need to remind you about the many advantages of *body heat!*

Take your time. Unwind. Talk — and most especially, *listen*. Let her tell you what's on her mind. And then reach into your pocket and pull out her gift —

A star. Uh-huh, a certificate for an actual star, named after her through the International Star Registry. You may not be able to see it, but your papers will tell you where it is. Make a wish on it, and seal it with a kiss.

The heavens may be as constant and unchanging as your love. (But I'll bet you know how to make the *earth* move!!)

INGREDIENTS

1 blanket • 1 personalized star (currently $45 through the International Star Registry 1-800-282-3333)

(BUDGET TIP: Pick any familiar star and create your own certificate!)

26 | *Call Me Sentimental*

FOR HER EYES ONLY.

CONVERSATION PIECE

ROMANCE 101 LESSONS IN LOVE
Gregory J.P. Godek

Homework: Defining "Love"

- Fill-in the blank: Love is _____."
  (More than one answer *is* allowed.)

- List 5 characteristics of love.

- Fill-in the blank: "Love is *not* _____."

- How is love defined by your parents, family and friends? How is love defined in our culture? What definitions do you agree and disagree with?

What is love? I don't mean that *philosophically*. I mean it practically. What is love to you? What *behaviors* make you feel cared-for and loved? What gives you pleasure? What could your partner do—*specifically*- to make you feel more loved?

- Love isn't *love* until it's acted-upon.

THE LOVERS' BEDSIDE COMPANION
Gregory J.P. Godek

Because romantic moments are charged with emotion they create positive memories that last a lifetime

The past is home to fond memories. The past is a vast and rich reservoir of experiences and learnings for us to draw from. Tapping into your past together can be a powerful romantic resource. If you honor your past, you can use it to help you appreciate the present and build a more fulfilling future.

Have you created any romantic memories recently?

101 NIGHTS
OF GRRREAT
ROMANCE

*Kiss
of the
Week*

KISS & TELL
KISS

*After kissing
your love today,
say he is a great
kisser and tell why.*

✂ *You fill in the blanks. He follows the coupon. You both get to play.*

Passion Coupon

SOMETHING SENSUOUS

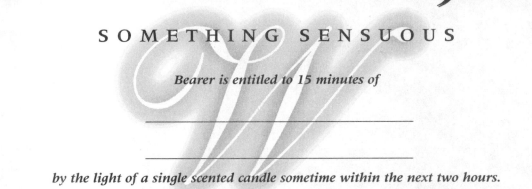

Bearer is entitled to 15 minutes of

_____

_____

by the light of a single scented candle sometime within the next two hours.

Call Me Sentimental

Truly great romance is about creating *moments*. Whether it's a gigantic, flashy production number or a tiny, sweet gesture, all romantic events have at their core a special moment that captures the feeling of love and caring that you share.

This week you're going to create one that's deeply intimate, and like all such profoundly romantic scenes, this one should be enacted near open flame. So gather up all the candles you can find. And then go buy some more. If you've got a fireplace, this is the perfect occasion to light it. And throughout the week —

Start stealing some of your lover's stuff!

Not just any old stuff, of course. What you're looking for is four or five objects around the house that have special significance to your relationship. Things that you associate with him; things that bring to mind important memories or illustrate some of his best features. Just pick out one a day, and when he's not looking, *sneak it out and gift-wrap it*. Make it beautiful. And then place it on your hearth or some other prominent spot.

If he asks, just tell him it's for *Show and Tell* this Friday night. One by one the presents accumulate, until he's got a pretty pile of them stirring his curiosity every time he walks by. Finally, when your evening arrives, make your living room beautiful — firelight and candles, cushions on the floor. Soft music and wine help set the mood. Let him start opening his gifts, while you explain the significance of each.

Well, that's my very favorite tie. You wore it on our first date and I've always loved it. Every time I see it I remember the butterflies I got the first time I laid eyes on you. Oh, your penny jar! Well, for some reason, it always makes me think of my dad, and I love that responsible side of you that puts money away for important things. It makes me trust you — I always feel like you have a plan for our future.

Your screwdriver, well, it's sort of the same thing. I kid you about your home improvement projects, but the truth is I love the way you take care of things. You take care of me. And this is the bracelet you got me for no reason at all two years ago; boy, what a perfect surprise that was . . . .

And so it goes. Tell a good story relating each item to one of his positive qualities and the guy will absolutely glow. Most important of all, *let him know that he makes you happy*. After all, that's the one and only job that means anything to him. This evening, you're going to convince him that he's a complete success at it. And the few dollars you spend doing it may be the best investment you ever make —

Because tonight he's going to feel like a million bucks!

INGREDIENTS

Lots of candles • Lots of wrapping paper • Lots of special memories

FOR HIS EYES ONLY.

$

CONVERSATION PIECE

BORN FOR LOVE
Leo Buscaliga

Each Day Offers a New Opportunity for Love

We are told that there is nothing new under the sun. I have found this to be a great lie. In fact, each day everything is new under the sun! All things are either in the process of growing or dying, but nothing is remaining the same. Each morning when we awaken we can expect the day to be another boring interruption of our sleep, or we can take it as another opportunity to circulate a few new refreshing ideas. Each day has novelty written all over it if only we will awaken to it.

We are offered opportunities to create anew, to see in a different way, to change a little from the day before. If at the end of a day we are no different from when we started, we should beware. Sameness will surely create boredom and when we are bored, we are certain to be boring. What a waste in our dynamic universe!

101 NIGHTS OF GRRREAT ROMANCE

Kiss of the Week

PHOTO KISS

Stage a photo session and capture a photo of the two of you kissing for posterity. Find a camera with a timer, or go to a photo booth.

✂ *You fill in the blanks. She follows the coupon. You both get to play.*

Passion Coupon

ANYTHING GOES!

The kitchen timer has just been set for 20 minutes. From now until it goes off, she must

_____

_____

and do it well!

You Oughta Be in Pictures

Do you have a pretty nice camera? Can you borrow one? You're going to need it to make this week's gift for your sweetheart. It's a simple present, really, but it's effect is priceless. You're giving her the one thing all women want more than any other — you're going to make her feel cherished.

Get plenty of film . . . at least two rolls . . . and start taking snapshots of your darling early in the day. Now, please, be sensitive about this! Not every woman likes to have her picture taken, especially before she wakes up! If you catch her while her face still looks like the pillow it was laying on, *she may have to kill you*. (And these days, no jury would convict her!) But as she goes through her day, click away, catching her from a variety of angles and in all her moods. Soon she'll forget about the camera following her around, and that's when you'll capture the most special images — unposed, and completely natural.

If she asks, you can tell her it's for a special secret project. If she's still not too keen on the idea of being photographed, fall back on the tactics you first used to get her to go out with you, which, I'm guessing, probably had as much to do with *begging and pleading* as with your natural charm, right? Okay, okay, so whining may not be especially dignified, but I promise, the end result will be worth whatever you have to do to get her to play along.

When it's all over, you're going to give your lover a chance to see just how beautiful she is *through your eyes*. Your gift is a beautifully matted and framed collage consisting of several of the nicest shots, with this note attached:

"I'm giving this to you, but it's really for me. It's a sort of shrine, you see; a place where I can stand and worship the woman I adore, looking all the ways I like her best. I will treasure it always . . . ."

Of course, *she's* the one who will truly treasure this present, not so much because it makes her look great, but because it's so obvious that you think she looks great! (And the next time that flash starts popping, she may be a bit more inclined to relax and play along with your impromptu photo session. *"Hey, big boy — is that a camera in your pocket . . . or are you just glad to see me??)*

INGREDIENTS

1 camera (auto-focus and auto-exposure are a good idea, and with a zoom lens you can be farther away and less intrusive) At least 2 rolls of film. (Takes lots of shots! Professionals know that's the best way to be sure you get a handful of great ones)

1 good eye • 1 beautiful subject • 1 nice frame

FOR HIS EYES ONLY.

CONVERSATION PIECE

DAVE BARRY'S COMPLETE GUIDE TO GUYS
Dave Barry

Probably the fastest-growing sector of the U.S. economy is the sector that conducts surveys asking women what is wrong with men. About every two days you read yet another newspaper article stating that 92.7 percent of American women find men to be pathetically inadequate in some way, What two major areas of male deficiency are revealed by these articles?

- Housework

- Orgasms

Why Men and Women Have Trouble Getting Along

At the risk of generalizing, I would say that the basic problem can be summarized as follows:

WHAT WOMEN WANT: To be loved, to be listened to, to be desired, to be respected, to be needed, to be trusted, and sometimes, just to be held.

WHAT MEN WANT: Tickets for the World Series.

LOVE NOTES FOR LOVERS
Larry James

LoveNote. . . One of the secrets to a healthy love relationship is to never take more than you give.

LoveNote . . . What you take for granted disappears!

LoveNote. . . Remember to flirt with your lover, the way you did when you first met. Toss out those subtle little signals that tell your lover you are still interested; signals that show you remember the real magic that lit the fire in the beginning.

✂ *You fill in the blanks. She follows your wishes.*

Passion Coupon

ANYTHING GOES!

*Recipient has twenty minutes to prepare for a private
fashion show, in which she will wear only*

_____

Draw and Get Lucky

Tolerance is a key to truly *grrreat* romance. No relationship survives long without it. I'm referring, of course, to tolerance of bad habits, and specifically *yours*. Sure, you're charming and clever and she's crazy about you, but face it, you're, well, a guy.

This means you have certain features, apparently built right in to your DNA, that makes you, in a broad and general sense, unfit for modern civilization. Your conviction that dishes simply clean themselves comes to mind. Your inability to see household dirt until there's enough to support *farm animals* is another.

But heck, she loves you, and she'll put up with these minor flaws as long as she knows you're trying. And this week you're going to try *real hard*. Better yet, you're going to let your love teach you which things she most wants you to work on. *Best of all, you only have to do one of them!!*

Find a decorative jar or canister and dress it up a bit. This, you will announce to your sweetie, is for the winning tickets in her Love Lottery. Every day this week she will write out one or two things she wants you to do, and put them in the jar. Saturday, you'll draw one at random and do it.

But every time you do she has to reward you with a kiss! *Positive reinforcement* — it's how we train dogs, too.

The cool thing is that she's basically handing you a *list of ways to make her happy.* Men throughout history would have killed for this knowledge. Keep the list for future reference, in case she gets unhappy and you can't figure out why. (But keep studying this book, and I'll bet you'll never need her list!)

Fix the burned-out light in my car. Oh, that's easy, and good for one kiss. *Come home earlier on Fridays.* Yeah, you have been working too late . . . that'd be a good idea even without a kiss. *Take me to a cabin in the mountains next weekend.* Oh, yeah! Now there's a great idea — and I'll bet there's more than one kiss in store for you up there! *Put your dirty clothes in the laundry hamper. Take me to a movie every single week. Get up earlier and walk the dog. Let's go to Cozumel!*

Could be fun. Might be hard. That's what makes it a lottery! But it's guaranteed to deepen your relationship and give you a better understanding of what your lover wants.

Unless . . . uh-oh . . . oh NO! She wants the remote control!! *Aaaaugh!! No, honey, please . . . . Anything but that! Honey . . . the game's on! . .*

INGREDIENTS

1 decorative jar • 1 open mind • several slips of paper

29 | Pinch Me, I Must Be Dreaming

FOR HER EYES ONLY.

CONVERSATION PIECE

HOT MONOGAMY
Dr. Patricia Love and Jo Robinson

If romance feels so good, why do we have so little of it in our long-term relationships? One of the main reasons is that ongoing romance requires *commitment and conscious effort.* It demands that we think, plan, compromise, change, and mature. It requires that we give up our hope of finding the "perfect partner" and turn our attention to the task of loving and honoring our real life mate. It forces us to transcend our preoccupation with our own needs and desires and view life through the eyes of our partners.

I view romance as an entirely different phenomenon. Romance is the way that you demonstrate your love and respect for your partner on an ongoing basis. Through your words and actions you let your partner know that he or she occupies a central place in your life. Every day we are confronted with examples of "special people" in the form of Hollywood stars, royalty, politicians, and lottery winners. We, too, want our day in the sun. When we're someone's sweetheart, we get to bask in that privileged position. Glen, fifty-eight, describes how he feels when his wife of sixteen years looks at him "in a romantic way": "Cyd has this particular way of looking at me that makes me feel so special. Her mouth has a certain smile that only I get on these occasions. It's not because of anything I did. It's just for who I am. I puff up and feel like a million dollars.

LOVE NOTES FOR LOVERS
Larry James

LoveNote... You never have time to do the things you do not want to do. Remember that the next time you get bogged down in unnecessary activities that keep you from doing what you know must be done to enrich your love partner. You always have time to do the things you want to do. Always. You always have choice. Think about it.

LoveNote... Random acts of thoughtfulness keep the graceful flame of love burning. They often dazzle our lover with their brilliance. They inspire a compassionate, warm, wonderful, and loving way of being together. Our capacity to love in this way ultimately defines who we are.

---

101 NIGHTS
OF GRRREAT
ROMANCE

---

*Kiss
of the
Week*

SHOULDER
MASSAGE
KISS

Open his shirt to expose his shoulders. Massage his left shoulder for a minute — and then kiss it. Rub the tense area between his shoulder blades — and then kiss it. Slowly work your way over to his right shoulder, kneading the tired, sore muscles all the way, and then — you guessed it — shower kisses all over every inch of the highly aroused skin you've been touching. Massage, nibble. Massage, kiss.

Passion Coupon

WILD CARD

*Bearer is entitled to have her wildest dreams
fulfilled for the next 30 minutes!*

Pinch Me, I Must Be Dreaming

Wagons are practical. Carriages are romantic. Heaters are practical. Fireplaces are romantic. What's the difference?

Well, mostly it's a question of intent! And as you go through this book I hope you'll develop the habit of *intentionally* looking at most things from a romantic angle. For instance, a Holiday Inn is an inexpensive way to keep a roof over your head when you're not home. It's practical.

Ahhh . . . but a *Bed and Breakfast* — now that's romantic! Not just because of the breathtaking views and off-the-beaten-path ambience most of them have. *They're designed from the ground up with romance in mind.* The beds are usually of the very highest quality. The rooms typically have fireplaces and jacuzzis. They're cozy — most B & B's only have a handful of rooms, so the proprietors are free to focus attention on their guests.

That's another reason a B & B can be so charming — the owners are professional conversationalists. If you and your mate find yourselves not talking as often as you used to, go hang out with a witty host and several other couples who also have love on their minds. You might be surprised at what your partner has to say!

That's your assignment this week. Book a stay at a Bed and Breakfast, not more than an hour or two from your home. Make it a surprise for your sweetheart — tell him only that he has to pack a bag for an overnight trip. Whether you've picked a rustic spot in the mountains or a rambling old mansion in a historic town, you'll want to explore, so bring casual clothes and comfortable shoes. And naturally, you'll want something, um, *interesting* to wear in the evening!

Oh, and I hope you find the same thing I came across during a recent stay — a journal written by all the room's previous occupants. Each of these couples had come seeking to renew their relationships, and each jotted a paragraph or two about the fun they had and the romance they found. It's a perfect conversation starter for you and your love. And that, ultimately, is why you should make a B & B weekend a fairly frequent treat — it's not the breakfast (which is outstanding), or the bed.

It's the talking. It's the chance to take yourselves out of your usual routine and focus completely on one another. It's — well, okay, who am I kidding?

It *is* the bed!

INGREDIENTS

1 romantic Bed and Breakfast

FOR HER EYES ONLY.

CONVERSATION PIECE

BORN FOR LOVE
Leo Buscaglia

Love Requires Effort

Love never dies a natural death. It dies from neglect and abandonment. It dies of blindness and indifference and of being taken for granted. Things omitted are often more deadly than errors committed.

In the end, love dies of weariness, from not being nurtured. We don't really fall out of love any more than we fall into it. When love dies, one or both partners have neglected it, have failed to replenish and renew it. Like any other living, growing thing, love requires effort to keep it healthy.

LIGHT HIS FIRE
Ellen Kreidman

Since most men aren't accustomed to hearing compliments about their bodies, they don't know what they're missing. Believe me when I tell you that the first time a woman tells him what gorgeous sexy eyes he has, or compliments him on his strong legs, he's gone! Although they are unaware of it, most men are starving for this kind of attention.

Notice Your Man
- Notice his muscular legs
- Notice his masculine chest
- Notice his handsome face
- Notice his gorgeous head of hair
- Notice his sexy eyes
- Notice his beautiful smile
- Notice his broad shoulders
- Notice his large, masculine hands
- Notice his deep voice
- Notice anything that makes him a male

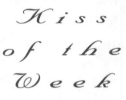
✂ *You fill in the blanks. He follows your wishes. You both get to play.*

Passion Coupon

ANYTHING GOES!

The kitchen timer has just been set for 20 minutes.

From now until it goes off, recipient must

_____

Countdown Fever

Okay, he *knows* you love him. You tell him all the time, right? In countless ways large and small, you always demonstrate how much he is in your thoughts, *right?* Uh, right??

Well, you're sure going to be doing it this week! Chemistry, as powerful as it is, can only blossom into real romance when two people learn to *show their feelings.* Your challenge for this Saturday: Come up with a fresh way to say "I love you" *every hour, on the hour,* all the way around the clock.

This is going to take a little planning, a sense of humor... and a timer! First thing Saturday morning, get up and fix your sweetie that ultimate symbol of indulgence, a *breakfast in bed.* After you set the tray on his lap, crank up your timer.

One luxurious hour later, the buzzer goes off. That's when you reach into your nightstand and pull out your love Coupon, good for *One Free Day With No Chores.* As soon as he's read it, set your timer again... and again, when it goes off in an hour, you're ready with another surprise. This one's simple — just a looooooong, passionate kiss and a whispered *"I love you."*

By now he's catching on — and you can bet he'll be wondering what romantic treats you have in store for him! Like Pavlov's dogs, he'll get excited just waiting for that bell to ring.

Write your names inside a huge heart, scribbled in chalk on the driveway . . . Hand him a carnation tied to his favorite candy bar . . . Put a slow song on the stereo and dance with him, right there in your living room . . . Read him a love poem . . . Sneak up from behind, wrap your arms around him, give his, uhh, soldiers a little five-finger salute, and ask him if he can guess next hour's surprise . . .

Now follow through with a little afternoon delight!! . . . Scrawl a love note on the bathroom mirror in shaving cream . . . Do you have a child's Jack-In-The-Box? Fix it up so that when the clown pops out, it's holding a tiny love letter . . . Snuggle into his lap and ask him to tell you all about his week at work . . . Make him his favorite meal, even if it is something disgusting like fried-baloney-and-ketchup sandwiches (Yikes!) . . .

Twelve hours. Twelve chances to express your affection. Twelve opportunities to *train your man to think of you* every time a buzzer goes off! I say keep that thing handy. You never know when you might need a good buzz....

INGREDIENTS

1 one-hour timer • 12 hours of romance

FOR HIS EYES ONLY.

♥ $

CONVERSATION PIECE

MEN ARE FROM MARS, WOMEN ARE FROM VENUS
John Gray, Ph.D.

Little Things Make A Big Difference

Some men may start out in a relationship doing the little things, but having done them once or twice they stop. Through some mysterious instinctive force, they begin to focus their energies into doing one big thing for their partners. They then neglect to do all the little things that are necessary for a woman to feel fulfilled in the relationship. To fulfill a woman, a man needs to understand what she needs to feel loved and supported.

The way women score points is not just a preference but a true need. Women need many expressions of love in a relationship to feel loved. One or two expressions of love, no matter how important, will not, and cannot, fulfill her.

This can be extremely hard for a man to understand. One way to look at it is to imagine that women have a love tank similar to the gas tank on a car. It needs to be filled over and over again. Doing many little things (and scoring many points) is the secret for filling a woman's love tank. A woman feels loved when her love tank is full. She is able to respond with greater love, trust, acceptance, appreciation, admiration, approval, and encouragement. Lots of little things are needed to top off her tank.

Beat the Clock

Years ago, when Richard Burton bought Elizabeth Taylor a single incredible diamond for more than one million dollars, women around the world swooned. And men around the world all had the very same thought—

Sure, it's easy to be romantic when you're rich...

And so it is. But it's just as easy to be romantic on a budget, and this little game proves it! You'll begin by leaving a long scarf tied to the refrigerator handle, with a note pinned to it. Hang on to this, it says, you'll need it tomorrow night.

Hmmm... already you've got her pretty intrigued. (And maybe a little turned on!) But the scarf is not to tie her up. That's covered in my other book, *101 Nights of GRRREAT SEX!*

No, this time you're just going to blindfold your partner, then tell her to sit still while you run all around the house making as much noise as you can. Stomp on the stairs; slam the closet doors. Then remove her blindfold and explain that you've just hidden fifteen presents, and if she can find all of them in an hour, she gets one more really special gift. The clock's ticking; now *go!*

What fun! And how romantic....

A beautiful card . . . a single rose . . . a small candle in a crystal holder . . . a hand-written coupon good for one long massage . . . another coupon for free kisses . . . a sample vial of perfume (free from most department stores) . . . a scented sachet for her panty drawer . . . a sexy panty! . . . a voucher for a week's worth of dishwashing . . . bubble bath. . . her favorite hard candies . . .

See? It doesn't take a million bucks. Just use your imagination, a little effort, and your knowledge of what she likes. She'll feel like a kid at Christmas as she dashes around digging into all the nooks and crannies of your home, and you can help out with hints— "You're getting warm! You're getting very warm! Now you're getting colder. Cold...."

She may not be able to get 'em all before the hour's up, but if she does, reach into your pocket and whip out one more coupon— *good for absolutely anything you want....*

If you've done your job well, what she'll want is you. Right now! And that's why this is my favorite game— the kind where everybody wins.

INGREDIENTS

15 small gifts • 1 hour • 1 blindfold

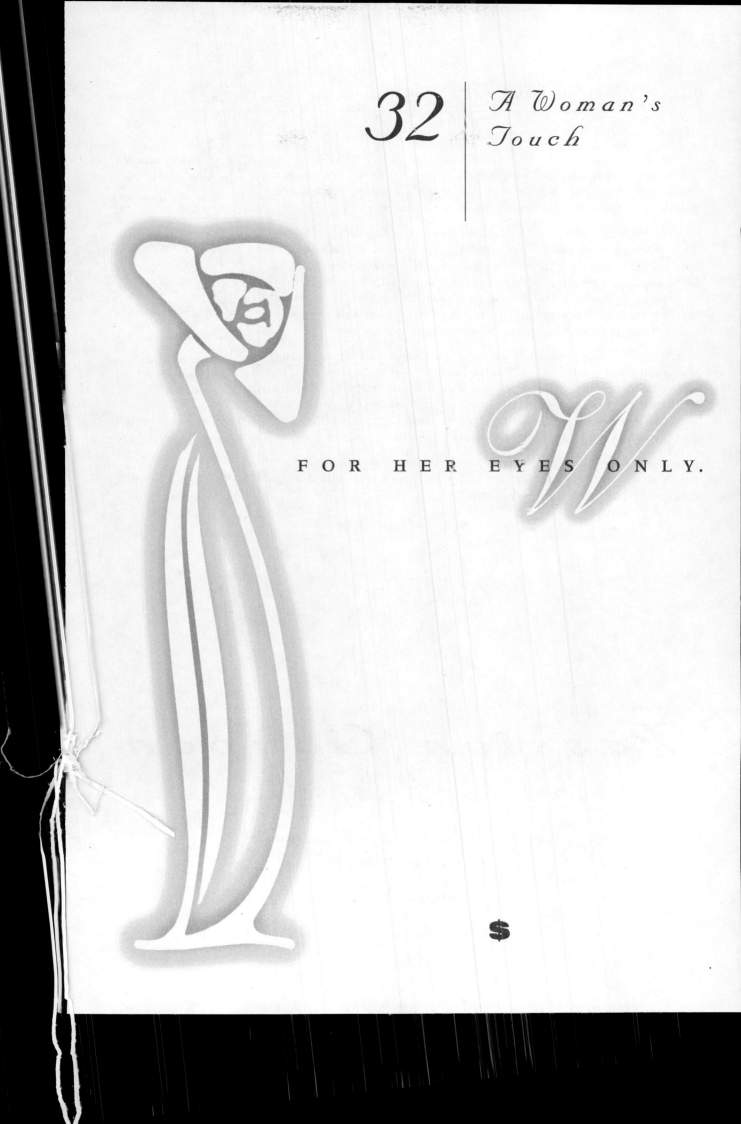

FOR HER EYES ONLY.

CONVERSATION PIECE

ROMANTIC MASSAGE
Anne Kent Rush

We all love to be touched with tenderness. Infants love touch. We hug our friends. We caress our lovers with special warmth. A loving touch is like no other; it exhilarates and renews the giver and the receiver.

You can say some things non-verbally that you can't say verbally. If you want to say I love you with intensity. If you want to affirm that you care for someone's comfort and well being. Even when you want to say I'm sorry. You can express these feelings beyond words with a touch. Central to romance is the desire for the touch of your loved one's hand. More thrilling than anyone's touch, the touch of your lover can change a moment into paradise now, becoming an unforgettable memory.

Simple acts of caring are often the most exciting part of romance. The phone call when it wasn't expected. The touch of your loved one's hand in a crowd of strangers to remind you of a shared private world. The flowers that arrive on your unbirthday. The love letter that comes in the mail from someone you live with. The back rub after a hard day at the office. The foot rub after a long hike. The full massage just to make you feel good.

Romance is these happy surprises that make us forget our everyday worries. Romance is feeling appreciated and pampered. Romance is sharing moments of pleasure with someone you love.

101 NIGHTS
OF GRRREAT
ROMANCE

*Kiss
of the
Week*

**GERMAN
MORNING
KISS**

Write on the bathroom mirror in lipstick or soap the following: "Morgenkuss" (German for "A morning kiss"). When your baffled love asks what is means, define it right on the kisser. ·

Passion Coupon

SOMETHING SENSUOUS

*Bearer is entitled to 15 minutes of creative kissing
on the body parts of her choice.*

Starting now!

A Woman's Touch

Most of the ideas in this book focus on the more cerebral and emotional aspects of romance. Improving communication. Getting in touch with feelings. Thoughtful and considerate gestures.

What the guys generally like to think of as *chick stuff!*

Which is not to say those things aren't important, even to men! Why, without the sweet and soft side of romance, the entire flower industry would collapse overnight. Hallmark stock would plummet. And try to imagine life if *neither* of the sexes wanted to express feelings, and *both* sexes wanted the remote control. What a nightmare! TV would carry football seven days a week.

But while it's vital to have that mental and spiritual connection to your mate, there *is* another facet to love. And if you've been wondering when we were finally going to look at romance from a more, um, *glandular* point of view — well, your wait is over. This week, you're gonna get physical!

Your gift is a massage, and I don't mean some little ol' backrub here. For starters, you're going to have professional instruction in the form of an excellent videotape called *The Lovers Massage*. (Or another called *Erotic Massage*. There's a mail-order number for both below.) In addition, you're going to create the perfect atmosphere for an intimate encounter.

You might need to visit your local adult love boutique to get one essential ingredient — *massage oil*. Early in the week, wrap it up and present it to your lover, but tell him he can't open it until Saturday night. When the evening arrives, set the scene. After dinner, light a few candles, and turn off all the lights. Lay out cushions covered by a sheet, and then invite him to open his gift.

Tonight, you'll explain, is an evening of total indulgence in the pleasures of the flesh. He won't have to do anything . . . except enjoy the treat you have in store. As he stretches out on the floor, pop in the video. This helps set the mood, too — there's great music, and two very attractive people showing you every stroke. You'll see exactly how it's done. All you have to do is follow along.

It's really quite sensual. (And towards the end of the tape, highly erotic! Believe me, you'll both find plenty to enjoy in it.) *Feeling* a massage while *watching* a massage means double the pleasure. Your sweetheart will be overwhelmed by the sensation. The temperature will definitely rise.

And so will *he!*

INGREDIENTS

1 bottle of massage oil • The Lovers Massage by Dr. Michael Perry, (818) 784-9212 or

Erotic Massage by Ray Stubbs, Vol. 1 and 11, (800) 500-KISS

Massage tapes also available at Blockbuster and other video stores:

Massage For Health by Sheri Belafonte, The Classic Art of Sensual Massage, Massage Your Mate,

Japanese Shiatsu, The Swedish Massage

33 | *Je T'aime*

FOR HER EYES ONLY.

CONVERSATION PIECE

CARE OF THE SOUL
Thomas Moore

Children paint every day and love to show their works on walls and refrigerator doors. But as we become adults, we abandon this important soul task of childhood. We assume, I suppose, that children are just learning motor coordination and alphabets. But maybe they are doing something more fundamental: finding forms that reflect what is going on in their souls. When we grow up and begin to think of the art gallery as much more advanced than the refrigerator door, we lose an important ritual of childhood, giving it away to the professional artist. We are then left with mere rational reasons for our lives, feelings of emptiness and confusion, expensive visits to a psychotherapist, and a compulsive attachment to pseudoimages, such as shallow television programs. When our own images no longer have a home, a personal museum, we drown our sense of loss in pale substitutes, trashy novels or formulaic movies.

As the poets and painters of centuries have tried to tell us, art is not about the expression of talent or the making of pretty things. It is about the preservation and containment of soul. It is about arresting life and making it available for contemplation. Art captures the eternal in the everyday, and it is the eternal that feeds soul.

Leonardo da Vinci asks an interesting question in one of his notebooks: "Why does the eye see a thing more clearly in dreams than the imagination when awake?"

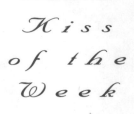
✄   *You fill in the blanks. He follows your wishes.*

Passion Coupon

SOMETHING SWEET AND HOT

Recipient is entitled to 20 minutes of sensuous stroking — 5 minutes of gentle kneading on both shoulders, 5 minutes of soft massage across her face, and 5 minutes

_____

_____.

Je T'aime (I Love You)

> *"Voulez-vous couchez avec moi, c'est soir?"*
> PATTI LABELLE , *Lady Marmalade*

Ah, Français! Eet ees ze language of l'amour. Ze French, zey *know* about romance. Zey eenvented a *trés* bon way to kiss!

And let's face it, if an actor who looks like that chunky Gerard Depardieu can be considered a national sex symbol, then *your* sweetie will feel as hot as Brad Pitt in France! So this week, take him to Paris, the romantic City of Lights.

Kidding! Only kidding! Tell your credit cards to calm down! Actually, you're going to bring *un peu de Français*, that is, the smell of France, to *your* town. Begin by taping an envelope to the steering wheel of your love's car. He'll be thrilled when he opens it and finds this invitation:

Bonjour, mon amour! Comment tellez-vous? Would you like to travel to an exotic land with me this weekend? Oui? Magnifique! The dress code, she is casual. Prepare to depart for the Land of Love this Sunday . . . .

Now, this is *not* an excuse to skip shaving your legs this week. But otherwise, think French as you put together an elegant picnic basket — french bread, a block of brie cheese, a couple of bottles of Evian water, and genuine imported French wine. As you and your cherie amour pack up on Sunday, grab his shoulders, pin him to the wall, and plant one of those great, spectacular, juicy French kisses on him! *Je t'adore*, you'll whisper in his ear, a phrase that sounds suspiciously like "shut the door" in English, so don't be surprised if he's confused.

Be sure to pop some appropriate music into your tape player while you drive. (Try to find one of Celine Dion's new French-language albums; I recommend *D'Eux*.) When you get to a secluded and striking spot, pull out your basket plus the big surprise you had hidden away — a couple of sketch pads and a set of watercolors! Lean back, relax, and attempt to capture the beauty around you. Okay, so you're no Matisse. It doesn't matter! You two will have a ball comparing your various masterpieces, and no matter how bad they are, they'll serve as a reminder of your vacation to Normandy.

Oh, and there is that one last little secret in your basket, guaranteed to get a rise out of him. It's what's commonly known as a French Tickler . . . *for ze stimulation of ze, umm . . . well, mon petit chou, would you lahk a leetle demonstración??? . . .*

LES INGRÉDIENTS

2 watercolor sets • 2 sketch pads or try coloring books! • 1 bottle of French wine

1 basket of French snacks • French music • 1 French Tickler!

FOR HIS EYES ONLY.

$

CONVERSATION PIECE

HOW TO ROMANCE THE WOMAN YOU LOVE THE WAY
SHE WANTS YOU TO!
Lucy Sanna with Kathy Miller

Tell her

Unless you tell her regularly that you love her, no matter how many times you may have said it in the past-unless you tell her now, today, she will think that you don't. So tell her. You have absolutely nothing to lose. She'll love you back. And how bad is that?

Whisper to her– in the kitchen, in the hallway, at a party. Sweet little nothings as "I can't wait to be alone with you," "You keep me wanting you," or just "Oh Sally" (if that's her name, of course...)

Write to her. Yes, even if you live under the same roof. **Write her a love letter. And watch her smile.**

WARNING! STOP!! *Guys, do not read the quote below to your sweetie! For your eyes only.*

1001 WAYS TO BE ROMANTIC
Gregory J.P. Godek

Do you feel silly trying to write a love letter? Do you think it's not cool to express your true/ passionate/insecure feelings? Maybe you'd feel more comfortable if you could only see someone's else's love letter, ? Here are selections from some love letters that may give you encouragement (and perhaps some ideas):

A letter from Napoleon Bonaparte to Josephine De Beauharnais: "I wake filled with thoughts of you. Your portrait and the intoxicating evening which we spent yesterday have left my senses in turmoil. Sweet, incomparable Josephine, what a strange effect you have on my heart!"

A letter from John Keats to Fanny Brawne: "Sweetest Fanny, you fear, some-times, I do not love you so much as you wish? My dear girl I love you ever and ever and without reserve. The more I have known you the more have I lov'd . . . The last of your kisses was ever the sweetest; the last smile the brightest; the last movement the gracefullest . . .

Passion Coupon

WILD CARD

*Bearer is entitled to have his wildest
dreams fulfilled for the next 30 minutes!*

Language of the Heart

Have you ever written a love letter to your mate?

No, not just a note, or a Hallmark card. I mean an honest-to-gosh, deeply felt, expensive-pen-on-elegant-paper *love letter*, the kind your great-grandpa may have written to his sweetie.

Gramps knew the secret, and so did his grandpa before him. *Women are turned on by what they read.* They buy about seventy-five percent of all books published in this country — and one hundred percent of the romance novels! Every woman's fantasy is to have a man feel such passion that he can't contain it, that he is compelled to pour out his deepest feelings for her. A woman can be seduced *by language alone . . .* and this week you get to put that to the test with a suitable-for-framing love letter.

If your own handwriting isn't up to par, find a professional calligrapher to lay the ink on the page. Make sure you purchase the best paper you can find — remember, your goal is to create art. Not so good with words? Then you may want to start with these:

I may not say it enough. But I think it all the time.

Every morning when I see your face, when those beautiful eyes first open and that smile starts to shine, I think about how much <u>I love you</u>. I love to watch you get dressed. (I get so <u>aroused</u> watching you dress!) I love the quick kiss we share before parting, and the gentle hug as we meet again.

I love you when you're not around. Sometimes, in the middle of the day, you cross my mind and I pause, my heart racing, my thoughts turning to our next moment together. I'll see a small gift, and wonder if you'd like to have it; I'll see a big house, and wish that I could get it for you; I'll see some sweet seniors, and pray that you and I will be spending our golden years together.

I love it when you walk in the door. I love to hear you clanging about in the kitchen. (And as much as I love to see you dress, there's nothing like the thrill of watching it all come off!) I love how you make me feel, the thousand ways you show me you're glad to be with me. That trust, that respect, makes a better man out of me. But of all the ways I love you, my sweet, my favorite is when you snuggle close at night, and the warmth of your body and the warmth of your soul seeps into me, nourishing me, sustaining me. Without that — without you — I would be lost. Just . . . lost.

And so even if I don't say it as often as I should, I know that you know it's true . . . . <u>I love you.</u>

Personalize it, of course. Include her name, and make sure you praise all her virtues — her beauty, her sexuality, her wit, her wisdom. Seal your envelope with wax and a ribbon, and then wrap it in a small, elegant box. Here's a cool move! Send it certified mail, so she has to sign for it, and include a note saying she is not to open it until dinner Saturday.

(Then - get ready to live inside a romance novel for a night!!)

INGREDIENTS

elegant stationery • 1 box • 1 dinner • Bonus Points for calligraphy

Major Bonus Points for recording it on tape, in your own voice, with her favorite music in background

FOR HER EYES ONLY.

$

CONVERSATION PIECE

1001 WAYS TO BE ROMANTIC
Gregory J.P. Godek

Romantics live in the moment: "Carpe Diem" - seize the day! Don't put it off until tomorrow! Do something passionate for your lover. Do it now! Do it with feeling!

- Do something unexpected for your lover *today!*

- Do something totally outrageous.

- Do something totally out of character for you.

- Do something sexy. Do something sensitive. Do something creative.

HEART AND SOUL
Daphne Rose Kingma

Cuddle Up

Cuddling is nurturing of the body and the spirit and we all profoundly need it. To be touched and held, to have our skin — that miraculous fine thin silken wrapper of our being — caressed, addressed, remembered, and cherished, is one of the greatest human requirements. It's a leftover need from childhood, when most of us didn't get cuddled enough, didn't get held, or kissed, or lovingly touched, or dearly nestled nearly enough. We wanted to lie up cozy, safe, and sweet near our mother's heart, to be tossed in the air in our father's strong arms, but it didn't happen quite often enough. We didn't get to sit on quite enough laps, didn't get our backs scratched, our tummies rubbed, our feet tickled, our curls brushed, or the backs of our necks kissed nearly enough.

That's why, now, we need to cuddle up, why we long to feel the gigantic embrace that grown-up cuddling is. We want to feel protected and safe. We want to feel nurtured and loved. We want to feel that there's more to life than just our chores and our work. We want to believe that having a body in a world full of bodies isn't a sad, lonely joke. We need to be cuddled so much, in fact, that if we're not, our hearts cry out — with tears, with overeating and alcohol, with the overwatching of television, with anxiety and depression. The truth is that we're all — every one of us — touch-starved human beings.

✂

Passion Coupon

SOMETHING SWEET AND HOT

Recipient will spend ten minutes simply holding the bearer, and then ten more minutes

Something Wild

Brad Pitt and Gwyneth Paltrow do it. John Tesh and Connie Selecca do it, too. So do Arnold and Maria, and Bruce and Demi, and John F. Kennedy Jr. and *his* current flame. It's hip, and hot, and if *you* do it you'll have the time of your life. What is it?

Ballroom dancing!

After years of confinement to professional competitions and PBS specials (public television's *highest-rated specials*, by the way), ballroom dancing is back in a big way. It's popularity is so great that it will be an Olympic event for the first time at the Games in Sidney in the year 2000! People are indulging in it for the pure fun and glamour and romance of it. They've discovered the truth behind the words of the immortal Fred Astaire — *"Something happens when you're dancing."*

Well, of *course* something happens when you can dance like Fred Astaire! The floor clears; women swoon. The magic he created with Ginger Rogers has universal appeal. I'll bet there's not a man anywhere on the planet who hasn't watched *Top Hat* and thought — *whoa, now that's cool!*

But sadly, most guys think that only Fred Astaire can look cool whirling around on a dance floor. That's too bad, because swaying to a samba beat with your lover held close is just about the most intimate thing you can do. Standing up, I mean.

What your guy needs is a little encouragement and a dose of self-confidence. Point out some role models. Robert Duvall has been spotted in a ballroom. Sting, Bon Jovi, Hootie — heck, even *Clint Eastwood* has learned to look smooth on the floor. There's no secret to it; all you need is a *dance lesson*.

There's a ballroom in every town . . . and an *amazing* number of people who are into ballroom dancing, young and old. Find a studio and arrange for a beginner's lesson, but don't tell your sweetheart right away. Instead, sneak his best dress shoes out for a serious shine. Put them back in a shoebox with a ribbon tied around it, and attach a note: *You're gonna make these babies work this week!*

Now, when you pull up in front of the studio, he may be a tad intimidated. That's why you need to be incredibly supportive. Say anything, make any kind of promise, just to get him through the door and onto the floor —

And then watch him come alive. He'll grin when he masters one or two basic steps. He'll positively glow with pride when he can finally steer you gracefully all the way around the floor. After just one or two lessons, believe it or not, he'll be ready for the Big Night — an actual evening of dressing up, and getting down. And what an experience you have waiting for you. For a few shining hours your problems will disappear and romance will fill the air. His dream will finally come true — you *are* Fred and Ginger.

(But if his fantasy is to be *Ginger*, you may have a new problem!)

INGREDIENTS

2 pair of dancing shoes • 1 private or group dancing lesson

*(Cool Tip: Most dance studios offer **one free introductory lesson!** See Yellow Pages*
Cool Choices: Swing, Salsa, Tango, Disco, Nightclub, Ballroom, ...)

FOR HER EYES ONLY.

W

$

CONVERSATION PIECE

MARS AND VENUS IN THE BEDROOM
John Gray, Ph.D.

When Mom said that the way to a man's heart was through his stomach, she was about four inches too high. Sex is the direct line to a man's heart.

"Men Only Want One Thing"

Women commonly think men only want one thing: sex. The truth is, however, that men really want love. A man wants love just as much as a woman, but before he can open his heart and let in his partner's love, sexual arousal is a pre-requisite. Just as a woman needs love to open up to sex, a man needs sex to open up to love.

As a general guideline, a woman needs to be emotionally fulfilled before she can long for sexual contact. A man, however, gets much of his emotional fulfillment during sex.

Women do not understand this about men. The hidden reason a man is so much in a hurry to have sex is that through sex, a man is able to feel again. Throughout the day, a man becomes so focused on his work that he loses touch with his loving feelings. Sex helps him to feel again. Through sex, a man's heart begins to open up. Through sex, a man can give and receive love the most.

When a woman begins to understand this difference, it changes her whole perspective on sex. Instead of a man's desire for sex being something crude and divorced from love, she can begin to see it as his way of eventually finding love. A woman's feelings about a man's preoccupation with sex can dramatically shift when she understands why a man needs sex.

Passion Coupon

WILD CARD

Bearer is entitled to a 20 minute massage on the body parts of her choice.

Starting now!

Twice On Sunday

I'll bet you've gotten better at making love over the years. It only stands to reason that sex, like any other performance, improves with practice. But have you gotten *wilder*, too???

I mean wild like when your were first falling in love. Wild like a couple of kids just discovering sex. *Wild!* Wild enough to stay all day in bed, just relaxing and fooling around. I'll bet you did it that way early in your relationship . . . now, get ready to do it like that again, because that's your assignment this week!

Passionate, untamed, uninhibited indulgence is one of the best gifts you can possibly give your mate. Not just because it's so much fun. *(And it is sooooo much fun!)* But also because, as John Gray points out in his wonderful book, *Venus And Mars In The Bedroom*, it makes a man feel strong and virile. It restores his self-confidence. It makes him feel like he can do anything. *(Hmmm . . . like pick his socks up off the floor?? Well, maybe not everything.)*

Now, spending a whole day in bed takes some planning. You might have to find something for your kids to do. Certainly you'll want to get a big, fat Sunday paper and some easy breakfast-in-bed food, like bagels or danish. And you'll need something to do during, um, *intermission*. Rent a couple of videos for your sweetie, and pick up a few of his favorite magazines.

But keep your preparations a secret. His only clue that he's in for something special is a small, neatly wrapped box left on his nightstand Friday afternoon. The card reads *Do Not Open Until Sunday Morning*. By then he'll be like a kid at Christmas, dying to tear into his gift! Which happens to be underwear — an elegant pair of silk boxer shorts, accompanied by a note:

This is all you get to wear today. We're spending Sunday in bed!

And when you re-appear with a pot of coffee and a tray full of goodies, you'll be wearing sexy new underwear, too. Don't be afraid to mess it up — that's the whole *point* of this exercise! And then, after eating and reading and watching movies and napping and having one great, glorious, perfectly relaxing day with your darling — *mess it up again!* Why do you think I call this "Twice On Sunday??"

(Oh, but I have a warning for you! Nobody believes in the power of romance more than Laura Corn, but even I have to admit that there are some Greater Forces out there. So whatever you do —

Don't schedule this seduction for Super Bowl Sunday!!)

FOR HIS EYES ONLY.

CONVERSATION PIECE

HOT MONOGAMY
Dr. Patricia Love and Jo Robinson

For maximum effect, romance involves an element of surprise. We rarely get surprises as adults. As children we had surprises birthday parties, surprise holiday presents, surprise events orchestrated by adults. Life was full of surprises. Not so in adulthood. This makes it all the more meaningful to be pleasantly surprised-especially by the one who loves you.

LIGHT HER FIRE
Ellen Kreidman

A wonderful place to begin to unravel the mystery, to begin to understand the complexity of a woman's needs, is the following list:

- She wants to be your first priority.
- She wants you to consider her needs above everyone else's.
- She wants you to think that no other woman comes close to being as wonderful for you as she is.
- She wants you to brag about her to your friends and family.
- She wants you to feel proud that she's your mate.
- She wants you to prove your love.
- She wants you to think she's the most beautiful woman alive.
- She wants you to think that who she is and what she does is nothing short of miraculous.
- She wants tender, loving care at that special time every month when her emotions are ruled by her hormones.
- She needs and expects to have daily reminders of how much you love her.

From her point of view, she needs to believe that you are constantly thinking of her and that you are counting the moments until she will be in your arms again. This may be only a fantasy for her, but with a little effort from you, it can come true. You, too, can join the ranks of great lovers, those men who are able to turn a woman's fantasy into reality.

Passion Coupon

WILD CARD

*Bearer is entitled to a 20 minute massage
on the body parts of his choice!*

Starting now!

Driven to Excitement

You only get a *little* credit for doing the things you're *supposed* to do. Dinner on Mother's Day? Been there, done that. A gift on your anniversary? Nice, but expected. Flowers on her birthday? Fella, you're up the creek if you forget about 'em!

Nope, the way to *really* score major points in the game of love is to do nice things for your mate *even when you don't have to*. Big or small, a romantic gesture from right out of the blue is the very best way to convince her that you think she's special.

Well, there *is* one way that's even better. That's if you do something incredibly romantic— *and do it in front of her friends!* They'll flip when you treat her like a queen. If you set them abuzz, you'll set her aglow. Nothing turns a woman on like a man who's knocked himself out for her. And the nice thing about this project is that it can cost *as little or as much you like.*

First, call a few of her best friends and let them in on your plans. Arrange for some behind-the-scenes help, and then, late one afternoon, hand your baby her sunglasses and ask her to go for a ride with you. But there's something very odd about the glasses—

The lenses have been blacked out! They've been taped over, and the opening along the sides of the frame are blocked off! (Black electrical tape works best, I think.) It's part of a big surprise, you'll explain; a magical mystery tour with a secret ending. Now, this will be the longest thirty minute ride of her life! She'll be dying to know what kind of treat you have in store, and of course she'll be trying to figure out just where you're driving her. (If she can tell where she is, you need to drive some more! The object here is to completely confuse her sense of direction.) Finally, pull up to her best friend's house. Lead her carefully through the door. Tell her to pull off her blindfold.

And watch her face as she sees several of her friends— yours, too, if you like— gathered for a small surprise party in her honor. No special event, no reason beyond the fact that you love her. This is just a chance for those close to her to celebrate their friendship and make her feel special for one golden evening. Your guests should be encouraged to make toasts to your love. You should make one, too! *"To the woman who took the dull and tedious thing that was my life and turned it into a party...."*

Of course, the party I'm thinking of here doesn't actually start until all the *other* guests have gone away!

INGREDIENTS

Blacked-out sunglasses • several friends • party snacks

1 friend's house (or your own, if everyone can get there while you're out)

FOR HER EYES ONLY.

CONVERSATION PIECE

LIGHT HIS FIRE
Ellen Kreidman

The Best Kept Secret About Men

A woman who knows that inside every man, no matter how old, how successful, or how powerful, there is a little boy who wants to be loved and to feel as if he's special is a woman who knows a powerful secret. A man wants to know that he matters to you more than anyone else in the world. He wants to matter to you more than your parents, more than your children, more than your friends, and more than your job.

If he could verbalize it a man would say, "Tell me why I make a difference. Tell me why I matter to you. Tell me over and over again. Don't tell me just once. Tell me every day of my life. Keep complimenting me and recognize my strengths. I want to be your knight in shining armor. I want to be your hero."

Men tend to fulfill our expectations of them and to become what they hear continually reinforced. The way to get positive behavior is to reinforce positive behavior constantly. The German author Goethe said: "If you treat a man as he is, he'll stay as he is, but if you treat him as if he were what he ought to be, and he could be, he will become the bigger and better man."

My husband constantly hears what a wonderful husband and father he is, which makes him want to be an even better father and husband.

101 NIGHTS OF GRRREAT ROMANCE

Kiss of the Week

THE SLIIIDE KISS

Start your kiss on the neck, just below your lover's left ear. Slowly sli-i-i-ide along the line of his jaw, and gently nip him on the chin. Now up his right cheek to his temple, then plant several quick pecks along his eyebrows, heading back to his left. Complete your circle of smooches. Glide your lips back down to mouth . . . and trace another tiny circle around his lips!

♥♥

✂ *You fill in the blank. He follows your wishes.*

- -

Passion Coupon

ANYTHING GOES!

Bearer is entitled to a 30-minute hot-oil massage — five minutes on her shoulders, five minutes on her neck, five minutes on her back, five minutes on her bottom, and five minutes on her

_____

_____ .

Pleasure Hunt

Romance is built from a thousand and one little things — kind words, gentle touches, quick kisses before parting. But every so often, just to spice things up, you have to throw in something *big*. Something extravagant. Something like this week's assignment — *one entire day devoted to the pursuit of romance*.

More specifically, your sweetheart is going to devote an entire day to the pursuit of *you!* Of course, he is a guy, which means you're going to have to give him a clue. *Several* clues, in fact, and the first one is hidden in the Saturday morning paper.

"Gee, honey, I checked your horoscope, and it looks like you're going to have a grrreat day! Really, you should see it!" Make sure he does see it, of course, even if you have to leave it right in front of him. He can hardly miss it, though — his "horoscope" is handwritten on a large sheet and taped into the newspaper.

"If you were born on (<u>fill in his birthdate here</u>), this is your lucky day! And if you follow all the instructions you receive, you'll get <u>even luckier</u> tonight!! According to the alignment of the planets, you must be at 4444 East Grant by three."

He'll sputter and laugh, but before he can ask any questions, give him a kiss, and *slip out the door.* You've got some work to do — and he has a mystery to solve! The address leads him to a local spa or massage center, where the staff is waiting to give him one of the greatest luxuries of our age. *An hour of therapeutic massage* will make a new man out of him. When it's over, his masseur hands him an envelope with another clue. *"Revitalized? Good — you're going to need that energy to keep up with me tonight! Next stop, The Wherehouse on River Road. Ask for the manager."*

Waiting at the music store is another envelope, this time containing a twenty-dollar gift certificate and another note. *"Pick out something hot. Something that makes you hot! Bring it to the Hilton by six. I miss you."* Now we're getting somewhere! You've been teasing the poor man all day long. It's finally time to end his suffering and let him get his hands on *you!*

Ah, but is there *enough* time? Well . . . maybe. The first thing you do when he walks in is put his new tape in your boombox. Second, light some candles. Third, explain that you just ordered dinner — *so he better <u>hurry</u>!!* Wow . . . passion is just so much more *intense* when you know you could be interrupted at any moment, isn't it? And if the bellman comes first — with your *meal*, I mean! — it's no problem. With the kind of "room service" you have planned for tonight, there's no charge for seconds. Or thirds. Or fourths. Or . . . .

INGREDIENTS

1 fake horoscope • 1 tape • 1 elegant hotel with room service

1 massage • candles • 1 portable stereo (borrowed, if necessary)

39 | *The Slow Surrender*

FOR HIS EYES *M* ONLY.

CONVERSATION PIECE

LIGHT HER FIRE
Ellen Kreidman

Sex is Giving

Sex for her is kindness, gentleness, devotion, commitment, caring, patience, and compliments. it starts in the morning with whether you said "I love you" before you left. It's telling her how much she means to you. It's going shopping with her. It's helping her with chores. It's noticing that she has a new dress or hairdo. It's asking her to dinner. It's whether you phoned to say you'll be late. It's bringing home a card or a gift. Real romance for a woman is letting her know she's special, appreciated and loved. It's you spending time reaching out to her in a very giving way.

So give her little things-your attention, your caring, your kindness-and you will receive more from her than you ever hoped for. Unlike most men, a woman will not be in the mood to make love just because you are there. She'll be in the mood because you are nice to her.

Emotional Versus Physical

If a woman's emotional needs are not being met, she can't respond to you physically. I also know it's hard for you to respond emotionally to her unless your physical needs have been met. We are so different, and yet someone has to take that first step. If you will learn how a woman wants to be loved, then she'll respond in a way you never dreamed possible.

I polled a group of men and women and asked them, "What is the most pleasurable time you spend to together with the woman or man you love?"

Most of the men responded, "When we were making love."

However, the women responded in a completely different way. Not one said, "Having sex." Their list consisted of hugging, touching, kissing, and talking. Not the sex act. The most powerful knowledge you can have about how to turn a woman on is to know that *a woman is receptive to making love only when her emotional needs have been met.*

✂ *You fill in the blank. She follows your wishes.*

Passion Coupon

ANYTHING GOES!

*The bearer of this coupon is about to stretch
out on the couch, where the recipient will*

_____

for twenty minutes.

The Slow Surrender

So much of romance is about *small gestures*. Tiny acts of consideration. Sweet things you do for your sweetheart, day in and day out; little courtesies performed so often that they become noticeable only when they're absent.

And then there are stunts like this one! Oh, it's a huge one. A home run, a smash hit, a plan so cool, so special, that she'll be telling her friends about it for months to come. (And they'll be telling *their* significant others all about it, with dreamy looks in their eyes. The guys may give you some flak for making them look bad, but don't sweat it— they're just jealous that they didn't think of it first!)

You'll have to gather up some supplies and hide them somewhere handy, ready for the next time she runs out to the grocery store. Now, as soon as she's gone — it's time for you to fly! Everything has to be prepared for that moment when she walks back in the door . . .

The first thing she'll notice is several elegant foil-wrapped chocolates on the floor. (The *second* thing she'll notice is that the kids and the pets are obviously someplace else, or there wouldn't be any chocolates on the floor!) A note on the refrigerator tells her to follow the trail of treats... *"and don't worry about the groceries! I'll put them away."*

One by one, the chocolates lead her to the bathroom, which has been transformed into a luxury spa. Candles cast a flickering glow about the room; soft music drifts through the door. On the counter there's a glass of wine and a book by her favorite author. And there's a little bookmark inside with an inscription.... *You deserve this treatment every day. I love you.*

The tub is steaming and full of bubbles. (No, it's not a coincidence! As soon as you heard her car pull up you ran to the bathroom, started the hot water, and lit the candles.) The room smells like a small slice of heaven, thanks to the bath crystals and skin treatments you'll have laid out. Sadly, though, you won't be able to stay and enjoy the setting yourself — as promised, you've got some work to do in the kitchen.

Or do you? Did she just say she'd like to see how fast you can finish with her pantry?

Or with her panties??!

INGREDIENTS

1 box of very nice, individually-wrapped chocolates (you can't go wrong with Godiva!)

Candles • 1 new book or magazine • Bubbles, oils and salts for the bath

40 | *Ohhh Yes!*

FOR HIS EYES ONLY.

$

CONVERSATION PIECE

BORN FOR LOVE
Leo Buscaglia

Love's Priorities

A successful way to determine how much we truly care for someone is to discern how high their happiness and welfare are on our priority list. This may sound mechanical and arbitrary, but it is a simple and reliable indicator for measuring our love.

We all have personal priorities, whether conscious or not, when it comes to how we apportion our time and the social choices we make. For example, how often do we place our own needs and desires over those of the people we love? Is our lover's desire to attend a dinner party on a specific evening more important than our missing a baseball game, a concert or a night out with the girls or boys? Do we keep loved ones waiting because we consider our time far more valuable than theirs? Just how willing are we to postpone our desires and reorder our priorities for their happiness?

This does not mean that we should be constantly readjusting our lives for the sake of others. It does suggest that we might be more able too judge how much we value our loving relationships by taking an honest look at our behavioral priorities.

HOW TO ROMANCE THE WOMAN YOU LOVE THE WAY
SHE WANTS YOU TO!
Lucy Sanna with Kathy Miller

Pampering Her

Simple pleasures, thoughtfulness. The smallest acts are often the most cherished. It doesn't matter whether you've been married to her for fifty years or you've just met-anything you do to pamper her will certainly be appreciated.

✂ *You fill in the blanks. She follows your wishes.*

Passion Coupon

ANYTHING GOES!

The bearer of this coupon has a sudden craving for

_____

The recipient must immediately satisfy it.

Ohhh Yes!

Romance, at it's very center, is nothing more than an extra effort to *make someone else feel special*. That's why you don't get any points for remembering your anniversary. It's not out of the ordinary; you're *supposed* to do that. Same goes for flowers on her birthday.

Ah, but flowers when there's *no special occasion* — now that's romantic. Writing a note to thank her for being in your life is very romantic. Fixing the john is not. Which is not to say that your toolchest can't *help* you be romantic. For example, building a special shelf so she can display those cute little whachamacallits she collects, that's really romantic.

Even ordinary activities take on romantic meaning when you're doing them just to make your lover happy. Like dinner on Friday night — who wants to cook after an exhausting week of work? Not her! You could fetch a pizza, which is . . . well, nice. You could take her out to a great restaurant, which is nicer, but you have to get dressed up and wait for a table and do all that driving.

What you're going to do *this* week, though, goes beyond nice. It's *seriously* romantic. And here's the really great part — as impressive at it is, it *actually doesn't require all that much work*. (And that's my favorite kind of seduction!)

Friday evening, when you come through the door, scoop your sweetheart up in your arms, give her a good kiss and then tell her to go to the bedroom. (Uh, I mean by herself. Oh, hold your horses; you'll get there eventually!) As soon as she disappears, you go to work. By the time she's freshened up and comes back out, your surprise should be ready.

There, on the patio table, is the *very same meal* she loves so much at your favorite restaurant. Right down to the fresh bread in the little basket and the radicchio salad — the entire feast has been hiding in your car. Include a tablecloth, scented candles, cloth napkins, perhaps a bottle of wine, all set up just the way she'd expect if you went out to eat. But here at Chez D'Amour, there is no crowd, no noise, no wait, and the service is delivered with a *very* personal touch.

Seat her and serve her. Treat her like she's your best customer. After the wine is gone and the candles have burned low, kiss her and tell her to go to the bedroom again. But this time you'll be joining her, since you're about to present the final course of the evening — the specialty of the house, *Triple-Chocolate-Between-The-Sheets-Cake*. With *nuts*.

(Now let's see just what kind of tip you earned!)

INGREDIENTS

*1 take-out meal from her favorite restaurant - The **good** dishes!*

*Patio table, living room table, or some other **unusual** spot to eat*

FOR HIS EYES ONLY.

CONVERSATION PIECE

HOW TO ROMANCE THE WOMAN YOU LOVE THE WAY
SHE WANTS YOU TO!
Lucy Sanna with Kathy Miller

Whisper in her ear. Even the most mundane statements take on romantic connotations if whispered: "Let's adjourn to the living room." "How about chicken for dinner." "You've got sauce on your lip."

Whispering connotes a special, intimate connection. Even "I'll take out the garbage now," when whispered, can sound pretty sexy. And a kiss on the neck, a tongue in the ear, or a slow sweep of your fingers through her hair adds flair to the flirting.

Move toward her with your best flirting smile and eye contact. Hold that gaze just a bit longer than she might expect. Back off quickly, suddenly preoccupied. Then come back slowly, smiling, whispering, touching. Wow! She'll be waiting for more. This can happen all within a few minutes, or it can happen within a few hours — flirt with her when you arrive home, then go change your clothes or start up the barbecue or watch the news and then come back with that great flirting style again.

WARNING! STOP!! *Do not read the quote below out loud. For your eyes only!*

1001 WAYS TO BE ROMANTIC
Greg J.P. Godek

Jim Rickert, "The Songsmith" will write and record original songs for you. (This guy is *really great*.) Tell him the type/style of song you want, the theme, occasion, and specific information you want included-and he'll customize an original melody that your lover is sure to love. He can give you songs that range from a solo singer accompanied by a guitar, to a singer with full orchestration!

Normal turn around time is two weeks. Call him at 617-242-8500 or write to The Creative Works/Songsmith, P.O.Box 484, One Thompson Square, Charlestown, Massachusetts 02129

✂ *You fill in the blanks. She follows your wishes.*

Passion Coupon

ANYTHING GOES!

The bearer of this coupon has just dimmed the lights, drawn the curtains, and turned on the stereo. The recipient will immediately begin to

_____

to the beat of the music.

Off the Charts

Most of what I've learned about romance has come from listeners who called my radio shows and shared their experiences. But it was the *hosts* of those shows who taught me one of the most important lessons. Because of their jobs, those talented deejays are intimately familiar with the *incredible seductive power of the human voice.* What they've told me can be pretty well summarized like this—

Men are seduced by what they see, women by what they hear.

Of course, that's not big news to Hugh Hefner — or Barry White! And it's a fact of romantic life you're going to use to your advantage this week when you *serenade your sweetie.* Uh-huh. You're going to *sing.* And before you say no, I want you to ask yourself one question: *Why do so many rock musicians score with stunningly beautiful women?* The answer is simple. Women love to be sung to! They can become seriously aroused when a man puts his passion into music. Even the *thought* of it is terribly romantic — it's a common theme in romance novels.

And I'm speaking from experience here. To this day I have a vivid, powerful memory of a stroll down Fifth Avenue in New York City with a boy I liked. It was my sixteenth birthday. Suddenly, without a word of warning, my friend dropped to his knee and broke into a song from *The Sound Of Music,* right there on the sidewalk — *"You are sixteen, going on seventeen . . ."* I was floored. And so impressed! I've long since lost touch with that guy, but I will *never* forget that magical moment. He made me feel like the star of my own movie. (And I'll bet he still remembers his *reward!!*)

To do it right, first find the proper setting. A park or garden will add to the impact, and nothing can beat the romantic beauty of an elegant hotel or resort. But even if you simply stand in your own yard and call her to the window, she'll absolutely *melt* when your show begins. As for gear, your best option is to rent a karaoke machine. They're not very expensive, and give you the advantage of a little *reverb* to, uh, "reinforce" your voice. (Hey, it works for Paula Abdul.) At the very least you need a good-sized boom box. And if turns out that you're just truly *awful,* well, take the Milli Vanilli approach. Lipsynch!

When a man loves a woman . . . I've been kissed by a rose . . . Unforgettable, that's what you are . . . I'll make love to you, like you want me to . . . I love you just the way you are . . . .

Hootie? Garth? Elton? *Pavarotti???* Whatever strikes your fancy, or hers. The key to success here is *enthusiasm,* because unless you're as good as Lyle Lovett, it won't be the performance that thrills her — it's the performer. (And Lyle got *Julia Roberts* to marry him! See! This stuff works!)

INGREDIENTS

*1 portable stereo • 1 tape of **grrreat** love songs • 1 full moon (the best time to get crazy!)*

OR 1 karaoke machine. Great sound, hooks into your TV so you can read the lyrics,

rents for about $60. See the Yellow Pages.

(Bonus points if you re-write the songs to include your sweetie!!)

FOR HIS EYES ONLY.

CONVERSATION PIECE

HOW TO ROMANCE THE WOMAN YOU LOVE THE WAY *SHE* WANTS YOU TO!

Lucy Sanna with Kathy Miller

Every woman is an individual. And there is no one formula a man can use to please all women. But there is a romantic attitude that any man can adopt to help decipher the mysteries of his partner's wishes — and fulfill her romantic desires. As Shakespeare once wrote, "They do not love who do not show their love." We call it a "romantic spirit."

From our survey, we learned that every woman needs to feel appreciated, wanted, and loved. Occasionally she even likes to feel indulged, "spoiled," and delighted with surprise. No matter how rewarding her everyday life, no matter how attractive, intelligent, and self-sufficient she is, she still needs caring and attention. Add a little romance to her life — it's such a simple thing if you know how — and watch the relationship evolve from something ordinary into something special.

Keep Her in Your Thoughts

Your partner wants to know that you think of her when you're apart- and that you long to be with her. You can satisfy this need by calling her frequently during the week, at her home or place of work. You can leave little notes for her to find after you've left for the day, for the evening, or on a business trip. You can phone her just before you leave work to let her know that you'll be home soon. If she's not home when you call, she'll enjoy coming home to find the message on her answering machine.

And what's the message?

Tell her over and over again, in a different way each time: "I'm longing to be with you." "I'm looking forward to seeing you." "I can't wait to hold you again."

✂

Passion Coupon

WILD CARD

(For the next 30 minutes, anything goes!)

Hidden Talents

True romantics know that it isn't *just* the thought that counts. In fact, the sweetest surprises are often simple ideas that have been dressed up with only a little bit of extra effort.

Balloons, for instance, are a pretty basic idea, and everybody loves them— hey, just watch the grins spread around the room when a big brightly-colored floating bouquet arrives. Too bad you won't get to be around for the real fun. That starts when your love discovers the second, *secret* part of your gift!

It's not one you can just order over the phone, though. You'll have to plan ahead and enlist the aid of an understanding balloon merchant, who is going to love the whole idea and give you some major points on the Big Romance scale. This trick is completely cool and very romantic; don't be surprised if he begins suggesting it to all his customers!

You start by writing love-notes on small slips of paper— *I still get lost in your eyes . . . You know that spot on the back of your thigh? I can't wait to bite it . . . Thinking of you makes me hot; seeing you makes me wild . . . I love you! . . . I want to kiss you. Everywhere. Especially there*— and then roll them up and tuck them into the balloons before they get inflated. If your budget allows, buy an elegant, small set of earrings (wrap them in plastic to protect the balloon!) and pop them in, too. The *pièce de résistance*, though, is a pair of tickets to a show she wants to see— a movie, a play, a concert, or whatever would appeal to her most. These go inside a special balloon, the only red one in the bunch. On the attached note, you explain that at a certain time she must pop all the balloons, saving that single red one for last.

Now have the bouquet delivered to her workplace. Her friends and colleagues will be thrilled for her, especially when she starts popping the balloons and your gifts fall out! You, sadly, will miss that part of the excitement— because you're waiting for her at the theater where her show is about to start. She won't be able to miss you. You're the only one in the crowd with a red balloon drifting above his head!

(Extra "guy stuff" bonus: One of the benefits of having a source of helium nearby is that you get to greet your date using that squeaky Munchkin voice! Oh, go ahead. Get a lungfull; you know you want to. All the other guys will be so jealous!)

INGREDIENTS

Assortment of love notes • A bunch of balloons • A pair of tickets • A sympathetic balloonist

(BUDGET TIP: Buy a pack of balloons, then stuff them with notes, blow them up yourself, and leave them in her car!)

FOR HIS EYES ONLY.

CONVERSATION PIECE

WHAT YOUR MOTHER COULDN'T TELL YOU AND
YOUR FATHER DIDN'T KNOW
John Gray, Ph.D.

"Judy used to really appreciate the places I would take her," Jim said. "Now it seems no matter where I want to go, she wants to go somewhere else. I don't even want to bother."

Jim doesn't understand that women need variety. Because men are so goal oriented, when they find a restaurant they like, they tend to keep going back. It is a sure thing. Why risk failure by trying something new?

Variety increases a man's chances of failure, while variety lifts a woman out of the boredom of routine. She looks forward to trying new things.

In the beginning, Judy could appreciate his choices in restaurants because they were all new to her. It was fun and exciting to discover his hangouts. But, later on, when his choices became routine, she was ready for a change.

1001 WAYS TO BE ROMANTIC (NEW & EXPANDED)
Gregory J.P. Godek

Dinner Plans

We had plans to go to dinner. Nothing unusual, right? Wrong! I'd gotten ready early, so that while my girlfriend was showering, I . . .

1. Quickly uncovered the fireplace and lit the wood that I pre-stacked.

2. Set-up a folding table in front of the fireplace.

3. Covered the table with a nice tablecloth, and set it with wine, two crystals glasses, a single red rose and one candle.

4. Heated-up the full-course dinner that I prepared before-hand! By the time she had finished showering, putting on her make-up, and getting dressed, I was calmly waiting for her at the dinner table. Her look of surprise was priceless! And the memory we created is timeless.

-J., Washington

Passion Coupon

WILD CARD

M

(For the next 20 minutes, anything goes!)

Do It in Public

"A rose by any other name would smell as sweet...."
WILLIAM SHAKESPEARE, *Romeo & Juliet*

A man can *never* go wrong with flowers. Funny thing about them, though — the very best time to present them is when the girl of your dreams *doesn't expect them*. It's the *surprise* that makes flowers so special, after all. Of course, there are some occasions where you just have to give flowers, and it's not a surprise at all. In that case, you might be afraid that they're unimaginative and way too conventional, but trust me — she'll still find them touching and traditional.

It's all a matter of perspective. Some guys, not you, of course, look at flowers and see an expensive gift that's just going to wither and die. Most women, on the other hand, see a sweet and loving gesture that's just *loaded* with sentiment. And they never have to be exchanged for the right size. Plus, no calories! No wonder women love them.

But *this* is a bouquet that's going to stand out from all the rest. This is the one she'll be telling her girlfriends about for years. If the sight of a delivery boy carrying a bundle of flowers makes her smile with anticipation, then this arrangement is going to make her go completely *weak at the knees*.

This special bouquet is going to spell out her name!

Here's an example: If her name is Carol, you'll use Carnations for C, Anthuriums for A, Roses for R, Orchids for O, and Lilies for L. Consult your florist, and buy as many as you can afford; if she's got a long name, one of each will do. Is her name impossible to spell out this way? Use a pet name, or a bedroom name, or even her initials. Have them delivered to the restaurant before your dinner date, or take them over yourself; either way, make sure the maitre d' will have them on your table when you arrive. After she's oohed and ahhed over them, start with your big tease.

These aren't just any old flowers. They were picked specifically for you, and for a *special* reason. Can you guess what it is?

This is a game that can last all through dinner! From time to time you can help her out by giving her the name of a flower. And eventually, if she still doesn't put it all together, hand her a card with the secret of her hidden name spelled out. She'll flip! She'll probably get the card framed — and it's certain that she'll treasure it for the rest of her life.

By the way, don't be surprised at the dreamy looks you might get from the staff at the florists. They get men in there all the time who are trying to impress the women in their lives, but few who put so much thought into their gifts. Fewer still manage to conjure up so much romantic magic with such a simple idea. "Say It With Flowers," the old advertising slogan used to advise . . .

Well, just wait until you're alone again. I'll bet your sweetheart will find an even better way to say, "Thank you." (After which, I think, you'll be thanking *me*!)

INGREDIENTS

1 full-service florist • 1 restaurant • 1 cool Maitre D

FOR HIS EYES ONLY.

CONVERSATION PIECE

IF . . . (QUESTIONS FOR THE GAME OF LIFE)
Evelyn McFarlane and James Saywell

If is the ultimate book about fantasy. Each of its questions is meant to spark and tantalize the imagination. They are a celebration of the human spirit, which loves to dream and needs to hope, but which can also fear and even grow angry. Our ability to imagine is the remarkable gift we have been given to lead us into joy and aspiration and out of despair or sadness, because common to all of us is the idea that there could be a different world, perhaps a better one.

How many times a day do we say, "if only . . . "? If we could create the perfect life, the perfect city, the perfect home, the perfect job, the perfect mate. We all fantasize, and we all dream. We dream of perfection, money, revenge, glory, change. We fantasize about both good and evil, about winning and losing, about our past and future. Fantasies are what inspire us all; to work, marry, raise families, create, improve our world. It is why we lose ourselves in books, go to movies, watch television, go to the ballgame and on vacation. We dreamed as children and we dream now because without our fantasies we would be lost. We imagine in order to learn, to understand, to strive, to attempt, to predict, to avoid, to correct, to describe, to solve.

This book is also a game. It was born of many dinner parties and gatherings, when just to throw out a provocative question and ask for each person's answer always led to the most surprising and fascinating discussions. Every time, a kind of synergetic and addictive momentum took over as answers led to other related questions, reasons were demanded, disagreements were unleashed, conditions were imposed, other's answers were predicted, and inevitable those involved were startled by the responses, at times even their own. No matter who is present it seems to be irresistible, whether we are at flagging party, on a long car or plane ride, among a group of students, within a family, or alone with someone very close to us. It is infectious and fascinating to watch and take part in.

"Nearness To Nature Keeps The Spirit Sensitive To Impressions Not Commonly Felt, And In Touch With Unseen Powers."

- Ohiyesa

✂

Passion Coupon

WILD CARD

(For the next 20 minutes, anything goes!)

Take Her in the Woods

I admit it. I was wrong.

For years I avoided any attempts to get me to go camping. Oh, I love nature, but eat there? Sleep there? *Voluntarily?!* No way!

Then one day I was kidnapped by my sweetie and taken to the pine country on top of Mt. Lemmon. This turned out to be an incredible experience, *maybe the most memorable night of my life,* and now it's a standard part of my romance repertoire. You can turn your lover on — and turn her on to the Great Outdoors — if you make her evening as unforgettable as mine.

Tease her with a written invitation early in the week. *Overnight trip on Saturday! Extremely casual. One small bag only.* Before the weekend, line up your gear. Sleeping bags with soft pads, backpacks, a lightweight tent. You can rent the whole package at an outdoor store for about forty dollars. There's one more fairly crucial item you'll need to make this really work —

A best friend or another couple. Why? Well, think about the best times you've had in your life. Didn't most of them involve talking the night away with a small group of friends? Everybody has a story. Laughter becomes contagious! Under the right circumstances words and ideas start to flow like water — and these are the *perfect* circumstances.

Camp Romance might only be a few hundred yards from the campground parking lot, but it might as well be a different world. It's a world where your *inner cave-man* can come out — much to the delight of your mate! She'll see you in a whole new light as you gather wood, set the tent, chase the bears away, and generally *protect her* from that slight hint of danger in the woods. No TV, no phone, no kids to distract you; there's nothing but starlight, a roaring fire, and a big adventure ahead. That's when you start with your questions — *If you could spend one whole night alone with anyone in history, whom would you choose? If you could suddenly possess an extraordinary talent in one of the arts, which would you like it to be?*

These questions come from a terrific book called "If..." by Evelyn McFarlane and James Saywell. I also recommend *"The Book Of Questions,"* by Gregory Stock; either of these will trigger hours of discussions. Believe it or not, that simple act of *talking* will help your mate unwind. At the same time, the night air and dark skies (and the occasional animal sounds!) will excite her, while the crackling wood and the twinkling stars conjure romance. It's a powerful — and powerfully *erotic* — combination.

So give her that gift this weekend. Let her get lost in a world of raw nature and fascinating conversation. And later, after the flames have turned to embers, after you've laughed yourselves silly and your friends have crawled off to their tent, if after all that your lover should decide it's time to, well, bare more than just her soul, then I have two words of advice for you —

Mosquito repellent. (And don't ask how I learned about *that!!*)

INGREDIENTS

1 light tent • 1 big fire • 2 sleeping bags • 2 good friends

camping supplies (food and toiletries) • Lots of questions

FOR HER EYES ONLY.

CONVERSATION PIECE

HIDDEN KEYS TO A LOVING LASTING MARRIAGE
Gary Smalley

Develop a Sense of Humor

It seems we all did more laughing in our premarital days.

You probably weren't somber and sad when your husband married you. So, if you want to be his best friend now, you may need to add a little humor to your relationship. No need to buy a clown suit. Just look for ways to tickle his funny bone. Clip those cartoons that strike you as funny and save them for his enjoyment during lighthearted times. Be willing to loosen up and laugh heartily when he tells a good joke. There are countless ways to add humor to your marriage. Be willing to set aside the serious quest for romance at times to enjoy just having fun together as friends.

1001 WAYS TO BE ROMANTIC
Gregory J.P. Godek

Romantics have a good sense of humor.

There's no such thing as a "humorless romantic." While the *foundation* of romance is a serious love, the nature of romance is lighthearted.

- Do you laugh together a lot?

- Do you let your True Self shine through? (Or are you playing a role? Favorite roles include The Responsible Provider, The Good Mother, The Big Shot Executive, The Long-Suffering Spouse. — Loosen up, for crying out loud!)

- Do something ZANY tonight.

✂ *You're the bearer. He's the recipient.*

- -

Passion Coupon

TICKLED PINK

Along with this coupon, the bearer will present you with a __feather__. You will use it to write your most erotic thoughts and sensuous fantasies on her __bare skin__, working your way up one side of her body and down the other.

But in order to turn her __giggles__ into __moans__, you may need to abandon your writing career and concentrate on __oral__ storytelling.

Endorphin Soup

"Love is the answer. But while you're looking for the answer, sex raises some pretty good questions."
WOODY ALLEN

Let's face it — all men think they're funny.

And guess what? Every one of them needs a good audience! In the course of putting together my book, *237 Intimate Questions Every Woman Should Ask A Man*, I asked one thousand men, "What one alluring quality draws you to a woman *and keeps you there?*" Seventy-five percent responded "sense of humor."

So it's not surprising that men buy most of the comedy albums in this country, just like women buy most of the romance books, and for the same reason — it serves a powerful, fundamental need. Men need to laugh — and you need to join 'em.

It's good for the soul, and absolutely indispensable for love. Chemistry and passion might ignite a romance, but it can't last long without the occasional bellylaugh to fuel it! Tonight, you're going to make sure your sweetheart falls asleep with a smile on his face. (And wakes up with one, too!)

Right after dinner, ask him to take you for a ride. Why? Well, you want to get some dessert, annnnd . . . you have a surprise for him, which you hand over in the car. It's an elegantly wrapped tape of his favorite comedian, either the newest release or an old classic he hasn't heard in a long while. His big smile will broaden into a full grin as he hears that familiar cadence, the comic rhythms, those *grrreat* punchlines.

He'll be roaring with laughter by the time you get to the ice cream store, where you gallantly suggest he keep listening in the car while you run in for a couple of scoops. Then — if he can still drive while splitting his sides! — it's off to a scenic spot for the end of the tape . . . and the beginning of the *real* fun!

No, I don't mean "that" kind of fun! I mean you should take advantage of all that good humor and start reminiscing about the wildest, funniest moments *you two have shared in the past*. All that laughter helps to cement a relationship, building a bond that can last through decades. It can also leave you both happily simmering in a kind of *endorphin soup* — those naturally -produced brain chemicals that make us feel so great.

Those are also the same chemicals we get when we're feeling highly *aroused*. Hmm . . . maybe it's time for "that" kind of fun, after all! (Well, I did say he'd fall asleep with a smile on his face!)

INGREDIENTS

1 funny tape — like Jeff Foxworthy's "You Know You're A Redneck If . . ."

(Try classics by Bill Cosby and George Carlin or recent releases by Adam Sandler, Weird Al Yankovich,

or (the very R-rated!) Andrew Dice Clay)

2 sweet desserts • 2 hours of love and laughter

FOR HER EYES ONLY.

CONVERSATION PIECE

LIGHT HIS FIRE
Ellen Kreidman

Behind Every Man Hides a Little Boy

Most men can't resist that vulnerable little girl who resides inside all of us, but I have found that most women who were only children or the oldest in the family have a tough time being playful or using baby talk. If you heard messages such as, "Grow up and act your age," or "Stop being a baby," it may be hard for that little girl to come out. You have to experiment with what feels comfortable for you.

Practice looking adorable in front of a mirror. I know that what I've said here feels foreign to some of you, but I'm convinced that men will react favorably to you if you can make them laugh or appeal to the little boy in them. Remember, inside every man, no matter how strong, how successful, or how powerful he is, is a little boy just waiting for permission to come out and play.

BORN FOR LOVE
Leo Buscaglia

Love is Enriched by Play

Too often we relegate playing to childhood. Adult games are usually structured, have defined rules and are played to win. Children play just for the joy of it.

Lovers who play together know the value of fun, laughter and surprise. When they indulge in make-believe, they find it opens areas of imagination that are often lost in the routine that most relationships fall into. Creative play can help us relate to people and things in new ways. Play encourages lighthearted cooperation and gets us away from the competitiveness of our society. There is no striving to win when we are playing for fun.

The sole purpose of play is to have fun, to be diverted and amused, to frolic meaninglessly and gleefully for a while, outside the realm of the intellect. When we do this, we discover a positive side of ourselves that celebrates life without analysis, one of the basic components of love.

✂ *You fill in the blanks. He follows your wishes.*

---

101 NIGHTS
OF GRRREAT
ROMANCE

*Kiss
of the
Week*

MANNEQUIN
KISS

*The next time
you see your love, strike
a pose and don't blink.
Have a sign around your
neck that reads:
"Breathe life into me by
permorming mouth-to-
mouth resuscitation."* *

Passion Coupon

ANYTHING GOES!

Recipient must immediately take off his

_____

use it to blindfold the bearer, lead her to the location of his choice and

_____

Winner Takes All

Once you get past all the flowers and candy — well, you should never *completely* get past all the flowers and candy! — Grrreat Romance comes down to this: Two people who can completely lower their guard around each other. Trust. Relax. Get silly. It's essential, really, for true intimacy. But it's not always easy.

Practice makes perfect, though . . . so this week you're going to practice at *having fun!* And you're going to start by challenging your mate to a contest. Leave a note under his wallet —

Feel like a little wager? We've both been way too busy lately, so I hereby declare a moratorium on all seriousness this Sunday afternoon. Nothing but fun for us, starting at three o'clock. And I'll bet I can come up with more fun than you! Here's the deal — you think of three games we can play, and I'll come up with three. Winner gets one looooong massage!

What man can resist an offer like that?! Expect to be challenged to guy things, like Risk, where he gets to take over the world . . . or wrestling, where he gets to take over *you!* Let him go first. And when his game is over —

Okay, now it's __my__ turn. Pull out a squirt gun, and blast away! Get off several shots, then toss him another water pistol, and *run!!* Tough to go fast when you're laughing so hard, but you're not going far — just to the backyard, where you've got a bucket already filled with water balloons! Grab 'em quick and *one two* three four five let him have it! At this point you can yell, "Game's over! I win, I win!" but frankly, I don't think you should expect him to stop until you're both good and soaked. No problem here — drying each other off is half the fun!

He'll have a game, then you'll have a game — a pillow fight. (You win, of course. Hey, it's your game, your rules!) Play his final game, then propose yours. Remember Jacks? The really big ones are my favorite! Or Jumprope. Or any game you were really good at when your were little, so you're certain to win. (And in the case of Jumprope, you'll win by default! I never met a guy who could do Double-Dutch without hurting himself. It's a girl thing.) The score is now tied at 3 and 3, which means you need a tie-breaker. Maybe a slightly more adult form of recreation this time.

Say, strip poker. A contest where there *are* no losers! *Let the games begin . . . .*

INGREDIENTS

1 free afternoon • several water balloons • 2 squirt guns

2 pillows • 2 free spirits • 1 deck of cards

47 | Come and Get It

FOR HER EYES ONLY.

$

CONVERSATION PIECE

WHAT YOUR MOTHER COULDN'T TELL YOU AND
YOUR FATHER DIDN'T KNOW
John Gray, Ph.D.

Romance for the Woman, Sex for the Man

Just as romance is important to a woman, sexual gratification is important to a man. He needs constant reassurance that his partner likes sex with him. Sexual rejection is traumatic to a man's sense of self.

HOW CAN WE LIGHT A FIRE WHEN THE KIDS ARE DRIVING US CRAZY?
Ellen Kreidman

In Defense of Men

Imagine what it must be like to live with a woman who is paying her dues or fulfilling an obligation. A man wants to feel loved, not endured. A woman who sacrifices her body for her partner's sake is not doing anyone a favor, including herself. A man whose mate simply tolerates sex feels diminished, both sexually and emotionally, and is likely to seek a sexually satisfying relationship elsewhere. We've all heard stories about successful politicians, actors, ministers, and other highly visible men who risk everything they've worked so hard to achieve for the sake of an extramarital affair. It doesn't matter who he is or how successful he is, every man wants to feel wanted and needed physically.

A woman who enjoys sex and is an active partner doubles the pleasure a man derives from sex. The men in my classes have told me that they really want their mate to be responsive: "Although it's great to have a woman be concerned about my pleasure and satisfaction," said Taylor, "I want the same for her. The ultimate turn-on for me is when she's turned on. I love knowing she wants me sexually."

✂ *You fill in the blanks. He follows your wishes.*

Passion Coupon

ANYTHING GOES!

*The bearer of this coupon is entitled to have her neck rubbed,
her back massaged, and her*

_____

for ten minutes.

Come and Get It

You say you want more than mushy love notes and flowers? You're ready to move past love songs and sweet phone calls? *You want some serious heat applied to your romance??* Well, you came to the right page! There's enough steam in this week's seduction to fog up mirrors all over your house.

Here's a universal truth — nothing in the world arouses a man like the thought of a woman who really, *really* wants him. It's every man's fantasy to have a woman take charge in the bedroom. (Or the bath!) And just seconds after he walks into the house this Friday, he's going to know *you mean business.*

His first clue is a long string tied to the doorknob. (Actually, I prefer something bolder, like that shiny metallic ribbon you can get at party stores. While you're there, grab some colorful invitations for your notes.) The string stretches over to one of the dining room chairs, and your first note is on the seat. *"Hey! We're home alone! And there's a big treat at the other end. But first sit down and take off your shoes."*

The string continues to the refrigerator handle, and there's another note taped to the door. *"Vital supplies inside. Bring the paper bag and the champagne. Oh, and take off your shirt and tie."* Wow! What's racing faster now — his imagination, or his pulse? The bag in the fridge, as you've no doubt guessed, contains his favorite hors d'oeuvres plus a couple of glasses.

Your mighty bare-chested hunter continues up the testosterone trail to the hall closet and your next clue. *"It's dark up ahead! Bring these candles. It's hot, too, so lose the pants. I did."*

Wheeee! This just keeps getting better and better! Next stop — the bedroom door, where your sign simply says "You're getting closer!" From the doorknob your string is draped across the room to the bathroom. *"Candles lit? Then come on in."*

You knew he was coming, of course. You could hear him as he entered the house, so you had plenty of time to warm up the shower and step inside — *still wearing your sexiest lingerie.* Clad in something exotic from Victoria's Secret, water streaming over the slinky fabric, lit only by the flickering candlelight, you must look to him like something out of a dream. Invite him over. Tell him you'll scrub his back if he'll wash your hair. Even if he's still got something on, grab him. *Pull him in.*

*And show him just how wet you **really** are!*

INGREDIENTS

1 very long string • notes • champagne and snacks • candles

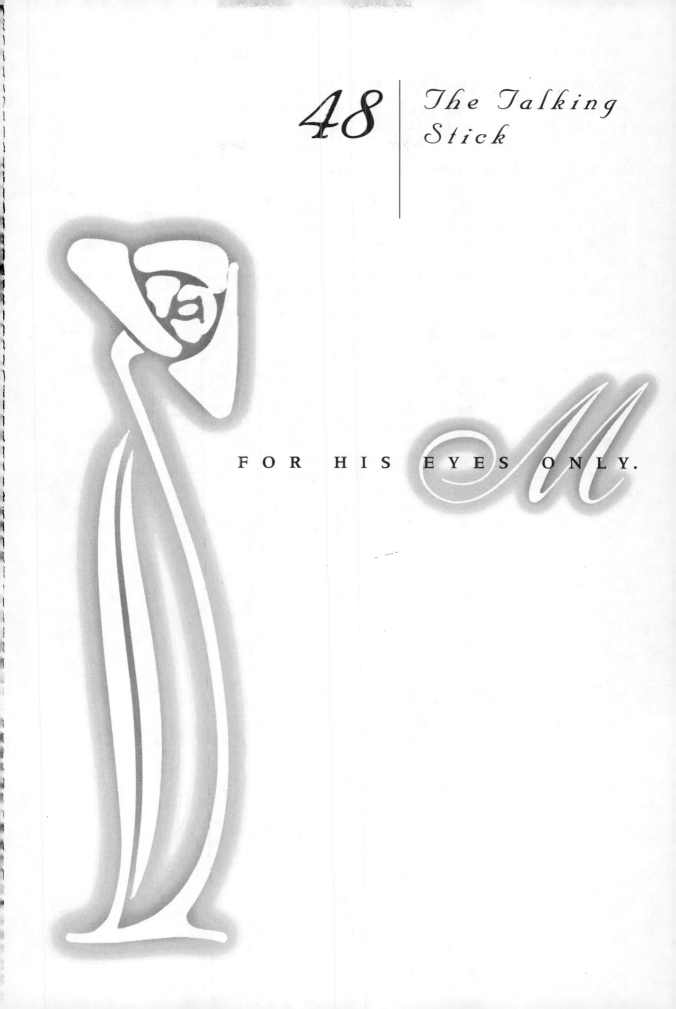

FOR HIS EYES ONLY.

CONVERSATION PIECE

MEN ARE FROM MARS, WOMEN ARE FROM VENUS
John Gray, Ph.D.

Mr. Fix-it and the Home-Improvement Committee

The most frequently expressed complaint women have about men is that men don't listen. Either a man completely ignores her when she speaks to him, or he listens for a few beats, assesses what is bothering her, and then proudly puts on his Mr. Fix-It cap and offers her a solution to make her feel better. He is confused when she doesn't appreciate this gesture of love. No matter how many times she tells him that he's not listening, he doesn't get it and keeps doing the same thing. She wants empathy, but he thinks she wants solutions.

Finding Relief Through Talking

When a woman is stressed she instinctively feels a need to talk about her feelings and all the possible problems that are associated with her feelings. When she begins talking she does not prioritize the significance of any problem. If she is upset, then she is upset about it all, big and small. She is not immediately concerned with finding solutions to her problems but rather seeks relief by expressing herself and being understood. By randomly talking about her problems she becomes less upset. When women talk about problems, men usually resist. A man assumes she is talking with him about her problems because she is holding him responsible. The more problems, the more he feels blamed. He does not realize that she is talking to feel better. A man doesn't know that she will appreciate it if he just listens.

✂ *You fill in the blanks. She follows your wishes. You both get to play.*

- -

Passion Coupon

ANYTHING GOES!

Bearer is entitled to be surprised with

_____

_____

sometime within the next two hours.

The Talking Stick

Every time I tell an audience about this technique, the men in the crowd light up. Not because it leads to better communication with your sweetheart (which it does), or because it's one of the cheapest plans in the whole book. (Which it is. And there are some guys who love it for that reason alone!)

Nope— men go for this one because they get to use their tools! And how often does your Black & Decker help you further the cause of Grrreat Romance?

The basic idea comes from Native American culture. Some Indian tribes keep the peace by using a Talking Stick— a simple stick with some powerful symbolism attached. *Whoever holds the stick gets to do the talking.* Each person gets a chance to explain what's on his mind without anyone else jumping in and derailing his train of thought. (Think Congress might get a lot more done if they used a Talking Stick to keep their arguments on track? Maybe. But I suspect those guys would probably just end up using the stick to whack each other on the head!)

So how's this stick going to help your relationship? Simple. *It has the power to stop small disagreements from becoming major romance-killing grudge-nursing battles.* Big problems can start from small resentments, and that's where your Talking Stick works it's magic.

"Sweetheart, I know there are times when you don't think I'm really listening to you. And sometimes, I have to admit, you're right. But I truly love you, and even when I'm distracted by other things, I always want you to be my first priority. That's why I made this for you...."

Make a big presentation out of it— nice wrapping, romantic setting, the works. *"If there's ever a time when you don't think I'm paying attention... if you think I'm ignoring something important... just pick up this Talking Stick. I promise to listen, without interruption, while you tell me what's up. This represents my commitment that I will always put you first, no matter what...."*

Wow! She'll flip. In one smooth move you've corrected the biggest single gripe women have about men. Aretha said it best— R-E-S-P-E-C-T. And you're getting what all guys want most, too...

A woman who'll grab your Stick when she wants your attention!

INGREDIENTS

1 wood pole, a foot or two long, whittled and sanded

Feathers, rope, leather, paint — anything you want to dress it up

FOR HER EYES ONLY.

CONVERSATION PIECE

BORN FOR LOVE
Leo Buscaglia

Creating Your Own Paradise

What do we expect from life and love, anyway? Few of us will discover a new continent, take a rocket to Jupiter, change history or become legendary lovers. Our life and our death will be of no momentous import, except to ourselves and those we love. Our days will probably be spent in eating, sleeping, working, washing clothes, growing gardens, raising children, getting sick and getting well, making new friends and saying goodbye told ones, dressing in the morning and undressing at night, brushing our teeth and combing our hair, saving money and spending it, crying, laughing, getting angry and frustrated, finding moments of happiness and beauty, growing up, growing fat, growing old, dying.

If there is to be any poetry, romance, or meaning, it will be because we created it ourselves. The life and love we create is the life and love we live.

THE LOVERS' BEDSIDE COMPANION
Gregory J.P. Godek

Intimacy is not required 24 hours a day. But it is required some time during every 24-hour period.

Don't let a day go by without connecting in a meaningful way with your partner. Hundreds of "little" gestures over time are more important than one "grand gesture" that attempts to make up for lost time.

Some small building blocks of intimacy: Private jokes, pet names, silly messages, "your song," love letters, love notes, bear hugs, gentle kisses.

101 NIGHTS
OF GRRREAT
ROMANCE

*Kiss
of the
Week*

ICE CREAM
KISS

Share an ice cream cone with simultaneous licking. If tongue movements and closeness don't get the two of you kissing, think of how cold and wonderful your love's mouth tastes and go in for a smooch.

Passion Coupon

WILD CARD

(For the next 15 minutes, anything goes!)

Joy Ride

*"It won't be a stylish marriage, I can't afford a carriage.
But you'll look sweet upon the seat of a bicycle built for two!"*

Half of romance is just planning. The other half, which may be loosely defined as chemistry, can only carry a relationship so far before it needs a little assistance. Fortunately, keeping the heat turned up in a romance is easy compared to, say, teaching your mate to get his dirty clothes *all the way to the laundry hamper.* And you don't have to wait thirty or forty years for it to work!

Nope, no waiting for results — there's an immediate benefit each and every time you plan a romantic activity. First, your partner is reminded that you're always thinking of him, and what man doesn't love to be the focus of a woman's attention? Second, you develop the really great habit of actually *doing things together,* as opposed to endless hours wearing out batteries in your remote control. Third, *you have fun!* And from time to time, you may also be lucky enough to discover new passions to share.

This Sunday, you'll indulge in an activity he's guaranteed to love. Make reservations for one of those fabulous all-you-can-eat brunches at a nice hotel or resort. *Mmm-mm!* Waffles and maple syrup, bacon and eggs, steaming bowls of oatmeal with brown sugar and cream. Mountains of fresh sliced fruit. Pancakes! That tiny, squeaky little voice you hear? That's your *will power,* saying goodbye to your diet!

But don't worry if you give in to temptation at a feast like this. You're about to work all those calories off, and in a most romantic fashion. Climb in the car and give your sweetie directions — but keep your destination a secret! You're heading to a local bike shop, where you're going to rent a *bicycle built for two.*

Get ready to have a blast! New technology has made bikes more fun than ever, and a lot more comfortable. All those gears means it's less work, and of course for you it's practically no work at all. *Hey, he ate more at breakfast; he should do most of the pumping!* Go for a leisurely ride around a local park. Stop and smell the roses. If you can do it safely, ride back to your own neighborhood — the view from a bike is different, more relaxed and pleasant, than anything seen from a car.

Your body will appreciate a little honest sweat and some heavy breathing. Uhh, I mean because of the bike ride. But that applies to certain *other* circumstances, too, and if those appeal to you, you've got a perfect opening to suggest them.

"Honey, my legs are so tired, and my heinie is really sore."

"Come kiss it and make it better!"

INGREDIENTS

1 grrreat big brunch • 1 bicycle built for two

FOR HER EYES ONLY.

CONVERSATION PIECE

LIGHT HIS FIRE
Ellen Kreidman

Although there are many things in life over which we have no control, all of us are capable of creating memories. Remember, when we are old and gray, and all is said and done, we are left with only our memories. And what we remember best are those events that had special meaning-those crazy, out-of-character experiences-not whether we served mashed potatoes or baked, how the house looked, or what we wore. As someone once said, "You'll never remember the test you failed, but you'll always remember who you were with the night you decided not to study for that test." Start now to create the memories you and your family will cherish in the years to come.

THE LOVERS' BEDSIDE COMPANION
Gregory J.P. Godek

One of the biggest dangers of married life is complacency. The security and comfort can lead to laziness. We longer take *risks*, we no longer stretch ourselves. It's no wonder the passion withers away.

Singles take much bigger emotional risks on a regular basis than marrieds do. The rewards are passion, joy, and wonderment. A little risk-taking within a marriage has the potential to energize your relationship in incredible ways!

Advice for marrieds only: "Think Like a Single Person."

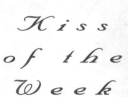

Passion Coupon

WILD CARD

*Bearer is entitled to anything she wants
for the next ten minutes!*

(As long she keeps her eyes on the road!)

Steaming the Windows

Some of the best times of your life happened at night, right? The first time the grownups didn't make you go to bed early at a big celebration . . . your school prom . . . talking all night with a new boyfriend . . . falling in love with your sweetheart.

So why in the world do we sacrifice so many of our nights to the remote control? Night time is the right time for *romance*, and if you need a little assistance to break the spell of the cable box, then call on a couple of higher powers —

Ice cream. And kisses!

They're two of the most fundamental forces of the universe, and together they're *irresistible*. Want proof? One night this week, right after dinner and before your love has time to get wrapped up in another episode of Baywatch (Hint: They all get rescued), climb into his lap and kiss him. *"Hey" you'll say, as you kiss him hard and snuggle close, "Let's go get some Cherry Garcia with chocolate syrup."* Another kiss. "I'm buying . . . ."

And then *pow*, plant another kiss on him as soon as you're in the car. And another at *every single red light* along the way. Think of it as warm-up exercises for your lips. No, not to burn off the dessert; everybody knows that ice cream eaten in the pursuit of romance has no calories. Nope, you need it to prepare your kisser for the real goal of your evening:

Lover's Lane. A place to park and watch the spectacular view. And feed little nibbles of ice cream to your sweetheart. *"Aww, I got some on your cheek, here, let me clean that up"* — with another kiss, of course! Every town has a place like this, and if you don't know where it is ask a teenager or call your local police department! They know all the hot spots.

Visiting a hot spot like this is a little different when you're a grownup, though. At first you feel, well, *really ridiculous*. I know I did, the first time I tried it! After all, you're sitting in a car, like a couple of kids on a date. And you're surrounded by adolescents who are all there for the sole purpose of making out!

But then something magical happens. You get caught up in it. You'll probably start to giggle (and if you're like me, you'll be giggling about it all week long!) *You become one of those kids again*, expressing a little innocent passion. It's just sooo much fun! So give into it. Kiss your guy. And kiss some more.

And kiss some . . . hey . . . wait a second . . . you're a couple of responsible adults, you shouldn't be . . . Hey! Get a hotel room, for crying out loud! Sheesh, you'd think you two were reading my other book — *101 Nights Of Grrreat Sex*. Well, you're old enough, I suppose. But whatever you do, don't forget the prime rule of safe sex in an automobile:

Always set the parking brake!

INGREDIENTS

1 ice cream parlor • 1 great view • 1 comfy front seat

FOR HER EYES ONLY.

CONVERSATION PIECE

THE ART OF KISSING
William Kane

Kissing can stand alone as a sensual pleasure that deserves to be enjoyed for itself without going on to other sex acts. Kissing can bring two people closer than ********* because it's a more personal interaction. Which is why many prostitutes won't kiss their customers. "I don't kiss my customers," said one prostitute during a recent Cinemax interview. "That's too personal of a thing." They'll ********** for hours but won't kiss because kissing is considered even more intimate than **********!

The past few years have witnessed a groundswell of new interest in kissing as a contemporary generation of lovers redefines what it considers romantic. Recent sex surveys indicate that modern lovers believe kissing is one of the most essential aspects of a relationship, yet men and women are increasingly reporting that there is not enough kissing in their love lives. For example, a recent survey of more than 4,000 men showed that of all foreplay activities kissing was considered the most enjoyable. At the same time another survey — The Hite Report on Male Sexuality — indicated that many men want more kissing in their relationships. And The Hite Report itself, just like the women quoted in this chapter, revealed that many women rated the pleasure they received from kissing higher than the pleasure they received from any other type of sexual activity, yet they frequently complained that there wasn't enough kissing in their love lives. Lovers take note.

✂ *You're the bearer. He's the recipient.*

- -

Passion Coupon

SOMETHING WILD

Bearer is entitled to 1 Clothes On Quickie!

Starting now!

(Try not to rip buttons!!)

Kiss Me Silly!

Remember those mad, passionate make-out sessions on the sofa that seemed to go on for hours? Has it been a long time since you indulged in one? Well, get out your lip balm, because you're about to do it again, and this time there's a prize at stake:

"I hereby challenge you to a duel. The rules? I'll tell you on Thursday. The prize? Whatever I can give you. Write out your secret wish and seal it in this envelope. The winner? Why, that will be me, naturally!"

That's the inscription on the front of an envelope you'll leave for your sweetie this week, and it's also his invitation to the best game show not on television! It does involve a TV, though, so plan your duel for a night when you'll both be watching a favorite show. Whatever that is, you're going to find it much *more* entertaining than ever before!

As the show gets ready to start, explain the rules. At the first commercial break, you're going to kiss your mate. He then has to give you the exact same kiss back, and follow it with a different kind of kiss. You repeat your first kiss, then his, and then add a third one, which he has to repeat back to you in order, after which he adds a fourth, and so on.

Chances are one of you will goof it up before the ads are over and your show starts again! That's when you break out the scorecard — a legal pad with both your names at the top will be fine — and put a mark under the name of the kisser who lost track of the kisses. (At the end of your show, lowest score wins.) As the next commercial break gets under way, he begins a whole new sequence of smooches.

Light peck on the lips . . . a nibble on the left earlobe . . . a butterfly kiss on the eyebrow . . . a deep, long, wet one that traces teeth with tongue . . . A sweeping flurry of kisses from one cheek to the other . . . an "Eskimo kiss," nose-to-nose . . . a vampire kiss on the neck! . . . a vertical swipe, forehead to nose to lips to chin . . . a lower-lip bite . . . and of course there are all those kisses that happen, um, elsewhere! Be inventive; use your imagination.

As you can see, this gets complicated — but that's what makes it a contest! A duel, fortunately, where there are no losers. (Except for America's television advertisers who, once this game catches on, will have no one left staring at their messages. A small price to pay for Grrreat Romance, if you ask me.)

Only one of you, however, gets the added bonus of having your secret wish come true. And isn't he going to feel silly if his was, "Turn the TV off all week!" *(Oh, get real, Laura! What guy is gonna say that??!)*

INGREDIENTS

1 envelope • 1 scorecard • 1 television set

FOR HIS EYES ONLY.

CONVERSATION PIECE

HOW TO ROMANCE THE WOMAN YOU LOVE THE WAY
SHE WANTS YOU TO!
Lucy Sanna with Kathy Miller

Court Her

Even if you've been with her for years, it's time you started dating her,
The whole idea of a "date" can bring new excitement to your relationship.

In her book The Erotic Silence of the American Wife, Dalma Heyn points
out the need for excitement in a relationship- and the adultery than can
occur when it isn't there. A woman seeks excitement outside marriage
when her own man doesn't think that excitement is important at home.

When carried out in a romantic spirit, dating your partner can create the
romantic spirit, dating your partner can create the romantic tension that
will have her wanting to be in your arms.

LIGHT HER FIRE
Ellen Kreidman

Grooming Habbits

Most women want to feel they are worth going to some trouble for. When
you make that extra effort in preparation for spending time with your
mate, she takes that as proving your love once again. When you first
dated, you got ready for the evening. You took pains to make sure that you
looked as good as you could for her. Being presentable for her was an
important part of the courtship, and courtship makes a woman feel as if
she's the most important person in your life. Even now, she'll accept nothing less than that and deserves the same thoughtfulness throughout your
life together.

Passion Coupon

SOMETHING WILD

Bearer is entitled to 1 Seat-Reclining, Window Steaming,

Just like High School Car Quickie!

Starting now!

High School Reunion

Save your pennies. Crack the piggy bank. Get a second job. Take out a loan. Pull out all the stops for this one, big spender, and you will create memories that will last a *lifetime*. You're about to take your sweetheart to the Prom.

And this time you're going to do it *right!* No borrowing the car from the folks, no sweating bullets out of fear that your date will order the most expensive thing on the menu. No cheesy powder-blue tuxedo! This will be the evening you *wish* you could have had, and now you get to do it with the woman of your dreams.

Make it formal from the start — get a fancy invitation from a stationery store. *Mr. John Doe requests the pleasure of your company for an elegant evening of cocktails and dancing next Friday the 24th. Festivities to commence at six.*

Now go rent a tux. Yeah, yeah, I know; they're not cheap. But trust me on this point— *there's not a man on the planet who doesn't look smashing in black tie*. And there's not a woman alive who doesn't have to catch her breath when she sees her man suddenly looking like Cary Grant. Get an elegant, classic style; nothing too trendy. Don't forget her flowers! (Me, I love a wrist corsage. It's terribly romantic, and so traditional.) When the magic evening rolls around, arrange to **pick her up at the front door.** Offer her your arm. Remember your manners.

Now, every town has a spot where the drinks are expensive, the lights low, the music live and cool and not too loud. It's probably a pretty nice crowd that hangs out there, but even in that sophisticated atmosphere heads will turn when you two walk in. Tonight, you're what everybody else *wants* to be — two good-looking folks who are obviously in love. You're the King And Queen Of The Prom. Your sweetie is suddenly a young girl again, and this time, she's a young girl who knows *exactly* what to do with all those hormonal urges running through her body. Gentleman, this wild child may chase you around the bases tonight!

Big-bucks bonus: hire a limousine. And you'll have a blast if you share the fun (and the expense!) with another couple. See if you can talk your best friend into springing this same surprise on his partner. Explain to him how this evening will be so much *better* than the original, now that you're grownups. No curfew, for instance. No zits. More cool. More dough.

And you have <u>much</u> better odds that you're gonna get lucky!!

INGREDIENTS

1 tuxedo • 1 elegant club • 1 bouquet

1 limo (optional) • 1 wad of cash

FOR HER EYES ONLY.

$

CONVERSATION PIECE

THE LOVERS' BEDSIDE COMPANION
Gregory J.P. Godek

Give your lover 15 minutes of undivided attention every day.

Warning: You just might fall in love all over again.

Note: The Surgeon General has determined that it is possible to succumb to infatuation at any age.

Fact: A passionate, one-minute kiss burns about 26 calories.

HOT MONOGAMY
Dr. Patricia Love amd Jo Robinson

It may also be wise to put more effort into how you look at home, a lesson a friend of mine learned a few years ago. She was newly remarried, and her first husband was over at the house picking up their children for a weekend visit. She went upstairs for a few minutes, and when she came back down, she overheard her first husband say to her second husband, "She may look good to you now, but just wait a few months. Soon she'll be wearing baggy sweatpants during the day and coming to bed in an old flannel nightgown. And you'd better get used to seeing her in curlers because she wears them *all* the time."

My friend got the message. To this day her second husband has never seen her look frumpy. She said to me, "It's not that I dress up at home. I wear casual clothes. But he's never seen me look *bad*."

Coming to bed freshly showered and wearing beautiful lingerie or elegant cotton or silk pajamas is another way to say, "I care about me."

✂

Passion Coupon

WILD ABANDON

*Bearer is entitled to 1 Evening Quickie to take place
anywhere except the bedroom!*

Starting now!

Five Card Stud

What do I want for my birthday? Oh, really, honey, you can just get me a card....

Ever have someone pull that line on you? It can make you crazy. You *know* they're hoping for more than that. And you know you'd better provide it, *if you can just figure out what it is!* Well, after this week's surprises, your sweetie's really going to mean it when he says he wants a card. If it's *this* kind of card, that is....

This extended seduction starts when he finds a small package on the seat of his car. In it are five greeting cards, individually sealed in envelopes marked with cryptic messages. *"Open Me On Tuesday"* . . . *"This Is For Wednesday"* . . . all the way up to number five, which says *"Not Until 4 PM on Saturday!"* I hope his job isn't too demanding, because this week his mind's going to be on you and your mysterious messages! The Tuesday card won't tell him much. It says— *Meet me in the kitchen tonight at nine.*

At the appointed hour, you'll show him a sweet treat— a cream-filled pastry, or maybe a fudge brownie. The gooier the better! *"Here,"* you'll say, *"I wanted you to taste this—"* Now pop it in his mouth. And before he can swallow— *"I want to taste it, too...."* Now kiss him! Make it a long and sexy kiss, and when you've *both* finished with that first bite, go back for more. Mm-mm-*Yummy!*

Wednesday's card instructs him to meet you in the bathroom, 7:30 sharp. Which is where he'll find you soaking in a tub of bubbles, illuminated by candles and sipping a glass of wine. *"Oh, I just wanted another kiss, that's all...."* (Hmm. I wonder if a kiss is really all you're going to get!) Thursday, his card simply says hall closet, 9:00. Open the door, step in, then *grab him and pull him in after you!* If you're feeling a little frisky, then this could be a chance to hand over your passion coupon! Men get so turned on by making love in unusual places. Now, Friday's plan is a simple one— *Tonight, 10:30, Patio,* and all you do is stretch out on a lawn chair with him and watch the stars wheel by. *Very* romantic.

Saturday... well, I'll leave Saturday to your imagination. But make it a big one— get a babysitter, make reservations, buy tickets, and get dressed up. Keep him in the dark about your plans, though. *Pick me up at eight,* your final card will read, *and don't be late!* Go out and have a ball— you'll be able to afford lots of nights out like this if you follow my investment advice, which is this: When your love tells his buddies about this very cool seduction, and all *their* sweethearts start to do exactly the same thing—

Buy stock in Hallmark Cards!

INGREDIENTS

5 nice greeting cards • 5 fun rendezvous ideas

FOR HIS EYES ONLY.

CONVERSATION PIECE

LOVE NOTES FOR LOVERS
Larry James

. . . Intentionally add a little pizzazz to your love relationship every day. Do it in a playful ways. Exercise your sense of humor. It enlivens your spirit, breeds happiness and causes you and the one you love to experience fully the love you feel for one another. Do things that make each other smile. Smiles and knowing nods from your lover create a sense of unity that adds longevity to your relationship.

MEN, WOMEN AND RELATIONSHIPS
John Gray, Ph.D.

Every day, a woman needs to receive some form of verbal reassurance that she is loved. This means saying things like, "I love you, I love you, I love you, I love you, I love you, I love you, I love you, I love you...." There is basically one way to say it and it needs to be said over and over.

Men sometimes stop saying "I love you" because they want to be new and original. They imagine that a woman would grow tired of it or become bored by it. But saying "I love you" is never redundant. Saying it is actually a process of allowing her to "feel" his love. He may love her, but if he doesn't say it she won't feel it.

Passion Coupon

HE'S IN CHARGE!

For the next ten minutes, recipient will fall under the bearer's spell and do exactly what he says.

The Velvet Hammer

When was the last time you wrote a poem for your sweetheart? Junior high school? Never?? That's too bad, because women are turned on by words. Want proof? Well, somebody's buying more than a billion dollars worth of romance books every year, and I'll bet it's not *you!* Good poetry can have the same effect.

Sadly, though, I am *not* a good poet, and the poem I'm suggesting here is pretty pitiful. But you can seduce your partner with even a bad poem if you can *just make it fun!* Here's how — first, plan a route around your neighborhood and pick some likely spots to hide your verse. Early one evening, take the pieces of your poem and nail them up in four appropriate places. Now invite your lady to join you for a stroll.

If she doesn't spot it right away, direct her attention to the folded slip of paper nailed to a nearby tree. It's got her name on it, and when she opens it up she'll see these lines —

*"I'm in love with a beautiful woman
Sheila is her name."*

Very mysterious, huh? (Of course, it'll be a real mystery if her name's not Sheila! Write it out with hers instead.) A half a block later, there's another piece of paper stuck on a wall —

*"I think she's the world's best lover,
And Sheila tells me the same."*

There's part three, tacked up on a fence —

*"I'd love to be nuzzling her body
In a way that's wild and untame."*

Part four is on the outside of an envelope —

*"But here we are in a public spot,
And ain't that a crying shame!"*

Okay, it's not Longfellow, but it's good for a laugh. And a laugh is always good for a seduction! Inside the envelope, another poem:

*"My poem is lame, but am I to blame?
My brain is aflame with thoughts of this dame!
The bedroom's my aim. So . . . . Are you game?"*

So. Is she?

INGREDIENTS

1 envelope • 4 slips of paper • Hammer and nails

(In a pinch, just use Post-It™ Notes around the house)

FOR HIS EYES *M* ONLY.

CONVERSATION PIECE

HOT MONOGAMY
Dr. Patricia Love and Jo Robinson

Another way to indulge your sense of sight is to put more effort into the decoration of your bedroom. When you go to bed tonight, look around the room. Do the colors soothe or excite you? Is the bed welcoming? Do you have mood lightning? The right artwork can help create a romantic or erotic mood, and strategically placed mirrors can give you a whole new perspective on your lovemaking. Buying a new bedspread, sheets, or duvet can both enhance your sensual pleasure and declare your lovemaking a major priority in your life.

1001 WAYS TO BE ROMANTIC
Gregory J.P. Godek

Pay Attention to the "Afterglow Effect."

After you've made a romantic gesture, there's a certain "afterglow" that lingers. Your partner appreciates you more, is nicer to you, and is likely to respond in kind. You feel more loved, and bask in the glow of having given something special.

Romance is not an end unto itself. It's about enjoying your life more fully—living passionately in partnership with your lover. The most successful relationships seem to be surrounded by a perpetual "afterglow."

✂ -

Passion Coupon

SOMETHING WILD

Bearer is entitled to 1 Just Before Going

Out On a Date Quickie!

Starting now!

The Perfect Frame-Up

"What four items should you *always* keep in your bedroom in order to enhance your sex life?"

I just love to ask that question when I appear on talk shows! It seems like everyone in the audience has a suggestion, and a lot of them are so good I've included them in this book.

But there are just four ideas that are universally recommended by the experts, and one of them is at the heart of your assignment this week. You need a very special picture — a sensual, suggestive work of art.

Actually, you need *five* special pictures, and your sweetheart should be in every one. Four of them can be simple snapshots — but take your time picking them out of the family album. Find photos that stir some really great memories . . . and then write a line or two about each photo on four nice cards.

I always loved this shot of you! Makes me think of that winter when we never left the ski lodge. I love you . . . Remember this? About seven months pregnant, and you've never looked more beautiful. Je t'adore . . . You'll need a fifth card, too, but this one will be a little different. It doesn't include a photograph —

I love all these pictures, but I think we're missing one. It should be really special . . . an intimate portrait of the two of us. Pick the date, and I'll arrange an appointment to have it made.

Each morning this week, your love will find an envelope with a card and photo somewhere in the house — on the bathroom counter, the refrigerator door, the coffee table. Each day, she'll be knocked out by your thoughtfulness. She'll be totally thrilled to find that you still think she's beautiful.

And she'll *love* creating that last, extraordinary portrait. This one is definitely not a standard, smile-and-face-the-camera shot. What you want, and what the experts recommend, is something that *sizzles* with erotic content. Not a nude shot — not *necessarily*, anyway! Instead, you want to create a portrait that drips with sensuality; a picture of the two of you nuzzling, kissing, embracing. It doesn't have to be expensive, but it should be *dramatic* . . . and *big*, because this picture is going up on your wall. Now, every single time she walks into the bedroom, your mate will be reminded of her sexual nature. She'll be thinking about intimacy. She'll be thinking about you.

Wow. A week's worth of foreplay and a lifetime of arousal, all for the cost of a few cards and one portrait.

I'd say you're getting a lot of *bang* for the buck!

INGREDIENTS

5 elegant cards • 4 snapshots of your sweetie • 1 portrait sitting • 1 perfect frame

FOR HIS EYES *M* ONLY.

CONVERSATION PIECE

ROMANCE 101 LESSONS IN LOVE
Gregory J.P. Godek

Creating romance is easy. It's re-creating romance that seems to give people a hard time. Most people come to Romance Class with great romantic memories. "He used to bring me flowers every week." "She used to surprise me with breakfast in bed." What happened? No, they didn't "fall out of love"— Life just intruded, that's all. The good news is that they (and most of us) are not starting from scratch—we have a good romantic base to work from. The bad news is that Life won't stop intruding—you have to deal with kids and jobs and deadlines and taxes and chores and committees and relatives and neighbors and dogs and crabgrass.

MARS AND VENUS IN THE BEDROOM
John Gray Ph.D.

Bill didn't understand that for a woman to feel sexual desire she needs love and romance. It is not enough for her partner to be provider and protector. She needs him to do the little "magic" things he did in the beginning—to sweep her off feet again and again.

During courtship, a man makes the romantic gestures to open a woman up to having sex. Once they are having sex regularly, he doesn't realize that she still needs to be romanced. Without romance, she can easily become so overwhelmed with day-to-day tasks and duties that sexual desire moves to the back burner.

101 NIGHTS
OF GRRREAT
ROMANCE

*Kiss
of the
Week*

CHRYSANTHEMUM
KISS

*Chinese say that if
you wipe your lips
with a chrysanthemum
after drinking wine
and then give the flower
to your love, he or
she will be yours forever.
Well...what are you
waiting for?*

♥♥

✂ *You fill in the blanks. She follows your wishes.*

Passion Coupon

SOMETHING HOT

Recipient is entitled to a 30-minute hot-oil massage.

Five minutes on his neck, five minutes on each shoulder,

5 minutes on his back, and ten minutes on

Compliments of the House

Oh, boy, is your florist gonna love you for this one!!

Actually, it doesn't have to be all that costly, because you're not presenting your mate with artfully arranged bouquets of flowers. She's had that before. (She *has*, hasn't she?? If not, then you *really* need this book!) And ironically, fancy, expensive arrangements *lose a little impact* when given for birthdays and other occasions when they're more or less expected.

Nope, single flowers can be much more meaningful (not to mention a whole lot cheaper!) if you just put a little imagination into their presentation. In fact, that's one of the Key Rules Of Grrreat Romance— *How You Do It Is More Important Than How Much It Cost.*

Sound familiar? Well, it's also one of the secrets to success in any business. Just think of yourself as the CEO of Romance, Incorporated, using a limited budget and a lot of creativity to dominate a *very* narrow market. When you've got a customer base of *one*, you gotta be a *full*-service company!

And today you're going the extra mile for your only client. She's going to wake up and find *rose petals* sprinkled over her side of the bed. The fragrance is intoxicating; she'll already have a smile on her face when she opens her eyes to see a single rose on her nightstand. In the bathroom, one huge geranium is floating in the sink! She'll find a few gardenias out in the kitchen, each blossom adrift in it's own snifter of water.

In a large bowl on the dining table, float a chrysanthemum. On the coffee table, leave another bowl with a lily drifting in water. Prop up a pretty card against each bowl. Inscribe them all with little love notes.

Come evening, when you're getting ready for bed, it's time to bring out one last special flower, one you've had wrapped up and hidden in the fridge. It's an orchid; one of the most beautiful, aromatic flowers on earth. And one with an interesting legend attached—

I've always heard that these things bear a striking resemblance to some part of the body, honey. Let's find out, okay?

Bet you never knew botany could be so sexy!

INGREDIENTS

Several big blossoms, stems removed • some bowls • some cards

(BUDGET TIP: Buy a bouquet from your local supermarket!)

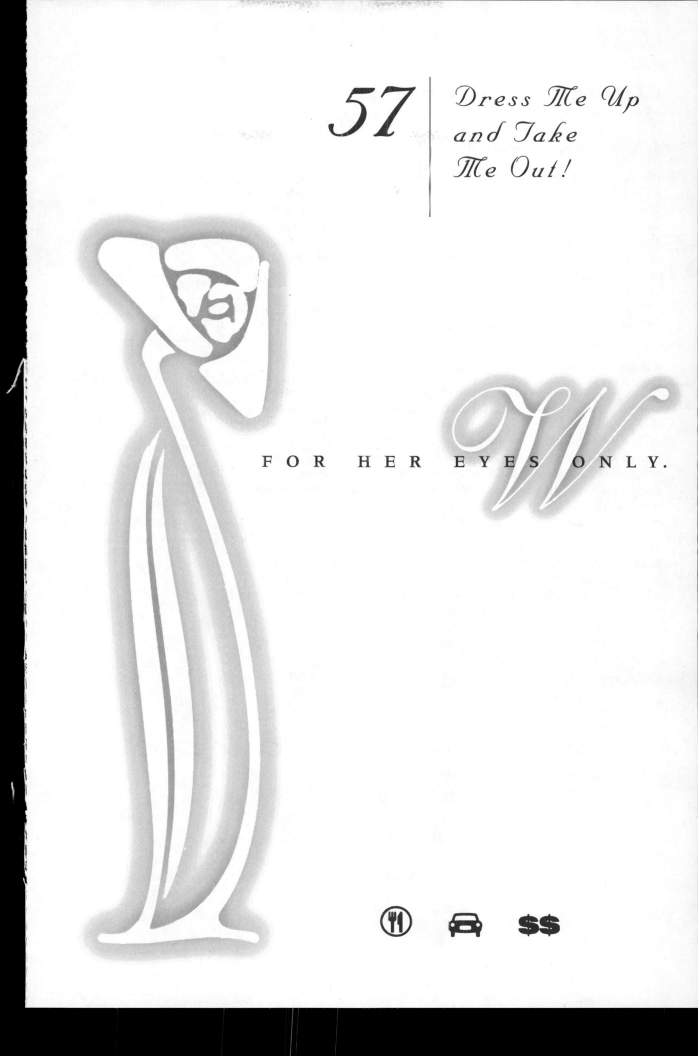

57 | Dress Me Up and Take Me Out!

FOR HER EYES ONLY.

CONVERSATION PIECE

HOT MONOGAMY
Dr. Patricia Love and Jo Robinson

This sales figure doesn't surprise me. In one survey a thousand men were asked what turned them on most: dirty talk, x-rated videos, pornography, female masturbation, sexy lingerie, or "other." Of the men surveyed, 92% said they were most turned on by sexy lingerie. In an interesting footnote, 73% of these men said they relied on stimulation such as this to sustain their interest in a long-term relationship. In essence, a man who asks his partner to wear a lace teddy to bed may be saying to her, "Please help me be monogamous."

TRUE LOVE
Daphne Rose Kingma

Kindle The Romance

Romance is the champagne and frosted glasses of love, the magic that gives love a tango to dance to, a fragrance to remember, and a fantasy-come-true to hold in your heart. Romance is the antidote to ordinariness, the inspiration for passion; Whenever you fold it into your relationship, you instantly elevate it to a more delicious state of being. Romanced, you feel beautiful or handsome; life becomes ripe with hope; the moon, stars, and planets bathe you in a cascade of beneficent light; and you believe every-thing is possible your sweetest, wildest, and most cherished dreams will certainly come true.

At least that's certainly how we feel in the rosy blush of new romance. But the feeling of romance doesn't just stick around all by itself. As time goes on, it takes effort, ingenuity, intuition, and sometimes even a will-ingness to feel foolish, to keep the moonlight magical. That's because somewhere along the line, without quite paying attention, we stop doing the things that kindled romance in the first place: we forget to bring the long-stemmed roses and to whisper the sweet nothings; we leave the lights on (or off), we trade in the black lingerie for flannel pajamas. In short, we start treating one another as roommates instead of passionate lovers.

Passion Coupon

WEEKEND WILD CARD

Bearer is entitled to 1 Thank God It's Friday Quickie.

Starting now!

Dress Me Up and Take Me Out!

Pity the poor Post Office employees. They're maligned in the press, made the butt of jokes, and all because some of them seem to react badly to stress. Okay, *very* badly. That doesn't change the fact that the post office has been responsible for a heck of a lot of *grrreat romance* over the years!

Don't believe it? Well, try to imagine life without love letters. There's nothing more exciting than getting an unexpected envelope in the mail filled with words of love and passion, don't you think? Small surprises like that make all the difference between a simple relationship and a major romance.

This week, you're going to send mail that goes way beyond "I love you." Your message says something more like this— "I want you, I need you. I'm going to have you!" Yep, the good old U.S. Postal Service is going to help you generate some serious heat— and I can't think of a better way to put your tax dollars to work!

You're going to practice one of the Big Rules Of Romance— *if you want to get your mate aroused, arouse his curiosity first.* He'll be scratching his head on Wednesday when he gets a mysterious package at work that contains a small box and this note— Do Not Open Until Friday. The next day, a similar package arrives with an identical note. (Okay, okay, so there's no guarantee the Post Office will get them there on those exact days. They do deserve that part of their reputation! So mail early. And pray.)

Yet another package will arrive, and on Friday your lover will finally get to open all three. I hope he has a private office, because he is gonna blush when he sees what you've sent. One package contains stockings. Another holds a brief pair of panties. And the third has the most elegant bra in the Victoria's Secret catalogue. *"Bring these home Friday night,"* your card says. *"I have plans for them. And plans for you."*

That squealing sound you hear, like tortured rubber against pavement? That'll be him, violating the speed limit, and a couple of laws of physics, in an effort to get home to you. Neither rain, nor sleet, nor gloom of night can keep this man away! But remember what I said about the importance of *curiosity*— keep your new treasures hidden under your dress while you two head out to dinner. (Well, maybe not *totally* hidden. The occasional and discreet little flash of lingerie will have your man bouncing in his seat. And skipping dessert.)

Then, it's home for a little, uh, *special delivery.*

INGREDIENTS

3 items of lingerie • 3 packages • 3 notes

FOR HIS EYES ONLY.

CONVERSATION PIECE

HOT MONOGAMY
Dr. Patricia Love and Jo Robinson

One of the fundamental pieces of advice I give couples about romance was underscored by a research project conducted by Arthur Aron, Ph.D., a researcher and lecturer at the University of California, Santa Cruz. But after twenty years of researching the phenomenon of love, he believes that the overwhelming predictor of whether or not you will love someone is the last one: *knowing that person loves you...*

What I have concluded from research such as Aron's and from my own training and clinical practice is this: If you want to create ongoing romance, *find out what says "I love you" to your partner and do it.*

*   *   *

A few days ago I was dragging myself into the house after spending six days conducting back-to-back workshops. It was nine o'clock at night, and I was tired, jet-lagged, and in no mood for romance. The smell of fresh bread drew me in the kitchen. There was my husband, ladling out a bowl of homemade cream of chicken soup, my favorite soup. It had taken my husband all afternoon to make the soup and the bread, and he had timed the bread so it would be ready to take out of the oven five minutes before I was due to walk in the door. I felt instantly revived. We had a late intimate supper, catching up on all the news. As we were heading for bed, I said to him, "Now *that* was my idea of foreplay." We went to bed and proceeded to make love — not because I felt obliged to him but because I truly wanted to make love to him. It was yet another example of the power of romance.

Passion Coupon

WILD CARD

(For the next 10 minutes, anything goes!)

Candlelight and Your Smile

Truly Grrreat Romance isn't about trips to Tahiti or diamond earrings. Not *always*, anyway! That's a good thing, too, or we'd all go broke in the pursuit of love. Of course, it's important to be extravagant on occasion— hey, Bill Gates rented *Hawaii* for his wedding! But the fact is that love is best expressed in small gestures, done every day. Every affectionate act helps build a stronger bond. Every kindness lingers in the air like perfume.

Or, more to the point, it lingers in the air like *spaghetti* sauce, which is part of the dinner you're fixing this week for your sweetie. Now, I can hear you asking— Laura, what the heck does spaghetti have to do with romance? The answer is, first, that even a complete amateur can successfully boil water and noodles. (Uh, you *can*, can't you?) Second, I've never met a woman who didn't just flip when a man offered to make a meal for her, no matter how simple. And third, all that pasta will do a great job of covering up your *real* gift—

Dishes.

Still doesn't sound romantic? Ah, but these are special *love dishes*. You can't buy 'em— you have to *make* 'em, and therein lies their magic.

Ninety percent of romance is attitude and atmosphere. So set the proper scene with a formal, handwritten invitation— *You're invited to the Grand Opening of a new work of art dedicated to the love of my life. Day: Tomorrow. Time: Dinner.* At the appointed hour, light a few candles and put on soft music. Now— watch her face as she starts to nibble at her salad. Underneath all the lettuce... there's some writing....

JP loves LC forever, it says, inside a big Valentine's heart! You don't need fancy tools to make it— colorful permanent markers will be fine. Just make it look as nice as you can.

There's more under the spaghetti, and she'll be mopping up sauce in a hurry so she can see it! *I love you . . . Free kiss when you clean your plate . . .* Use your imagination and your heart. Her smile will become a wicked grin when she gets to the bottom of her dessert plate and finds this message—

Ready for another dessert? No calories in the next one! Um, I think I'll leave that particular menu up to you. Bon appétit!

INGREDIENTS

2 sets of inexpensive dishes • *1 set of permanent markers* • *candlelight*

A dash of artistic flair (or a mate with a sense of humor!)

FOR HER EYES ONLY.

CONVERSATION PIECE

FROM THIS DAY FORWARD
Toni Sciarra Poynter

How You Dreamed It Would Be

"But there's nothing half so sweet in life/ As love's young dream."
Clement Clark Moore, "Love's Young Dream"

We begin marriage filled with dreams. At first there is only the dream. Then reality of marriage consumes us. It's easy to get lost in the maze of day-to-day survival, losing sight of the ideals we held at the start. Don't be swayed from your dreams and aspirations. Staying in touch with your dreams gives you a framework for shaping each detail of daily life. Without dreams marriage becomes a collection of grunts and groans; a scrapbook of grievances; a formless space.

Take time to recall the hopes that birthed your life together. Let them help you place your hand wisely in the midst of conflict

BORN FOR LOVE
Leo Buscaglia

Nothing is so fatal as predictability. Dull routines have a way of insidiously creeping into our lives: Sunday morning breakfast after church at the same restaurant; Wednesdays with the in-laws; Fridays at the movies. This thread of habit is woven into our lives until we find ourselves bound, limited only to experiencing the same small slices of life over and over again. What is so desperately needed in such situations is a serendipitous act, a surprise dinner, an unexpected gift, a little craziness to shake up this deadly, habitual existence.

Love withers with predictability; its very essence is surprise and amazement. To make love a prisoner of the mundane is to take way its passion and lose it forever.

Dessert First

"Life is short. Eat dessert first."
DOROTHY PARKER

Big dreams are a big part of romance.

In the beginning, of course, relationships don't consist of much *besides* dreams! And even when two people have been together a while, they'll always have hopes for a bigger, brighter future. They *should*, anyway — because without something to aspire to, terminal boredom is right around the corner.

Besides, dreaming is so much *fun!* Haven't you and your sweetheart spent hours discussing the house you'd like to design one day? Or the car you wish you could have? The vacation of a lifetime? Inheriting millions from a long-lost relative? It's not out of a sense of greed. (Well, not completely!) *It's because you want the best for your partner.* And he wants the best for you — that's what love is all about.

This week, you're going to totally indulge those fantasies. And you're going to create a wonderful new memory to treasure, because your assignment involves something I'll bet you've never done before. (Hey, if variety is the spice of life, it's the very *soul* of great romance!

Saturday night, before dinner, go out for dessert. Uh-huh; dessert *first.* (Believe it or not, it actually tastes *better* when it's your main course!) Pick a favorite restaurant or ice cream shop and order the most sinfully delicious treats you can imagine. Mm-mmm . . . *Cherries Jubilee . . . a Banana Split . . . Chocolate Decadence . . .* (Wow! I'm starting to get hungry just writing about it. I think I have to go out and do this seduction again tonight!!)

While you're indulging in sweet excess, bring up those dreams again. Talk about starting a business (*then give him a quick kiss!*), or buying a ranch (*Mm! Bite of chocolate!*), or riding a motorcycle across the country. What do you want your kids to become? (*Bi-i-i-g kiss!*) Where would you like to retire? (*More dessert, and this time feed it to him.*) If you hit the lottery, what's the first thing you would buy? The second thing? The fifth?

If you're still hungry after dessert, then it's time, naturally, to think about supper. For that, I suggest a place with a little more privacy, and *very* comfortable seating. Grab a movie and some take-out and then *snuggle into your bed for dinner!* Dress code: casual. Extremely casual. Where else could you be considered overdressed in pajamas?

And where else could you be on the menu??!

INGREDIENTS

1 restaurant or sweet shop • 2 fancy desserts

1 take-out dinner (optional) • 2 lovebirds with great imaginations

FOR HER EYES ONLY.

🍴 $

CONVERSATION PIECE

WHAT YOUR MOTHER COULDN'T TELL YOU AND
YOUR FATHER DIDN'T KNOW
John Gray, Ph.D.

A Man's Primary Goal

When a man loves a woman, his primary goal is to make her happy. Through history, men have endured the competitive and hostile world of work because, at the end of the day, their struggles and efforts were justified by a woman's appreciation. In a very real sense, his mate's fulfillment was the reward that made a man's labor worthwhile.

Today, because women are overworked, they often and understandably feel unfulfilled. Now, at a long day's end, both she and her mate are looking for love and appreciation. "I work as hard as he does," she tells herself. "Why is it my responsibility to appreciate him?" Exhaustion now prevents her from giving her man the emotional support he knows he has earned. If a man is not appreciated, he feels his work is meaningless; his wife's unhappiness confirms his defeat. To him, her unhappiness signals that he is a failure. "Why should I bother to do more?" he asks himself. "I'm unappreciated for what I do already." The harmful effects of this relatively new pattern are greatly underestimated by both women and men.

1001 WAYS TO BE ROMANTIC
Gregory J.P. Godek

Romantics are passionate (#1).

I'm not talking about sexual passionate here, but about a passion for *life*. Romantics don't allow their lives, or love lives, to slide into boredom— the deadly enemy of all relationships.

- Express the true depth of your feelings for your lover.

- What is your lover passionate about? Recognize it, act on it.

Romantics are passionate (#2).

- Yes, as a matter of fact, romantics *do* tend to be more sexually passionate than the average mortal. (Just another of the many side-benefits of the romantic lifestyle!)

The Royal Treatment

The world can be a cold, cold place. That, I think, is one of the reasons nature designed us to fall in love — we *need* a person we can count on when times are hard. We all want to have someone who will console us and cuddle us and comfort us when life laughs in our faces. We'd like a kind word now and then.

Of course, that's not always possible. He has troubles, you have troubles. He's busy, and so are you. But fortunately, you don't have to smother your mate with affection every single minute to get the full romantic effect. As with so many of the things that build intimacy in a relationship, you *just have to do it often enough*. Often enough to remind your partner that you can devote yourself to his needs; that you *love* doing it. And is he in for a surprise — because this is his weekend to be spoiled!

Thursday evening, ask him about his job. Tell him you're worried; you think he's been working too hard lately. He won't be able to argue with that, I'll bet, not wholeheartedly, and so you tell him you've come up with a stress-relief plan just for him. Tomorrow night starting at six. Don't be late!

As soon as he walks in the house Friday evening, you smile and grab him and push him up against a wall. *Tonight* (kiss!), *my sweet prince* (kiss!), *you are going to get* (kiss kiss kiss!) *the royal treatment you deserve....* Now pop his favorite hors d'oeuvre in his mouth. He'll need to unwind for several minutes, so hand him a drink and a newspaper, and lead him to the bath. Take a few minutes to slowly, sensuously *undress him.* Button. (Kiss!) Button. (Kiss!) Zipper. (Kiss kiss kiss!) *Ahhh!*

While he soaks, you bring other exotic appetizers, and prepare your next offering. Would His Lordship be interested in a bite of dinner? Served, perhaps, in his bedchamber? Forgive him if he doesn't answer right away. The sight of you standing before him in a flowing, silky robe that seems to open *just a wee bit* when you move may leave him stammering. Dinner in bed is followed by a massage — and not just a little pat on the back, but a full, get-out-the-oils, dig-into-those-muscles, head-to-toe *rubdown.*

Now, you might think the King Of His Castle would be ready to fall asleep here. He's full, and clean, and totally relaxed after a long, hard week. But he's with his one and only Queen, after all, so don't be surprised if there's a lot of life in the old boy yet.

You might find *yourself* getting some special attention from His, uh, Highness!

INGREDIENTS

1 lucky man • 1 dinner in bed • 1 newspaper • 1 bath

1 sexy robe • massage oil • 1 tray of hors d'oeuvres

W

FOR HER EYES ONLY.

🚗 $

CONVERSATION PIECE

ROMANCE 101 LESSONS IN LOVE
Gregory J.P. Godek

If you are an average American, and you live to be 75 years old, during your life *you will watch a total of 14 uninterrupted years of TV.*

Just *think* about this fact for a moment . . . I don't care if you're watching PBS, documentaries and *Masterpiece Theater* the whole time – it's *still* not a great way to use-up your life, is it? Take a holiday from your TV for a week. (Okay, *okay*. . . .You can tape your three favorite shows on the VCR for future viewing. Are you happy now? Can you please turn your attention back to your partner?) Many couples who try this experiment are pleasantly surprised to rediscover the art of conversation. And without the easy distraction of the boob tube, many of them rediscover each other.

IN THE MOOD
Doreen Virtue, Ph.D.

The Look of Love

If you're a woman, you can set the mood for romance by trying to look your best, whether you're relaxed in front of the television set or out on the town for dinner and a movie. You're giving your man a gift equivalent to a dozen red roses when you take care of your appearance. You can be in jeans and a sweater and still look great, just by checking your makeup and hair, and by choosing a flattering outfit.

Throw away your ugly flannel nightgown and replace it with a feminine night. Your man will appreciate it if you dress in lingerie and other sexy outfits, as well. Believe me, you don't need a perfect body to arouse a man with lingerie. They love skimpy, lacy outfits, and their eyes will focus on your best features.

By taking the time to look attractive, you are speaking volumes of love to your man. Then, after you look great, be sure to look at your man. He needs your eye contract while he's talking, just as much as you need him to tell you that he loves you. Give him your full attention, as you did on your first date. Smile at him and laugh at his jokes. You're not being passive or manipulative by engaging in this nonverbal communication. You're simply speaking his language!

✂

Passion Coupon

WILD CARD

Bearer is entitled to 1 Afternoon Quickie to take place anywhere except the bedroom!

Couch Dance

Henry David Thoreau was really onto something at that Walden Pond where he used to hang out. "Simplify," he said; advice that's better today than ever. We're surrounded by labor-saving devices and we're *still* too busy! That's tough on romance.

So . . . simplify! Create time to indulge in the basic pleasures of life. If you two can enjoy quiet, unadorned moments together, your relationship has all it takes to last a lifetime. Here's a good way to practice — read together. This week, leave an envelope on your sweetie's dresser with this inscription: *Let's do it this Sunday! Right after breakfast!*

Inside is a gift certificate to your favorite bookstore, and Sunday, after a lazy brunch, go use it. And don't rush! There's something really soul-satisfying about browsing through stacks of books and magazines, don't you think? Once you've grabbed a pile of interesting stuff, go home and explain the rules to your mate:

You can spend the whole afternoon reading and relaxing, *but you <u>always</u> have to be touching!* Set out snacks and drinks, and throw lots of pillows on the sofa. Take the phone off the hook. Put on soft music, snuggle in at opposite ends of the couch, and entwine your legs.

Now read. Unwind. Put the world out of your thoughts. And every so often, *wiggle*. Play footsie with your love. No need to break the spell; just let him know you're thinking of him. And if you've got kids around the house — *don't chase them off.*

In fact, you should probably pick up some books for them, too. Because while they're reading and enjoying "family time" with you, they're also learning one of the essentials of great romance. *Let them see you touching.* Show them that two people in love can express their affection in simple, quiet, intimate ways. They don't have to grow up with any bad romantic habits — they'll show the same sort of affection to their own partners down the road, thanks to the example you set for them today, and everyday.

Of course, if you *do* have little ones running around, you might have to tone down the kisses. Oh, did I mention the kisses? That's the *other* rule in this little game. Every sixty minutes or so, the kitchen timer will buzz, and that's your signal to slide over to your mate and give him a big smooch. You'll need a little break anyway, so get up, stretch, refresh your drinks, and before you dive back in to your books — *talk*. Ask him what his book's about. See if he likes it. Did he learn anything new? Does he like the author? Ask if he'll read his favorite part to you.

And then go back to the quiet luxury of reading and touching. *Always* touching, remember — shoulder-to-shoulder, head in his lap, maybe cuddled under his arm. And don't forget to set the timer! You've got more kisses coming.

And maybe a lot more than kisses, if you picked up a copy of my other book. *It's called 101 Nights Of Grrreat Sex.* But, uh, you'll definitely want to put the kids to bed *before* you open that one!

INGREDIENTS

1 bookstore gift certificate • 1 quiet afternoon

(REALLY COOL TIP: To spark a really fun and grrreat conversation, get two copies of the same book and read them together. Talking about it while it is fresh in both your minds will add extra excitement to your couch dance!)

FOR HIS EYES ONLY.

CONVERSATION PIECE

ROMANCE 101 LESSONS IN LOVE
Gregory J.P. Godek

How do you express affection? How *often* do you express affection? Do you express affection? Affection is the first cousin of Romance. While romance is the expression of love, affection is the expression of caring. Another definition, from Marisa G., a Romance Class participant, is that affection is "little romance." Many people, especially the workaholics and skeptics among us, who are somewhat threatened by the enormity of romance, feel they can manage to squeeze in a little affection. Great! You gotta crawl before you can walk.

*   *   *

Are you giving your lover leftovers? Do you give her whatever time is "left over" from the rest of your life? If you don't consciously put her at the top of your priority list, she'll automatically drop to the *bottom* of the list. It's a Rule of Nature. "People take for granted those who are closet to them." Our culture is not structured in a way that supports love. As a matter of fact, much of society actively resists your effects to make time for your partner. Your career could easily absorb all of your "free time" if you allowed it to. Your chores and other responsibilities will consume you — *if you let them.* Here's the secret: You must fight back. You must set boundaries. You must limit the encroachment of the rest of the world into your relationship.

✂

Passion Coupon

WILD CARD

(For the next 10 minutes, anything goes!)

Romancing the Remote

There is a funny scene in *Sleepless In Seattle* that shows some friends watching an old movie on television. It's *An Affair To Remember*, and the women are crying because it's just so . . . so romantic. The men are unmoved, and as the women try to explain their deep involvement in the film, Tom Hanks turns to his pal and sums the whole discussion up —

Chick Picture!

It's a big laugh with a touch of irony, since it comes from one of the great Chick Pictures of the nineties! Did your sweetheart love that movie? Ask her. And while you're at it, ask her about romantic movies in general. You want to find out what films inspire her, because this week you're going to put together a *Grrreat Romance Film Festival*, customized for the love of your life!

This is not simply to reward her for letting you hog the remote control all year long. And it's not just a chance to let her indulge her hopeful, sentimental side, although the Grrreat Romance Film Festival certainly *is* saturated with high-gloss Hollywood passion. No, this weekend's video extravaganza is mostly about showing your mate *how much you're thinking about her*. You're going to take care of dinner, and then let her unwind while you clean up the kitchen. This evening, *she* gets to channel-surf while you whip up a bag of popcorn and her favorite snacks. Then shut the phone off, light a few candles, and snuggle in for some serious seduction.

When Harry Met Sally, Moonstruck, or While You Were Sleeping. Dr. Zhivago and The Way We Were. Anything with Cary Grant. Anything with Hepburn and Tracy. Casablanca . . . and my own favorite, Don Juan de Marco, with Johnny Depp and Marlon Brando.

There are some big advantages to having your own private screening room, of course. The experience can be a bit more, well, *sensual* than anything you'll find in a theater. After the opening credits roll past, pull your mate's feet into your lap and give them a long, slow, delicious massage. I'm speaking from personal experience here when I tell you that the combination of great romance and a great footrub is absolutely electrifying!

Oh, and your manly skill with the remote control will come in handy tonight, too. Each time a film gets to a big kissing scene, hit that pause button for a moment — and duplicate the kiss! This usually leads to some interesting discussions at the end of every Grrreat Romance Film Festival. *Yeah, that was a terrific picture, hon, but I'm confused. That scene at the railroad station? Did he kiss her like this?? Or was it more like this?? Or perhaps . . . mmm . . . this?!!*

(Hey, the movies may be PG-13 . . . but there's nothing that says the Festival itself can't be rated R!!)

INGREDIENTS

2 or 3 grrreat movies • 1 VCR • 1 television

1 bag of popcorn • massage lotion

CONVERSATION PIECE

ROMANCE 101 LESSONS IN LOVE
Gregory J.P. Godek

Romance *itself* — being the expression of love — is, in fact, a celebration. Romance isn't a chore, a responsibility or something imposed on you from outside. Romance is a celebration of the life you live as part of a couple. It springs naturally and joyful from inside of you...*if* you'll give it access to your creative energies.

Don't wait for some *reason* to celebrate. The fact that you're alive and reasonably healthy, fairly good-looking, adequately wealthy — and *fabulously* in love are reasons enough to celebrate! The calendar is full of dates when you're supposed to celebrate. True romantics create their own calendars, and celebrate whenever their hearts are singing.

HOT MONOGAMY
Dr. Patricia Love and Jo Robinson

Reserving a one hour block quality time once a week for sex may increase your satisfaction with your lovemaking more than any other change you can make. You don't have to use this time for lovemaking if neither of you is in the mood. Think of it as an "opportunity" for sex. If you choose, you can spend the time massaging each other, going for a walk, or having an intimate conversation. But if conditions are right, you will have enough time for a sensual, satisfying experience.

✂ *You fill in the blanks. He follows your wishes. You both get to play.*

Passion Coupon

ANYTHING GOES!

**This Sunday morning, the recipient will present
the bearer with one hour of**

_____

Morning Yummies

It's not just flowers and candy. *Romance*, I mean. A lot of women seem to have the idea that they have to get gifts or take trips to exotic locations in order to feel romantic. But that's looking at it backwards, if you ask me. We shouldn't need a thing or a place to be romantic. We should *learn to find romance in everything*. We can experience it in every place.

And here's a grrreat example. You and your partner won't have to go more than a mile or two from your home, and the objects you require are as common as dirt. Well, common as rocks, anyway!

Wake yourself up early on Saturday. Instead of starting your usual morning routine, though, snuggle up close to your sweetheart and wake him gently with nuzzles to his neck. *"Good morning, sleepyhead. Looks like a beautiful day. Hey, that gives me an idea..."* Now kiss him. Make it a *grrreat* one, a kiss he'll remember as you slip out of bed and head to the kitchen.

Mmm — the aroma of hot java and warm sticky buns will serve as his final wake-up call. But to get those special treats, he has to join you on a morning stroll. Toss the pastries and your thermos full of coffee into a bag or backpack and head outside to watch the morning unfold. You really don't have to go far — just head for a pretty spot under a tree and set up your *sunrise picnic*. Caffeine and a little light exercise will clear his head.

Talk to him. Ask him questions. Men absolutely love being asked for their opinions on things. It makes them feel important when someone wants to know what they think — and that feeling of importance is at the very core of romance for guys. When you want to make a man feel special, ask him to solve a problem. The Need To Explain is built right into his psyche. (Along with slightly less meaningful things like the Need To Hold The Remote and the Need To Look Under The Hood As If He Actually Has Any Idea What's Wrong With The Car.)

On the way back, keep your eyes open for a *walking memory* — something you can pick up along the path as a memento of your adventure this morning. Encourage him to grab something, too, and then set aside a special place for the souvenirs of this and all your future strolls. Men seem to like sticks, but I suggest you look for stones. Why? Because you can send a rock to a *lapidary* and have it cut and polished, usually for under ten dollars. What's most remarkable is how even ordinary ones can turn out to be real gems when they're treated properly.

Kind of like men, huh?

INGREDIENTS

Sunrise • 1 thermo • 1 backpack • French Pastries, muffins, sweet rolls

64 | *Recipes Your Mother Never Told You About*

FOR HER EYES ONLY.

W

$

CONVERSATION PIECE

THE SEVEN SPIRITUAL LAWS OF SUCCESS
Deepak Chopra

Applying the Law of Giving

I will put the Law of Giving into effect by making a commitment to take the following steps:

(1) Wherever I go, and whoever I encounter, I will bring them a gift. The gift may be a compliment, a flower or a prayer. Today, I will give something to everyone I come into contact with, and so I will begin the process of circulating joy, wealth and affluence in my life and in the lives of others.

(2) Today I will gratefully receive all the gifts that life has to offer me. I will receive the gifts of nature: sunlight and the sound of birds singing, or spring showers or the first snow of winter. I will also be open to receiving from others, whether it be in the form of a material gift, money, a compliment, or a prayer.

(3) I will make a commitment to keep wealth circulating in my life by giving and receiving life's most precious gifts: the gifts of caring, affection, appreciation, and love. Each time I meet someone, I will silently wish them happiness, joy, and laughter.

✂ *You fill in the blanks. He follows your wishes. You both get to play.*

Passion Coupon

ANYONE GOES!

Here's a special time-delayed coupon. Tape it to the lamp on your nightstand so you don't forget the bearer's wishes. The moment the alarm goes off in the morning, recipient must immediately _____

When you finish — go into the kitchen and _____.

Then come back to the bedroom and _____!!

Recipes Your Mother Never Told You About

I'll let you in on a secret. You've got some big surprises coming your way. I know, because I've put them in the chapters I wrote for your mate elsewhere in this book! Sorry, I'm not going to tell you which chapters. It's the secrecy that makes it so special, after all. And when he gets to surprise you, it's special for *him*, too. Don't you think he'll be thrilled when he sees how happy he's made you? Won't he get a real kick when he watches you light up at the sight of his treat?

Well, you get that same thrill this week when you astonish your mate with a *surprise party!* And he gets the joy of finding out that the woman he loves went to a whole *lot* of trouble for him. Well, okay, strictly speaking it's not a lot of trouble. (For a woman, I mean. *Sticking candles in Ding-Dongs* seems to be a lot of trouble for some men, but take heart — your guy is reading this book! So his intentions are good! Even if he still can't remember your anniversary.)

There's a good reason why it's not much trouble: It's not a gigantic event. *You shouldn't have to wait for birthdays* in order to have parties. Instead, come up with simple occasions to celebrate much more often — like *Sweetheart's Day*, a holiday you can declare any time you feel like it! It's not an extravaganza. Sweetheart's Day is just a simple, romantic, unexpected treat for your sweetheart, the kind of thing that reminds him how much you appreciate him. It keeps your relationship from getting predictable. And if you need any more incentive to try this out, let me say just one word —

Chocolate! Mm-mm-Yes! Yep, Sweetheart's Day is a *grrreat* excuse for making a truly decadent chocolate cake. Start working on it the day *before* your little party. Give him twenty-four hours to meditate on the rich, gooey frosting and the dense, dark sweetness inside. *No touching!*

Already he'll be looking forward to coming home the next day, but that cake is only a small part of the pleasure you have in store. On the wall, you've hung a Welcome Home banner; candles and a few flowers rest on a tablecloth. When he walks in the door, toss some confetti his way! And invite him to open his presents — little, inexpensive items from a five-and-dime. Pass out the party hats, and get ready to dive into that incredible cake. It's neatly decorated with a heart enclosing his initials and yours. Sweetheart's Day — You should celebrate it *often*.

Now, I'm going to let you in on yet another secret. *You are about to be kissed*, in a major way. No, it's not because of any other chapter in the book. This time, it's because of *you*. (And all that chocolate!)

INGREDIENTS

1 chocolate cake • 1 banner • 2 party hats • confetti

a few small gifts • 0 special occasions!

FOR HER EYES ONLY.

CONVERSATION PIECE

MEN ARE FROM MARS, WOMEN ARE FROM VENUS
John Gray, Ph.D.

Going Out With the Guys

Each week, Craig has a ritual of going to the movies or doing something with his male friends. They generally go and see a "guy" movie, the kind of movie his wife, Sarah, doesn't like.

Although at first this kind of ritual may not seem support their relationship, but it does. Spending time with the guys keeps him from expecting to get all his support from Sarah. Time away helps him to feel completely free to be himself. As a result, he begins to miss her and want to be with her even more.

Sarah understands this because she greatly appreciates the support he gives her to spend time with her women friends. He recognizes that it is eventually important for her to get many of her needs met by women friends so that she is not looking to him for everything.

When he goes out with the guys, her accepting attitude about it really makes him feel her support. It used to be that she would look at him in a hurt way whenever he went out with the guys. Now she even reminds him to go out when he forgets.

No Girls Allowed

Scientists have learned enough to paint a sorry picture of our distant forefathers. Hunting in packs, defending territory, bonding over roast ox... it was a cruel and uncivilized life. The amazing thing is that, if left to their own devices, *men would live exactly the same way today*, except with pizza instead of wild animals. If you have teenage sons you know what I mean.

Clearly, man has an inborn urge to hang with his pals, engage in armchair battles, and swap stories. So why fight it? Instead, encourage your man indulge his, uh, inner chimpanzee. Let him have his *guy time*. This week, drop him into the middle of his own personal Budweiser ad. He'll love you all the more for understanding his primal needs, and for turning these occasions into thoughtful, romantic *gifts*....

Find out when this week's big game is going to be on the tube, and *get him to agree to have brunch with you* during that time. Then, without tipping your hand, call his buddies and arrange for a surprise sports party! Make sure they keep it a secret, and tell them to be on time. An hour before game-time—

Oh, honey, I'm in the middle of a recipe and I forgot some stuff! Would you run down to the store for a dozen eggs and some half-and-half? Pretty please? As soon as he's out the door, whip out all the party stuff. You'll need guy food, of course, this being defined as any product that can be eaten with fingers and has absolutely no nutritional quality. Stock up on guy drinks, by which, of course, I mean beer. In case the game gets dull, leave a pack of cards on the table and a couple of rented videos next to the TV— the Three Stooges, or anything starring Jim Carrey.

And don't forget the party decorations! For a real *Tool Time* touch, make a manly man's centerpiece. Put his electric drill and power saw into a big bowl. In the center, stuck in a small block of Styrofoam, arrange a bouquet of his screwdrivers, surrounded by baby's breath. Tape a tiny banner to a couple of the tool handles— *Have a blast, guys! Try not to spill any blood!*

And when your sweetie gets home and realizes what's up, he'll be grinning like a monkey. Grunting like one, too, I imagine. Be sure to hang out until some of his pals show up, so he can brag about *how his little sweetie did all of this just for him*....

Then make a little speech wishing them well, kiss your love goodbye— and *go see a Brad Pitt movie with your girlfriends!!!*

INGREDIENTS

a bunch of guys • a bunch of guy food

party decorations • 1 deck of cards • 2 stupid videos

FOR HER EYES ONLY.

$$

🚗 $$

CONVERSATION PIECE

DAVE BARRY'S GUIDE TO GUYS
Dave Barry

Guys vs. Men

THIS IS A BOOK about guys. It's *not* a book about men. There are already way too many books about men, and most of them are way too serious.

Men itself is a serious word, not to mention *manhood* and *manly*. Such words make being male sound like a very important activity, as opposed to what it primarily consists of, namely, possessing a set of minor and frequently unreliable organs.

But men tend to attach great significance to Manhood. This results in certain characteristically masculine, by which I mean stupid, behavioral patterns that can produce unfortunate results such as violent crime, war, spitting, and ice hockey. These things have given men a bad name. And the "Men's Movement," which is suppose to bring out the more positive aspects of Manliness, seems to be densely populated with loons and goobers.

So I'm saying that there's another way to look at males: not as aggressive macho dominators; not as sensitive, liberated, hugging drummers; but as guys. And what, exactly, do I mean by "guys"? I don't know. I haven't thought that much about it. One of the major characteristics of guyhood is that we guys don't spend a lot of time pondering our deep innermost feelings. There is a serious question in my mind about whether guys actually *have* deep innermost feelings, unless you count, for example, loyalty to the Detroit Tigers, or fear of bridal showers.

But although I can't define exactly what it means to be a guy, I can describe certain guy characteristics, such as:

(*You'll have to get the book to find out*!)

Neat Guy Stuff

Every man thinks he's funny. Guys tell jokes, or become the class clown, or even become comedians all for the same reason —

Women!

Women love to laugh. *And men love to hear women laugh.* It's built right in to us, I think — I've never seen a successful long-term relationship that wasn't solidly grounded in a shared sense of humor. If you two can make each other laugh, there's a good chance you'll still be having a good time together in your rocking chairs watching the great-grandchildren play.

And you *will* be laughing together when you read Dave Barry's "Guide To Guys." It's a huge bestseller, so you won't have any trouble finding it. Pick up a copy early this week, have it gift-wrapped, and present it to your guy with an attached note. *"Save this for Saturday. I have plans for it . . . and for you!"*

Saturday evening, ask him to get the book and read some of it to you — specifically, the chapter called "Tips For Women. How To Have A Relationship With A Guy." Dave — and I have a feeling he wouldn't mind you calling him "Dave" even though he's an internationally respected writer. He's still a Guy, after all — Dave has an incredible gift for zeroing in on the foibles of Guys and presenting them in a fashion that is absolutely hilarious

I've heard men stop in mid-sentence to shout *"Yes! YES!! This is so true!!"* when reading through the part labeled "Guy Vision." This is a rigorously scientific examination of the fact that men cannot simultaneously *look at breasts* and *still think.* Invite your mate to take the Guy Test in the book — it's Dave's quiz to determine his Guyness Quotient. There's a Guy inside every man, no matter how formal or sensible he might seem on the surface. Bring that Guy out from time to time, and you'll both have a ball. (Assuming you can ignore the Guy's unusual craving for Three Stooges videos. That, I'm afraid, is a mystery forevermore hidden in the Gender Gap.)

Now spring the second part of your surprise on him. Hand him tickets for tonight's show at your local comedy club. By the end of the evening, your guy will be *glowing.* He's had a huge bellylaugh. He got a couple of nice gifts. And the woman he loves was laughing at his material for more than an hour. Life doesn't get much better than that! (Believe me, he'll be more than willing to disregard the fact that it was really Dave Barry's material. Hey, was Dave here getting the laughs? Is Dave going to get lucky off this stuff tonight? No! But he will, won't he? And so will *you!*)

INGREDIENTS

1 copy of Dave Barry's "Guide to Guys" • *2 comedy club tickets*

FOR HER EYES ONLY.

CONVERSATION PIECE

MEN ARE FROM MARS, WOMEN ARE FROM VENUS
John Gray, Ph.D.

The Art of Empowering a Man

Just as men need to learn the art of listening to fulfill a woman's primary love needs, women need to learn the art of empowerment. When a woman enlists the support of a man, she empowers him to be all that he can be. A man feels empowered when he is trusted, accepted, appreciated, admired, approved of, and encouraged.

Like in our story of the knight in shining armor, many women try to help their man by improving him but unknowingly weaken or hurt him. Any attempt to change him takes away the loving trust, acceptance, appreciation, admiration, approval, and encouragement that are his primary needs.

The secret of empowering a man is never to try to change him or improve him. Certainly you may want him to change - just don't act on that desire. Only if he directly and specifically asks for advice is he open to assistance in changing.

HOT MONOGAMY
Dr. Patricia Love and Jo Robinson

People project much more positive images when they put conscious effort into their appearances. When the color of your clothes flatters your coloring, when your clothes fit well, when your clothes are well cared for, you make a strong first impression. It doesn't matter if you are old or young, tall or short, fat or thin, plain-looking or beautiful. The effort you put into looking good says, "I care about me. I'm worth the effort." When this attitude is reflected in your posture and the way you walk, the effect can be stunning. People are drawn to you. They think you must lead an interesting, full life. They want to spend time with you.

You were given only one body. Whatever its present size or shape, it's the only body you have. Dress it up and take it out! When you look as good as you possibly can, you will feel better about yourself, which will ultimately make you feel more sexually alive.

✂ -

Passion Coupon

SOMETHING WILD IN THE FALL

Bearer is entitled to 1 Half-time Quickie!

Starting now!

(She passes, he scores!)

Sports Babe

"I'm not big on social graces, Think I'll slip on down to the Oasis Oh, I've got friends . . . In low places!"
GARTH BROOKS, *Friends In Low Places*

Skip all the psychology. Blow off the analysis. You wanna know why men really go to sports bars?

Because it's a heckuva lot of fun!

Now, you might think you're doing your mate a favor by letting him indulge in his guy stuff without you. And some of the time, you'd be right. You might also think you're avoiding a lot of really dumb stuff that guys do together. *Most* of the time, you're right about that!

Remember, though, you're not just one of his pals — you're his *best* pal. He loves to hang out with you. He loves *you!* But if it's been a while since he invited you to hoist a few at his favorite club, it's not because he doesn't want to share the experience. He's just afraid you'd be bored.

Well, prove him wrong! Show him you can enjoy his company under any circumstances. This week, make a date to shoot pool, drink beer, and tell stupid jokes at his favorite joint. (And if he hasn't hung out in a place like this since his school days, well . . . find one and take him with you! He'll have a blast polishing his rusty bar skills.) If there's music, dance. If there's a dart board, throw. If there's foosball, uh, well, *foos*. (I know. Weird name. But fun game — and that's what they play every week on *Friends!*) You don't really have to understand sports to get a kick out of a sports bar. You just have to know that this is what the *guys* do — and *your* guy is going to have a ball showing you around.

Especially if you dress for the occasion! And by that I mean dress *casual/sexy*. What men really like to see is a great fitting pair of *jeans* and a pretty blouse or sexy T-shirt! Thousands of them told me so in the interviews I conducted for my first book, *237 Intimate Questions Every Woman Should Ask A Man*. Over and over again, they said that they love to see a woman who knows how to be comfortable. A woman who can relax and have fun is a *huge* turn-on.

So turn him on. Show him a different side of you. Laugh and swap stories. Bet him a drink on a game of foosball. Friday night, you get to be one of the guys.

(But Saturday morning — take a little time to remind him that you're *all girl!!*)

INGREDIENTS

1 sports bar • 1 foosball or pool table • 1 dartboard

FOR HIS EYES ONLY.

CONVERSATION PIECE

IN THE MOOD
Doreen Virtue, Ph.D.

Women search for evidence that their boyfriends or husbands love them, aching for written or spoken words of endearment. Every little "you're the greatest" or other compliment means so much to women. They replay these verbal hugs and kisses in their minds and relive the good feelings they evoke.

Women are auditory. They repeatedly replay answering machine messages that their men leave for them, analyzing and relishing the words and inflections in their voices. Pillow-talk and whispers of love are the equivalent of oral sex for women — sincere, loving words are the equivalent of a warm tongue caressing them into erotic arousal.

Women who aren't told "I love you" enough times, or who feel wounded because their men use harsh, critical, or sarcastic words, will feel unloved. They'll feel sorry for themselves, like little girls abandoned by their Daddies. They'll pull back and withdraw their own show of affection, thinking, "Well, if he isn't going to show love, then I'm certainly not, either."

1001 WAYS TO BE ROMANTIC
Gregory J.P. Godek

Recapture the fun in your relationship by viewing romance as "Adult Play."

Some people—especially men—tend to view romance as a serious (somber!) and difficult activity. Nothing could be further from the truth! True romance is easy because it's simply an expression of what's already inside you: your feelings of love, care and passion for your partner.

The concept of adult play is a reminder to loosen up, be creative, and remember the fun and passion you had early in your relationship.

✂ -

Passion Coupon

WILD CARD

For the next 10 minutes, recipient must join the bearer — bare — on top of the bed!

Play of the Day

"Oh, my love, my darling... I've hungered for your touch a long, lonely time...."
THE NUMBER-ONE REQUESTED SONG ON OLDIES RADIO STATIONS, *Unchained Melody*

If you owned your own radio station, wouldn't you fill the playlist with all her favorite songs? If you were a music-industry mogul, you'd put out an album of tunes that sang her praises, wouldn't you?

Well, until you acquire the resources to pull off tricks like that, try one of my favorite ideas— turn her answering machine into a customized Jukebox of Love!

You're going to call her number when you know she's *not* around and fill her answering machine with bits of special songs. You can't go wrong with the one at the top of this page! "Hi, sweetie... I was just listening to a song that made me think of you... here it is...." And then those powerful lyrics, made famous by the Righteous Brothers: *"I need your love... I need your love... God speed your love tooooooooo meeeeee...."*

There are a million great love songs to pick from, played on stations in every town. "Kissed By A Rose," by Seal . . . "Wonderful Tonight," by Eric Clapton . . . "I'll Make Love To You," by Boys II Men. If you like the old standards, check out anything by Frank Sinatra or Tony Bennet. Does she have a taste for rock music? Try "You Shook Me All Night Long," by AC/DC. A country girl will just melt when she hears "The Dance" by Garth Brooks. Or, for that matter, almost anything by Garth.

Need a simple (and slightly sloppy) way to pull this off? Keep a radio turned up one day while you work, tuned to her favorite station. When a great love song comes on, call her number, make a little introduction, and then stick the phone up to the stereo speaker for thirty seconds or so.

For a little more control and much better quality, buy or borrow the actual recordings of these great songs. Cue each one up to the "hook" (the best part of the song with the lines you especially want her to hear) before placing your call. You'll fill her tape with six or seven terrific, romantic, meaningful messages.

And you'll fill her heart with love.

INGREDIENTS

1 radio or stereo • 1 telephone • 1 answering machine

1 terrific radio station, or a bunch of great tapes

F O R   H I S   E Y E S   *M*   O N L Y .

$

FOR HIS EYES ONLY. *M*

CONVERSATION PIECE

MARS AND VENUS IN THE BEDROOM
John Gray, Ph.D.

Why Romance is Important

Romance is so important today because it assists a woman to come back to her female side. For most of the day, she is doing a traditionally male job that requires her to move more to her male side. To find relief, she needs her partner's help to return to her female side.

Romance clearly places the woman in the feminine role of being special and cared for. When a man passionately focuses on fulfilling her needs, she is able to release her tendency to take care of others. For romance to stay alive, however, eventually there must be good communication.

MEN, WOMEN AND RELATIONSHIPS
John Gray, Ph.D.

Often in relationships, a woman ends up feeling unloved because her man stops giving her the same quality of attention he did in the beginning of the relationship. When the quality of attention changes, she, not understanding men very well, assumes he's unhappy with her and doesn't care for her. *The quality of attention is the most important sign of love.*

✂ -

Passion Coupon

SOMETHING HOT

*Bearer is entitled to a 30-minute hot-oil massage:
five minutes per foot, five minutes per leg,
and ten minutes recipients choice.*

Starting now!

Mr. Grrreatwrench

Sometimes spontaneity takes a little planning!

Ahh, but it's worth the effort. Always. Every romantic surprise reminds your sweetie that she's on your mind. Each little act of love and respect leaves her with a kind of *afterglow*— a warm feeling she'll carry with her even when you're out slaying dragons, or whatever it is you do for a living. (And here's the best part! Do it right, and that afterglow will still be waiting for you when you walk back in the door! *Wheee!*)

You know those wildly romantic moments in the movies that seem so impetuous and off the cuff? Guess what— *they're scripted!* And sometimes, so are the best parts of real life, like this one....

It starts so innocently. You invite your love to go for a late afternoon cruise. A slow drive brings you to a scenic spot in a nearby park, when suddenly— (Wow, can't you just hear the sinister music creeping up?!)— the engine starts to misbehave! (You are your own Special Effects Department on this project, Mr. Speilberg. Some light taps on the brake pedal, some dancing on the gas.... And put on that serious face you guys get when you want us to believe you know what might be wrong!)

Hmmm... might be a clogged framistat. I better take a look. Ooh! The suspense builds as you get out and pop up the hood. Stare intently, and poke at a few things— hey, you know what to do! Head back around to the trunk—

Hang on, honey... I think I can fix it.... Yeah, right. She's thinking about hiking to a pay phone and catching a cab home. But she loves you, and as women have done since the first wheel fell off the first axle, she's willing to let you try. For a while.

But a *little* while is all you need to grab the picnic basket you hid in the trunk! Quickly toss a table-cloth on the nearest bench; set up a couple of candles. You'll need two glasses and a drink, of course. (And if it's wine, put it in a thermos. Might be against park rules!) Some light snacks and a little sunset-watching music on a boombox complete your Instant Romance package. *Hey, love, come take a look! I got it fixed!*

Watch her smile grow wider, first in relief, then at the dawning realization that you *had this planned for her all along....* She'll be thrilled. She'll toast your brilliance. I bet she'll volunteer to treat you to, um, dessert, once you get home! Assuming your car doesn't "break down" again on the way.

Check your oil, ma'am?

INGREDIENTS

1 false alarm in the car • 1 picnic basket in the trunk

FOR HIS EYES ONLY.

CONVERSATION PIECE

IN THE MOOD
Doreen Virtue, Ph.D.

Think about your partner for a moment. What is it about him or her that is special? Why have you chosen to be with this person, over every other potential lover in the world? Even if your partner is not your ideal mate or dream lover, something is keeping you with this person. Why? What are those special qualities?

Once you've written down a list of your partner's attractive characteristics, it's time to express your appreciation. You will reinforce and encourage your partner to display these positive qualities every time you tell him or her what you like. This is not manipulation. You are simply rewarding your lover for his or her attractive characteristics, and in this way, making your lover feel good. When your lover, in turn, appreciates your appreciation, a positive cycle follows.

There are many ways to express these feelings. Of course, showing your approval through loving actions is the best way to let your partner know how you feel. But it is also important to spell it out.

1001 WAYS TO BE ROMANTIC
Gregory J.P. Godek

Make a list of all your past excuses for not being romantic.

- Repeat the following in a whiny voice: "I'm too busy." "I'm too tired." "I'm just not very creative." "Maybe next week." "I want to be romantic, but I'm just so forgetful." Now, repeat the following in a macho, belligerent tone: "Real Men aren't romantic!" "I have a career to think about!" "It's too expensive." "What the hell do you want from me, anyway?!") Good. Got it all out of your system? . . .

- Now, write your own list of excuses down on paper, put a big"X" through it, and give it to your lover with an attached invitation for a romantic dinner out.

✂ --

Passion Coupon

WILD CARD

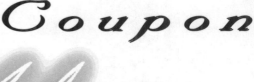

(For the next 15 minutes, anything goes!)

The Handy Man

Alright, guy, get out your toolbox. It's time for a *project!*

And the best part is that you get to decide just what kind of a project it will be. Are you good with a computer? Then you can produce the entire thing with a graphics program. Handy with crafts? Head down to the hobby shop and pick up some wood-burning supplies. You can whittle designs into a plank, or build a pretty frame, or simply get a handful of colored felt-tip markers and a nice, heavy sheet of parchment or posterboard. However you approach it, make it the best you can.

The technique you use is not as important as the concept, which is this—

Put her name in the center of your page, written nicely and quite large. Around it, write down words that come to mind when you think of her. Start with fond memories, like places you've been and things you've done together— *"Hiking in Vai." . . . Disneyland . . . The houseboat on Lake Powell . . . Cabo San Lucas."*

Add in some of the roles she plays— *"Incredible Mom . . . Math Whiz . . . Supreme Ruler of the PTA . . . Best Friend."*

How else would you describe her? *"Timeless . . Radiant . . . Charming . . . Alluring . . . Her smile just melts me . . . Fabulous Legs!"*

Make a real show out of the unveiling. Here's my favorite method— take her to a nice restaurant, where you've made arrangements with the waiter to bring a menu to you... and your gift-wrapped present to *her.* Don't be surprised if you get a round of applause from the other guests! And don't be surprised if she's speechless when she sees what you've created.

It's *her*, summed up on a single page, and believe me, it really doesn't matter if it comes out looking like a great piece of art. (You *should*, however, go to the trouble of getting it neatly mounted or framed.) It's the effort— and the sentiment— that will appeal most to your sweetie. And whether the finished product belongs on a museum wall, or stuck on your refrigerator door, it's certain that she'll look at it and admire it for years.

And how many of your handyman projects can you say *that* about? Warning: If she starts asking you to constantly fix and change things around the house, you have clearly demonstrated *too much skill* with your toolbox!

INGREDIENTS

Some tools and craft supplies— whatever you're best at

1 frame • a little imagination (Extra points for calligraphy!)

FOR HIS EYES ONLY.

FOR HIS EYES ONLY.

CONVERSATION PIECE

MARS AND VENUS IN THE BEDROOM
John Gray, Ph.D.

Why Romance Works

When a man plans a date, handles the tickets, drives the car, and takes care of all the small details, that is romance. When a man takes responsibility to take care of things, it allows a woman to relax and enjoy feeling taken care of. It is like a mini vacation that assists her to come back to her female side.

1001 MORE WAYS TO BE ROMANTIC
Gregory J.P. Godek

Here are the Top Ten Reasons Why You Should Be Romantic:

10. The Rose-Growers of America need your help.

9. You'll stay young-at-heart.

8. You need all the help you can get!

7. Love makes the world go' round.

6. Your wife will let you back into the house.

5. Romantics lead more interesting lives than mere mortals.

4. Why *not?*

3. Your partner *wants* it — What more reason do you need??

2. You'll score points with your mother-in-law.

1. It will improve the quality of your life.

✂ *You fill in the blanks. She follows your wishes. You both get to play.*

Passion Coupon

ANYTHING GOES!

Bearer of this coupon is entitled to five minutes of _____,

followed by five minutes of _____,

and five more minutes of _____.

Starting now!

Touch of Class

What's your R.Q? No, not I.Q.— I mean your *Romance Quotient*. It's a completely non-scientific measure of your ability to figure out *what's romantic and what's not*. Candlelight dinner on a small boat in the middle of a lake? Very romantic. Now, same lake, same boat, but it's full of beer, bait and bass. Romantic? Probably not. Moonlit drives with the top down on the car? Romantic, definitely. Same drive while redlining a thirty-two valve fuel-injected V8 with turbo boost and titanium con rods? *Not* romantic. Pretty cool, sure! But not romantic.

Know what else is romantic? *Culture*. No, not those stuffy Sunday morning shows on PBS— I mean art and music and dance and all the very best things that the most talented humans know how to do. (Of course, that can be hard to define precisely. Michael Jordan can leap right over Baryshnikov's head, but it's the Russian who's considered a true artist. Why? Money! *If the creator ain't broke, it ain't real culture*. It's a rule. You could look it up.)

Anyway, women love the stuff. You're impressed when a woman can explain the difference between an incomplete pass and intentional grounding? Well, women are *really* impressed when a man knows a little bit about art. You're going to learn a little bit about it this very week, and amaze your sweetheart with your hidden depths. First, though, you've got to find some, and I don't mean the kind that unfolds from the centers of magazines. No, you need a gallery or a museum, and with any luck you'll find one that has a special exhibition going on. Stop by early this week and pick up a brochure. Learn a thing or two about the featured artist. Memorize what the critics have had to say about his work. And when you think you can carry it off— ask your sweetie out for an afternoon of romance and enlightenment.

You'll astonish her. You'll dazzle her. Okay, you'll have to B.S. her a little, too, but she'll love the beauty of the gallery, and she'll love you for making such an effort. It doesn't have to be paintings— you might want to try a symphony or a ballet, or any kind of event where you're not supposed to wear Nike's. Hey, you might love it too, and if not, keep this in mind— *Women get turned on by guys who are a little smart and a little cultured.* So think of this as a kind of highbrow foreplay. (Hey, even William F. Buckley has children, so there must be something to it!)

But just because you get turned on by the smell of burning kerosene doesn't mean she's going to accompany you to the tractor pull. Remember your R.Q? Well, *hers is higher*.

INGREDIENTS

1 museum, gallery or concert hall • 1 special event
1 pair of shiny shoes, and maybe even a tie • 1 cheat sheet

FOR   HIS   EYES   *M*   ONLY.

CONVERSATION PIECE

IN THE MOOD
Doreen Virtue, Ph.D.

Love Stories and Mushy Movies

In romantic movies and novels, the heroine is pursued by a man who is hopelessly in love with her. Without her, he can't go on living, and he tells her so through tears, gifts, words, cards, and actions. He must be with her. She resists at first, but eventually capitulates to the strength of his ardor. In the end, they passionately kiss and ride off together into the sunset.

The books and novels don't take us beyond this moment, so we never get to see if the man continues his romantic pursuit once he's "got the girl." But in real life, the chase and the romantic words usually stop, or slow down, at this point.

Females are raised to believe that a man who really loves her is very vocal and persistent. Women not only enjoy being chased, they need it to feel loved. Being chased fits the mental image of true romance.

LIGHT HER FIRE
Ellen Kreidman

Take Me Away From All Of This!

For most women, home represents work. She's always looking at the refrigerator that needs restocking, the floor that needs to be cleaned, the wash that has piled up, the dust that has accumulated, the dinner that needs to be prepared, the vacuuming that must be done, and possibly the children, who need to be bathed. This is not an environment that makes for a sex goddess.

On a routine basis, you have to take her away from all of this. Your car can be your horse, and you'll be her knight in shining armor who rescues his princess from the daily stresses that come with running a household.

Remember, you will have to sacrifice time, money, and effort, but I'd rather see energy spent on wonderful future memories than time, money and effort spent in a marriage counselor's office.

✂ -

Passion Coupon

WILD CARD

(For the next 30 minutes, anything goes!)

King of Hearts

One day, your grandchildren will be bragging about this night as The Legend Of Our Sexy Old Grandpa and Gran. It's fun and exciting and romantic and, by the way, also expensive. Potentially *very* expensive. But you only need to do it once to prove you are the King of Romance, a title your sweetie — and your offspring! — will crow about for years to come.

It's looong, and hard, and you can play with it for hours. It comes today at five o'clock, and you'll want to be dressed up when it does. What is it? She may not guess the answer — the correct answer, I mean — but she'll spend all morning thinking about the clue you left taped to the bathroom mirror! At four, the answer pulls up to her door. It's a limousine, and the uniformed driver hands her an envelope holding your next clue.

It's hard to improve on perfection, but if it can happen, it'll happen here. Your appointment's at 5:15. Well, that can only be one place — her favorite salon. Her stylist has instructions to pull out all the stops — hair, nails, makeup — and then hand over another envelope.

This one contains an address . . . and a rhyme. *You look great! Now don't be late. One more stop and I'll see you at eight.* The address is for a lingerie store, where she'll find an elegant gift-wrapped box. The card simply says — *Come to me. I need you.*

The driver knows the way. He takes her to the Hyatt, where she's greeted by the concierge, who hands her a single long-stemmed rose. *"Madame, you look lovely,"* he says. *"Surely we must preserve a moment of such beauty . . . ."* at which point he pulls out a camera and snaps a picture of her in all her decked-out, made-over, flower-holding glory. He then escorts her to a room with a view — and a table, candles, dinner, and *you*, in your Sunday best.

He'll take some more shots of the two of you, but be sure to get the camera back before he leaves! You'll want to get a few more pictures of your baby tonight, especially when she opens your present, which, as you probably guessed, contains something *slinky* and *slightly daring*. These particular photos may not be the kind you'll want to include with all the others in your album.

(But then again, these pictures may be *exactly* the way you want the grandkids to remember you. Hey, Hugh Hefner is in his seventies now, and what's he best known for? Not the *articles*, that's for sure!)

INGREDIENTS

1 limo, 3 hours • 1 beauty appointment • 1 hotel suite • 1 rose
1 gift • 1 camera • 1 dinner • 1 understanding hotel staff

(REALLY COOL BUDGET TIP: Rather than the limo and beauty treatment, hire a violinist — only $60!
— to serenade your love during dinner in the hotel suite. Look under "Musicians" in the Yellow Pages)

75 | An Enchanted Evening

FOR HER EYES ONLY.

$

CONVERSATION PIECE

REAL MOMENTS FOR LOVERS
Barbara De Angelis, Ph.D.

Looking <u>into</u> someone's eyes is not the same as looking <u>at</u> him. When you look <u>at</u> someone, **your intention is to stay separate from that person, to view him while your awareness remains in your own space.** That is what makes him so uncomfortable — you are seeing him, but he cannot *feel* you there with him. The distance between you is what might give him the sensation that he is being judged or analyzed.

Looking <u>into</u> your lover's eyes, your intention is that the boundaries between you will temporarily dissolve, and for a moment, your souls will touch. You are look-ing into him, and opening yourself so he can look into you at the same time. It's as if your eyes are connected to your heart, allowing it to "see" your beloved. **This is what I call the "loving gaze."**

*   *   *

Your eyes don't merely see — they give off energy. Have you ever had someone give you a look that made you tingle all over with pleasure, or made you feel as if you'd been stabbed with daggers, or filled you up with strength and courage? Their eyes didn't just passively see you...they passed an energy to you, an energy you took in through your eyes.

In this same way, how you use your eyes in your relationship can have a positive or negative effect on your partner. Each glance you send his or her way can create more love, or more mistrust and distance, between you. You won't have to say anything — he will feel loved or not loved by the way you look at him. **Your eyes cannot lie.**

✂
- -

Passion Coupon

WILD CARD

(For the next 20 minutes, anything goes!)

An Enchanted Evening

From time to time I come across a book or video that's so well done, so on target, so perfect for advancing the cause of romance that I have to recommend it to my friends and my radio audiences. I feel that way about the game in this seduction — I only wish *I* had been the one to think it up. (Especially since it's sold over half a million copies! I think it's creators deserve every dollar they've earned from it, and then some.)

They're going to earn a few more dollars this week, because I want you to go out and buy a copy of *An Enchanted Evening*. (If your local game stores don't have it, you can get it through the mail-order number listed below. If you have to wait for it to arrive, you are, as always, on your honor to come up with *another* seduction this week!)

The ideal time for your new game is Sunday night, I think. If you're about to face another week of work, you might as well face it with a smile! And here's how you'll do it — Sunday at breakfast, leave a note for your love. *Meet me in the bedroom at ten. No kids, no phone. Very few clothes!*

And before gametime, set the scene. Candles, soft music, your best sheets. When he strolls in, he'll find the bed bearing a tray of snacks, the *Enchanted Evening* board, and you, wearing your most sensuous robe. Invite him to sit down, and explain the rules.

You both get to fill out secret wish cards — anything that you want, so long as it can be done that night. That's the prize you're playing for, but getting to the finish line is *so* much fun! There are several pretty hokey love games available (and a lot of sex games!), but this one genuinely gets couples talking and thinking about *romance*. As you work your way around the board, you draw cards with some very intriguing questions.

You're looking forward to a romantic weekend away with your partner. What two articles of clothing do you hope your partner will bring? . . . First impressions often last. If you saw your partner at a party, what might first attract you? . . . The "How Much Feeling Can You Put Into A Kiss" contest has just begun. Give your partner the winning kiss.

Communication and contact. What more can you ask from a game? I can also highly recommend "*Getting To Know You*" and "*Scruples.*" And then there are the old standbys — *Spin The Bottle Of Massage Oil* and *Where's Dildo*? Oh, and do you remember Post Office? Wait 'til you try *Federal Express!!!*

INGREDIENTS

An Enchanted Evening Call 1-800-776-7662 • An enchanted evening!

(or check your local toy store or game shop!)

FOR HER EYES ONLY.

CONVERSATION PIECE

IN THE MOOD
Doreen Virtue, Ph.D.

When I began surveying men about romance, I expected to read many answers that connected sex to love and romance. I was pleasantly surprised to find that the men's answers were much more removed from the act of intercourse than I expected.

Here's a list of the actions most often cited by men as turn-ons leading to a romantic mood, listed in order from most to least frequent:

1. Being with a woman who looks good or dresses seductively

2. A home-cooked dinner

3. Non-sexual touching, such as hugging, massaging, or caressing

4. Eye contact or a special way of looking at each other

5. Low lights or candlelight

6. Having a partner who makes a special effort to make a romantic evening

7. Having a partner who is spontaneous or who surprises me

8. Kissing

9. Soft music

10. Wine or champagne

11. A woman who smells great

12. A quiet atmosphere

All these turn-ons strike me as gentle, tender expressions of male and female bonding. A romantic setting is very important to a man —- he enjoys dimmed lights, soft music and a quiet atmosphere. His romantic mood is aroused when his female partner puts a special effort into making him feel like a king.

101 NIGHTS
OF GRRREAT
ROMANCE

*Kiss
of the
Week*

THYMELY
KISS

Thyme, according to the Greeks, is the herb which makes one irresistibly kissable. Prepare a meal for your love using the herb. Moments after the first bite, rush to your love's lips with a passionate kiss. Come up for air, announce the Greeks were right, then rush back with another passionate kiss.

♥♥

✂

Passion Coupon

WILD CARD

Bearer is entitled to anything she wants for the next twenty minutes

(As long she keeps her high heels on!)

Something's Cookin'

Little things mean a lot in the world of Grrreat Romance. Small gestures, thoughtful acts — they help sustain the warmth and respect two lovers feel for one another.

But hey — sometimes you just gotta pull out all the stops! *Big* things are important, too; huge romantic events make up the most special memories you'll share with your partner through the years. So this week you're gonna *knock his socks off.* (Yeah, as if he's going to be wearing any socks by the end of *this* night!)

Early in the week, leave a note for your mate. *New restaurant I want to try this Friday. Reservations at eight. Dressy! Will you wear that grrreat tie I like so much?*

Don't you just love all the excitement when you and your love are getting decked out for a big event? The bathroom smells like showers and shampoos and delicious colognes. The two of you are dashing about nearly nude, slowly pulling on your sexiest underwear, your nicest clothes, your best jewelry. It's as if you're wrapping up a couple of presents for each other. Well, I guess you are wrapping up a couple of presents for each other! But the unveiling has to wait for later. Right now, you've got to get your guy out the door and off to an upscale bar for a cocktail or two.

And while you're gone . . . .

Your best friend comes over to your house to set an elegant table. She lets in your personal chef — okay, actually, he's a caterer, and he'll have most of your meal already cooked, but make sure he warms some things up on your stove!

That way, the aroma of incredible gourmet food will fill the house, which is, of course, where you take your sweetie right after your drinks. Candles are lit; soft music is playing on the stereo. (And *boy*, are you going to owe your friend for all this! But settle up some other time. This is her cue to make a graceful exit.) Watch your lover's face light up when he sees your surprise . .

Now sit down. Relax. *Indulge yourselves.* It's the world's most private restaurant tonight, and you have nothing to do but gaze into each other's eyes while your meal is served. After dinner — some dancing, of course, while your chef cleans up and leaves. Now that you're alone, take it slow, like you did when you were first dating. A little kissing, some touching, pop a few buttons. And when things get *really* interesting, well . . . this private restaurant happens to have a private room right upstairs . . . .

And *you* know the owner!

INGREDIENTS

1 great caterer or Chef • 1 sexy new outfit

*1 **very** understanding friend*

FOR HIS EYES ONLY.

CONVERSATION PIECE

LIGHT HER FIRE
Ellen Kreidman

Verbalize Your Love

Many men don't say "I love you" very frequently, or they don't say it at all, because they're thinking, "She knows I love her. Why do I have to tell her?" A woman needs to hear "I love you" at least three times a day. Usually when I've made this statement, men and women who have been happily married for many years agree immediately.

Herb said, I've been married for forty-three years and can't imagine leaving in the morning without kissing Bess and saying `I love you' and certainly at night before we go to sleep. We also speak on the phone several times a day and always end with `I love you.'"

Howard, who was about to be married, said, "I can't even count how many times a day we say `I love you.'"

Lowell said that Karen finally broke up with him because he never said "I love you." It used to drive her crazy. I always told her that it was difficult for me, because I came from a family who never said they cared, but that was really no excuse. Now I wish I had another chance."

Too many people use their past as an excuse for ruining the present. You have to make a conscious decision to love someone in a way that you know makes that person feel good. It may not be important to you, or it may be difficult for you, but if the woman in your life needs to hear those words, and such a simple request is denied, then she thinks, "Do I really want to spend the rest of my life with someone who makes me feel so empty?"

Tell her, over and over, again and again, those three little words that mean so much to her: "I love you." She'll never get tired of hearing them.

✂ -

Passion Coupon

SOMETHING HOT

**Bearer is entitled to 1 Just Out the Shower,
in Front of the Mirror, Quickie!**

Starting now!

Building a Fire

There are fireplaces even in the hottest parts the country. Why? Not for warmth— at least, not the kind you can measure with a thermometer! It's *atmosphere*. A crackling fire stirs us. It inspires us. It draws us closer together. And then there's Reason Numero Uno why all those trees get incinerated every year—

They make women hot!

Are you thinking temperature again? Uh-uh. I mean seduction, and a fire will do half your work for you. Toss in a pinch of charm and you'll be *hauling ashes* before the night is through.

First, though, you've got to find one. Check out the hotels and clubs in your area, and when you've found a romantic spot with a functioning fireplace, make reservations for a table by the hearth. Not fancy— the key here is *cozy*. And don't forget to *ask your sweetie for a date*. Even if you've been together a long time, she'll appreciate an actual invitation for an evening out, delivered a few days before the fact. Sure, she knows you don't take her granted. But it doesn't hurt to remind her!

Once you're there, sit down and relax. Look into her eyes and tell her how much you love her and how great she looks by firelight. Then, part way through the evening, reach onto your pocket and pull out a card— a simple three by five note card. On it you've written a single word: Cabin.

"Mean anything to you, honey?" Let her think for a moment. *"I was thinking earlier this week about some of the fun things we've done together— remember that cabin we rented up in the mountains? Wasn't that just great?"* Go on, talk about it. Laugh about it. Freshen your memory of it. Then pull out another card with another single word— *Boardwalk*.

"Remember that one?" Sure she does... It was that romantic trip to San Diego and the stroll you took down by the beach. Ask her if she knows the significance of the words on the next cards. *Balloons. Hootie and the Blowfish. '68 Mustang Convertible.* (Obviously, you should be picking words that have meaning to *your* relationship! Quote my words to her, and she'll think you're nuts. I'll think you're nuts!) Do your homework this week and you'll have hours of memories and laughs to share. She'll be flattered you went to the effort, and thrilled to find that you think so much about her. This entire evening will be devoted to reinforcing the bond between you—

And generating a little fire of your own. (Keep your hose handy!)

INGREDIENTS

1 fireplace • several note cards • several 1-word memories

FOR HER EYES ONLY.

CONVERSATION PIECE

WHAT YOUR MOTHER COULDN'T TELL YOU AND
YOUR FATHER DIDN'T KNOW
John Gray, Ph.D.

Honey Do's

"When I get home I am barraged with a list of 'honey do's,'" Sam groused. "As soon as I sit down, Lisa starts giving orders. It is like she waits for me to relax and then she needs more. When I get home, I feel like I have to hide from her. It is not just me, because when I talk to other men they also feel this way about their wives. I don't want to come home to another boss. I have to go on fishing trips just to get away."

Women don't realize that men need to relax and do nothing responsible for a while in order to recover from the day's stress. Particularly when she is overwhelmed, a woman feels that everything has to be done before she can relax. She mistakenly assumes that if she reminds her mate of what to do, then they will both eventually be able to relax.

✂

Passion Coupon

WILD CARD

(For the next 20 minutes, anything goes!)

Between Venus and Mars

"And the words like silent raindrops fell...and echoed in the Sounds of Silence."
SIMON AND GARFUNKEL, 1966

Did you ever stop to think just how much *noise* there is in our lives? From the moment the radio goes on in the morning until we pull the plug on Leno or Letterman, our days are filled with voices. People try to entertain us, and persuade us, and sell us.

And it drives men crazy!! As John Gray points out in *Men Are From Mars, Women Are From Venus*, guys are designed for action. Evolution has bred them to do things, to *fix* things. They do not always enjoy *yakking* about things. So when a man is ready to unwind, he just wants to climb into a cave and stare at a fire. He's looking for a little peace and quiet. He *needs* it.

So pick one special evening this week and give it to him. When he walks in from work, don't say a word. Just wrap your arms around him, hold him for a minute, and then hand him a card —

"I know you had a busy week. I'll bet you could use a little downtime. So tonight, no talking. I've got the kids, and they know they can't bother you. And if you need anything, well, check out the special room service menu in the living room!"

Once there he'll find soft lights, quiet music, and a copy of the newspaper. The remote control, that symbol of modern man's mastery of the universe, is perched on the coffee table right next to a small bell and your custom-made menu. *"The living room is yours for the night,"* it says, *"and no one will interrupt you. But if there are some things you want, here's how to get them —"*

Need a fresh drink? Ring bell once.	
Tortellini and Caesar Salad served at eight. Want some? *Check this box.*	
Ice Cream served any time you want! Ring bell twice.	
Bailey's and decaf with that? *Check here.*	
Want robe and slippers? Ring bell 3 times.	
Want some company? Ring bell 4 times.	

Now, keep in mind, he may not want any company at all, and you can't let that bother you. After all, you're giving him an extremely rare and precious gift; let him enjoy his solitude. And who knows? After a few hours of "cave-time," he may be ready for something more, um, exciting. If so, he knows how to get it. The instructions are listed right at the bottom of your menu.

Want anything else? Blanket? Backrub? Lingerie show? *See concierge, in bedroom.*	

INGREDIENTS

1 card • 1 hand-written menu • 1 bell • 1 newspaper • 1 remote control

(Cool Tip Especially If You Have Kids: Leave a note telling him dinner's in the oven and
the house is his for the evening.)

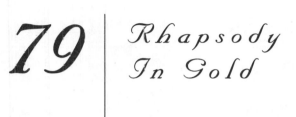

79 Rhapsody In Gold

FOR HER EYES ONLY.

CONVERSATION PIECE

LOVE NOTES FOR LOVERS
Larry James

A satisfying love relationship is one of the most rewarding aspects of our humanity. Even love partners who view themselves as people who are in good relationships know that to choose to be in a relationship where the romance continues; where love abounds, requires constant attention to the relationship. *Love partners with open minds know that their love relationship can always be better.*

LoveNote. . . Words of love make the music of the heart. They resonate love and cause my heart to dance. "My heart is dancing! Come teach it how to sing! The song of love is all there is to sing!"

LOVE IS LETTING GO OF FEAR
Gerald G. Jampolsky, M.D.

All That I Give is Given to Myself

The world's distorted concept is that you have to get other people's Love before you can feel Love within. The law of Love is different from the world's law. The law of Love is that you are Love, and that as you give Love to others you teach yourself what you are. *Today allow yourself to learn and experience the law of Love.*

I was mistaken in believing that I could give anyone anything other than what I wanted for myself. Since I want to experience peace, Love and forgiveness, these are the only gifts I would offer others. It is not charity on my part to offer forgiveness and Love to others in place of attack. Rather, offering Love is the only way I can accept Love for myself.

THE LOVERS' BEDSIDE COMPANION
Gregory J.P. Godek

A gentle touch; a simple gesture; a kind word; a wink of an eye; a simple gift; a big surprise; a little surprise; a dinner out; an evening alone; a hot bubble bath; a moonlit stroll; a walk on the beach; a day in the park; a night at the opera; a secret message; a special song. *The Expressions are myriad, the meaning is one: "I love you."*

✂ *You fill in the blanks. He follows your wishes.*

Passion Coupon

ANYTHING GOES!

The bearer of this coupon has just turned on her favorite music. Recipient must

Rhapsody In Gold

Even couples who met because they had similar tastes in music hardly ever like *exactly* the same thing. She relaxes to Kenny G; he wants to hear Charlie Parker. She likes her opera with an Italian accent; he prefers gigantic Germans spitting consonants all over the stage. Mariah Carey versus Whitney Houston in a Battle Of The High Notes. (And boy, wouldn't *that* shatter some glass!) Skinny Elvis versus Fat Elvis — you get the picture.

But if your collection is split down the middle by some kind of Irving Berlin Wall, you're really missing out — because you can learn a lot about your guy by *tuning into his music*. Who taught him to appreciate it? What moves him? What songs make his heart race, and why? You'll discover all that and more this week when you make your sweetie *The King Of The Stereo*. (Assuming he can fit it in between his other jobs as *Emperor Of The Remote Control* and *Chairman Of The John!*)

Early in the week, dig through your old recordings and casually ask your mate to name his very favorite cut on each of his favorite albums. Make a game of it — *and remember what he says*. (If you can do it without tipping your hand, take notes.) Then, Saturday afternoon before dinner, plan a trip to the record store. Don't just shop — *hang out for a while*. Slap some CDs into the listening centers and simply *groove* together. It's a great feeling; almost like dancing with your lover. But without all the sweat. Let your partner do most of the picking — and then buy him the disc he likes most.

But his biggest gift has to wait until you're home Saturday night. That's when you hand him his special, customized cassette — one that includes *all those old favorites* he named for you earlier in the week. For him, it's the *ultimate* tape, and an extremely thoughtful, personal gift.

(It's also *amazingly* easy to do, even on the simplest home stereos. And if you don't want to mess with all those buttons, I'll bet you can get a friend to help.)

So crank it up. Light some candles, pour some drinks, and let him tell you why he loves these tunes. Every one will bring up a great memory, and a revealing story. You'll watch the years melt away from his face as he drifts back to the times he first fell in love with each song. For one special night, he'll be a boy again.

(Ooh! That means you get to fool around with a *younger man* tonight! And for no more than the cost of a few tapes! This could become a regularly scheduled program at your house.)

INGREDIENTS

1 tape or CD at record store • 1 custom cassette

FOR HIS EYES ONLY.

CONVERSATION PIECE

WHAT YOUR MOTHER COULDN'T TELL YOU AND
YOUR FATHER DIDN'T KNOW
John Gray, Ph.D.

In the famous best-seller, Think and Grow Rick, Napoleon Hill interviewed five hundred of the most successful men in America about the qualities that created success. Remarkably, all of the men were sexually active in a passionate, monogamous relationship of over thirty years' duration.

These powerful, successful men had somehow learned to maintain passion with one woman for decades. Their sexual fire had not burned out, nor did they require the stimulation of an affair to be turned on. As they grew in passion through sharing their love in a sexual way with their wives, they grew in personal power and made a difference to the world.

Greater drive and success are waiting for those men who realize this simple secret of love. Through creating and sustaining a passionate monogamous relationship, not only can a woman grow in sexual passion but a man can be more powerful and effective in his work.

✂ *You fill in the blanks. She follows your wishes.*

- -

Passion Coupon

ANYTHING GOES!

Sometime in the next 30 minutes, the recipient will
surprise the bearer with a slow, sensuous and

_____

Newlywed Game

This is a great, fun way to spend an evening, and in spite of the title, you don't need a marriage certificate to play this game! In fact, this gem works best if you *aren't* newlyweds. All it takes is a little bravado, and a partner with a great sense of humor.

Whether you're long-since married or just dating, the best way to approach The Newlywed Game is to make it a surprise to your sweetheart. As you pull up to a new restaurant (one with valet parking — more on that later), give her a hint — *"You know, there's something I've always wanted to try . . . come on in . . . ."*

Then, when you get to the maitre d', proudly mention that you and your blushing bride are newlyweds, out for your first married dinner! And you were wondering . . . *"Is there anything you could do to help us make the evening really special?"*

You'll learn a lot about your little darling by her reaction to this announcement. Does her jaw hit the floor? Does she stammer and blush a deep crimson? Or does she just give you a little elbow in the ribs and play along with your game?

Go ahead — act out your part. Use sweet, silly terms of endearment. Carry her over the threshold! When was the last time you grabbed her and kissed her passionately in public? And here's a public display of affection she'll never forget — sometime during dinner, excuse yourself from the table. Make a quick stop at the valet stand and bribe one of the attendants to fix up your car. (All the necessary ingredients should be in the trunk.) When you and your sweetie are ready to leave, your ride is waiting — *with a string of tin cans attached to the bumper and "Crazy In Love" scrawled across the back window!*

Pull this off convincingly and you'll be the center of attention all night. Bistros will trot out their best desserts; nightclubs will send over champagne. All the world loves lovers, after all. And your new "wife" will be delighted! If you've been together for years, she'll be impressed that you still see your romance as fresh and new. If you haven't gotten around to marriage, she'll be thrilled that, unlike most men, you're not afraid to at least *talk* about it.

And remember, this is her "honeymoon." After a night like this, all the talking will be in *body language!*

INGREDIENTS

Long rope with tin cans • White shoe polish or a banner (If shoe polish is too wild for you, then leave a rose and a thoughtful card on the dashboard instead!)

1 elegant restaurant • a sense of humor

FOR HIS EYES *M* ONLY.

CONVERSATION PIECE

1001 WAYS TO BE ROMANTIC (NEW & EXPANDED)
Gregory J.P. Godek

He always did have a tendency to "overdo" things. One year he rented a limousine for her birthday. She enjoyed it so much that the following year he rented the limo again but this time he rented it for an entire week! So in addition to their fancy night on the town, she got chauffeured to the super market, to the dry cleaner, to church; the kids got chauffeured to school, to soccer practice, to the playground. A memorable experience for one and all!

CARE OF THE SOUL
Thomas Moore

A general principle we can take from Freud is that love sparks imagination into extraordinary activity. Being "in love" is like being "in imagination." The literal concerns of everyday life, yesterday such a preoccupation, now practically disappear in the rush of love's daydreams. Concrete reality recedes as the imaginable world settles in.

Love releases us into the realm of divine imagination, where the soul is expanded and reminded of its unearthly cravings and needs. We think that when a lover inflates his loved one he is failing to acknowledge her flaws — "Love is blind." But it may be the other way around. Love allows a person to see the true angelic nature of another person, the halo, the aureole of divinity.

Passion Coupon

SOMETHING WILD

Bearer is entitled to 1
"One-for-the-road" Quickie

Starting now!

Once in a Lifetime

What could be better than the undying admiration of one special woman? Well, how about the respect and veneration of several women, all of whom will proclaim you the Grand High Sultan Of Romance For Life? That's your reward — the first part, anyway! — when you treat them all to a spectacular *girls night out.*

Early in the week, leave a note propped up on the kitchen counter. Sweet Thing, I have a surprise for you! A big one — so big you're going to need some help with it. Call Susan, Laury, and Maggie and see if they can all get here by 5:00 Friday afternoon. And keep that evening open . . . .

Wow! Your mate and her best friends will spend the whole week burning with curiosity. And they'll be just floored Friday at 5:30 when a beautiful stretch limousine pulls up at your house.

"Ladies," you'll announce, *"I wanted to give the love of my life an evening to do whatever she wants, and a chance to share the experience with her dearest friends. So go — the car's yours for three hours. My only request is that you make a stop at Victoria's Secret and hand this letter to the manager . . . ."* Now kiss her, hand her an envelope — and wish the chauffeur good luck!

Away they go, four babes in a limo, drinking champagne and feeling spoiled. Maybe they'll take a tour of the hot spots in town. Perhaps they'll pop into a few shops along the way. (You get a whole different attitude from those snooty shopgirls when you exit from a limo!) And at Victoria's Secret, the staff will read your note and hand over the box they've been holding . . . the one that contains a sleek, sheer and extremely sexy black teddy.

Back home, hors d'oeuvres and more champagne await your Queen and her court. (Or coffee! Remember, her guests have to drive themselves home in a while!) And here comes your true test, the part that separates the Men from the Guys — you have to *sit and listen to them for a while.* I know, I know; this can be sheer torture. But believe me, these women will worship you if you smile and ask questions while they giggle and recount their big adventure. If they went shopping and want to show off their new stuff, remember *The Rule* — it all looks great. Repeat after me: It All Looks Great. Try to sound sincere.

Warning — *Even if your sweetheart says it's okay,* do not let her friends model any new lingerie they might have purchased. She's lying. It's not okay. (Tempting, yes! A good idea, no.) Ahh . . . but after the rest of them go home . . . *it's showtime!!!*

(And if your limo has curtains . . . *take the show on the road!*)

INGREDIENTS

1 limousine • 1 black teddy, waiting at the lingerie store

FOR HIS EYES ONLY.

CONVERSATION PIECE

AWAKEN THE GIANT WITHIN
Anthony Robbins

The Morning Power Questions

Our life experience is based on what we focus on. The following questions are designed to cause you to experience more happiness, excitement, pride, gratitude, joy, commitment, and love every day of your life. **Remember, quality questions create a quality life.** Come up with two or three answers to all of these questions and feel fully associated. If you have difficulty discovering an answer simply add the word "could." Example: "What could I be most happy about in my life now?"

1. What am I happy about in my life now?

2. What am I excited about in my life now?

3. What am I proud about in my life now?

4. What am I grateful about in my life now?

5. What am I enjoying most in my life right now?

6. What am I committed to in my life right now?

7. Who do I love? Who loves me?

In the evening, sometimes I ask the Morning Questions, and sometimes I ask an additional three questions. Here they are:

The Evening Power Questions

1. What have I given today?

2. What did I learn today?

3. How has today added to the quality of my life or how can I use today as an investment in my future?

✂ -

Passion Coupon

WEEKEND WILD CARD

Bearer is entitled to 1 Sunday Night Quickie!

Starting now!

Sunrise Dreamer

Star light, star bright, Last star I see tonight....

So how good a salesman are you?

You're going to get your skills of persuasion put to the test this week, fella! You have to convince your sweetheart to experience something that's exquisitely beautiful, soul-stirring, exhilarating, thrilling, and highly romantic — all of which will strike her as an incredibly bad idea!

At first, anyway. That's because you'll be proposing this little adventure in the wee hours of the morning, while the roosters are still snoring. You'll need some ammunition to break through her middle-of-the-night stupor — so set the alarm, get up first and brew a fresh pot of coffee. Heat a couple of cinnamon rolls in the oven.

Then, about forty-five minutes before the first light of morning, light a candle and place it on her nightstand. Gently — *very* gently! — kiss her awake. Tell her not to worry; everything's fine, and you have some special treats for her. First, a cup of java and some warm cinnamon rolls. Mmm — that incredible aroma alone will stir her sleepy brain cells. The tray you bring them on also holds a single rose. Now that you've got her attention... and put a smile on her face... announce your big surprise. You're going to watch the sunrise together and *talk!* Wrap her up in some warm clothes and lead her out to greet the dawn.

Don't go far — just find a nearby spot that offers a view of the eastern sky. Your surroundings don't really matter; all sunrises are gorgeous. Snuggle close and say goodnight to the stars as they fade away in the approaching glow. Listen to the sounds of the birds as they start about their business. Take advantage of all that peace and solitude to tell her how much you love her. Kiss her. Hold her hand.

And above *all* — do not make fun of her morning hairstyle! Not if you want to live to see *another* sunrise!

Once the sun has made it's debut for the day, head back in and start making breakfast for your love. Serve it to her in bed.

And if you can't quite get back to sleep after all that, well, I imagine you can think of *something* to do with a free morning in bed. (And if not, see *"Morning Glory"* in my other book — *101 Nights of Grrreat Sex!*)

INGREDIENTS

1 beautiful morning • 1 rose • 1 alarm clock

good coffee • great buns • breakfast in bed

CONVERSATION PIECE

THE ROAD LESS TRAVELED
M. Scott Peck, M.D.

Since true listening is love in action, nowhere is it more appropriate than in marriage. Yet most couples never truly listen to each other. Consequently, when couples come to us for counseling or therapy, a major task we must accomplish if the process is to be successful is to teach them how to listen. Not infrequently we fail, the energy and discipline involved being more than they are willing to expend or submit themselves to. Couples are often surprised, even horrified, when we suggest to them that among the things they should do is talk to each other by appointment. It seems rigid and unromantic and unspontaneous to them. Yet true listening can occur only when time is set aside for it and conditions are supportive of it. It cannot occur when people are driving, or cooking or tired and anxious to sleep or easily interrupted or in a hurry. Romantic "love" is effortless, and couples are frequently reluctant to shoulder the effort and discipline of true love and listening. But when and if they finally do, the results are superbly gratifying.

✂

Passion Coupon

SOMETHING SENSUOUS

Bearer is entitled to 1 Quickie by Candlelight.

Starting now!

What Money Can't Buy

Men are from Mars. Women are from Venus.

That's John Gray's theory, anyway, and it sure helps explain why it seems like we're speaking two different languages! And don't pretend you haven't noticed. Even in this politically-correct world, men still talk about *stuff* and women still talk about *people*.

Just another stereotype? No, it's real, there's a reason for it. Dr. Gray goes right to the heart of the matter when he points out that *talking is the way a woman comes to grips with her world*. Women simply *need* to talk — it makes us feel better. You might have to retreat to a quiet place when you want to think, but your mate solves her problems by bouncing them off of her friends. It's therapeutic. Really, one of the best things you can do for your lover is *listen to her*. And that's your assignment this week.

It's pretty simple — and it's the least expensive date in this book! Just ask her to take a short stroll with you late one afternoon. Grab a couple of blankets and head for a scenic spot. Stretch out, relax, and enjoy the glorious glow of the setting sun. Now *talk*. Or, more specifically, *ask questions*. And then listen.

"How's work these days? That manager giving you any trouble? Hey, I heard you mention that one of your friends just got engaged." I know, I know. From a guy's point of view, these are really fluffy questions. Chick stuff! But believe me, she'll have plenty to say, and she'll love sharing her feelings with you. From time to time, snuggle up next to her and kiss her. Stroke her hair. Point out the first of the stars as they begin to pop into the darkening sky. And then move on to some more meaningful questions.

"So how's your Mom these days? Mmm-hmm. She getting along with your Dad? Do you remember them fighting at all when you were little? Did they fight fair? Do you think we fight fair? Do we get along better than they did? What could we do better?"

You can pay your lover no greater compliment than to *listen to her*. She wants your respect — and by giving her what she needs, you're forging a deeper intimacy. Speaking of which....

"Do you know how turned on I get when I touch your hair like this? You don't mind if I nibble on your neck like this, do you? No? Mind if I touch you... Right here? Hmm? Mind if I take you home and make out with you on the sofa?"

Now *those* are questions a guy can understand. (And you're just gonna *love* the answers!!!)

INGREDIENTS

A bunch of questions (on a cheat sheet if necessary!)

2 blankets • A beautiful sunset

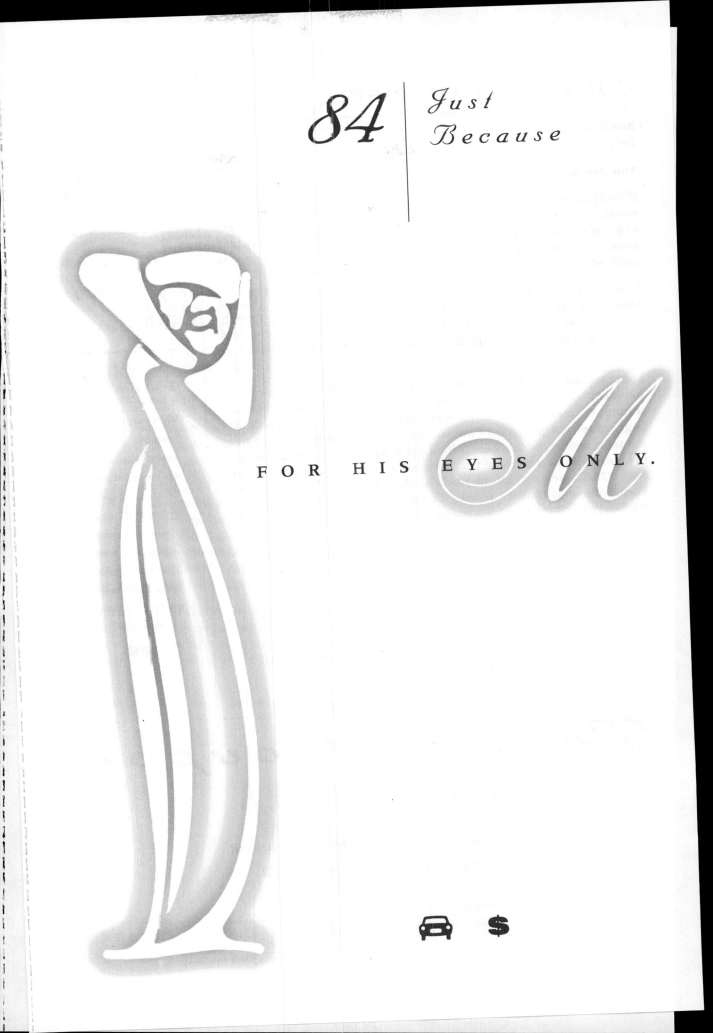

FOR HIS EYES ONLY.

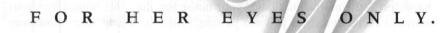

FOR HER EYES ONLY.

FOR HIS EYES *M* ONLY.

$

CONVERSATION PIECE

ROMANCE 101 LESSONS IN LOVE
Gregory J.P. Godek

SPONTANEITY

Big guy in the back of the class. He's been sitting with his arms crossed all evening, looking like he's swallowed something unpleasant. He suddenly brightens, and says, "Doesn't it kill the spontaneity in my relationship if I'm following pre-written lessons, or doing just what my wife instructs me to do?" With a smug look he settles back in his chair. (I should have expected this!) Do you think spontaneity happens spontaneously? Hah! Spontaneity requires commitment, preparation, flexibility, creativity, time and purpose. Think about the "spontaneous" creations of a jazz musician playing a solo, or a comedian doing improvisation. A lot of time and effort goes into creating these experiences. If you want to experience the fun, creativity and joy that spontaneity can bring to your relationship, you have to work at it. It's not hard work, but it does require some effort

THE GUIDE TO GETTING IT ON
Paul Joannides

Long term relationships can sometimes be a challenge to keep fresh and vital unless both partners make a constant effort to enjoy each other.

For instance, think about all the extra things you did to impress each other when you first met; you probably even cut your toe nails or trimmed your bikini line. Why would there be any less need for romance and wooing after you've known each other for a number of years? If anything, mature relationships require more rather than less effort at romance and improvement—from cards, flowers and special dates to extra attempts at tenderness and even reading books like this.

Save It for a Rainy Day

"I'm singing in the rain, just singing in the rain What a glorious feeling, I'm happy again..."
GENE KELLY, *Hoofer Extraordinaire*

Well? Is it really raining right now? If not, then glue this thing shut and put it back in the book! No kidding— this one requires wet weather.

Actually, it's not so much that this seduction needs a rainy day. Instead, I think that *a rainy day desperately needs a touch of romance.* A lot of people look at rain and can only think of all the fun it's spoiling. Some folks even get depressed. But hey, you're the King of Romance, right? (Well, you're reading this book, so you're on your way!) *You* can turn nature's worst into an opportunity for a *whole lotta lovin'!* It's really pretty easy— mostly just a matter of attitude. Plus a willingness to get wet.

Oh, yeah; you're gonna get wet. But first, think cozy. Dig out some games or a deck of cards. Find a big blanket or comforter. You might need to make a quick run to the store for some essential supplies— hot chocolate. Favorite snacks. *Some strawberry-scented shampoo.*

Now grab your sweetie and your umbrella and head outdoors. Then, when you're away from the house and ready to turn back — close the umbrella. Don't give it back! Smother her squeals in kisses.

Wheeee! Most of the time, a walk in the rain is an unpleasant surprise. But this one, like Gene Kelly in *Singing In The Rain,* is a celebration. It's a chance to have some fun, to laugh at the elements, to create a romantic memory. And, although your partner doesn't know it yet— it's foreplay!

Once you get back home, run to the shower, get it hot and steamy, and *pull your sweetie in with you.* Uh-huh, I mean clothes and all. Hold her and kiss her while the warmth soaks into your bones. Slowly— and I do mean slowly!— pull off those wet things. Volunteer to wash her hair with your sexy new shampoo. (I've never met a woman who didn't completely melt at the thought of a strong, loving guy running his fingers through her hair. Trust me.) When it's over... or when the hot water runs out....

Take your time drying each other. Throw on your robes. Spread that blanket, make the hot chocolate, set out the snacks and the games. It's time for some good, clean fun.

By which I mean that *you're* clean. And *she's* good. The fun can be as messy as you want!

INGREDIENTS

1 rainy day • 1 warm shower • hot chocolate or hot tea

sensual shampoo • blanket for indoor picnic

cards and games (Pick out a something fun at your local game store.)

CONVERSATION PIECE

REAL MOMENTS FOR LOVERS
Barbara De Angelis, Ph.D.

Have you been putting your lover on a *"verbal love diet"* without realizing it? Are you doling out little tastes of love that leave your lover hungry and always wanting more? Or perhaps it's your lover who's been starving you by controlling the amount of love words he gives you.

Most of us need to learn to use *more* words of love, and not *fewer* words. And most of us need more verbal love from our partners. Words of love will feed your partner's heart and nourish her spirit. How many more of our relationships would survive and flourish if only we were more generous with our words!

1001 WAYS TO BE ROMANTIC (NEW & EXPANDED)
Gregory J.P. Godek

Sally used to complain that Jack never complimented her. After pondering this, Jack realized, "It's not that I don't love you, or that I don't have nice things to say. It's just that I never think to say them on my own." With that insight, he instituted "Dial-A-Compliment" just for her. Sally could call him any time of the day or night and receive a spontaneous and heartfelt compliment!

✂ *You fill in the blanks. She follows your wishes.*

- -

Passion Coupon

ANYTHING GOES!

Bearer is entitled to be surprised with

_____

_____

sometime within the next two hours.

Love in a Secret Place

What is it that will make her melt with passion, always leave her smiling, and yet costs you virtually nothing?

It's her Box! And you, you lucky dog, get to stuff it with love on a regular basis.

Try to find a small, decorative gift box — something really nice she'll want to leave out on a shelf and admire. Card shops, department stores, and bed & bath shops all carry them. Early in the week, set it on the kitchen counter with a small, simple sign on the front: *"Surprise in progress. No peeking!"* Your girl is going to be burning with curiosity, but she'll just have to wait until Saturday to see what's inside.

By then you'll have composed five short love notes, no longer than a sentence or two. What's that you say? You hated creative writing assignments in high school? Yes, well, the kids who really worked at it are sure getting rich now — women spend more than *one billion dollars* a year on romance novels. Clearly, they're getting turned on by what they read! This is your chance to tap into that powerful, primal force; an opportunity to *seduce your love the way she wants to be seduced* — with words of passion and love. To make it easier, I've started some love notes for you. Just write them out on small slips of paper, finish the thoughts, and then place them in her Box. Tie a nice ribbon around it and deliver it to her in the middle of dinner on Saturday night.

You'll never know how often she'll open her Love Box, but I promise you that it will become a regular romantic ritual for her. Especially since you'll keep adding new thoughts to it from time to time! The beauty of this gift is that she will be surprised and delighted by it even when you can't be around... and when you *are* home, you'll always be welcome to open up her Box. *Uh-huh!*

Here's a little romantic homework. They don't have to be Shakespeare; remember, *it really is the thought that counts —*

- *Your beautiful, sparkling eyes make me think of:*

- I think the kindest thing you've ever done was:

- You look the most beautiful to me when:

- I love to see you dressed in:

- I get <u>so turned on</u> when you:

INGREDIENTS

1 box • several small slips of paper • A pinch of imagination

W

FOR HER EYES ONLY.

CONVERSATION PIECE

HEART AND SOUL
Daphne Rose Kingma

Play

It's no big secret that we all need recreation, relaxation, diversion, distraction, surcease even, from the deadly dailiness of life. There's even a section every Sunday in the newspaper to lure, cajole, and entice us into the travels and leisure's that represent a categorical departure from the mundane because we all need diversion so much.

But real play is more than simply stopping the doing of what you do too much of. It's a ridiculous, imaginative, creative approach, a new way of looking at life and entering into it magically — upside down, sideways, or backwards. It's the rabbit in the hat of your usual Saturday night.

When we were children we knew how to play. Play came easily, almost without thinking. It was a gift, a sort of spiritual inheritance. We understood then that doing nothing or making up something to do — anything — out of the whole bright cloth of our rich imaginations would nourish and restore our spirits. So a mudpie was a birthday cake, a stick a sword, and green crepe paper a deadly dragon.

But now we don't know how to play. Not like that. So much of what as adults we call play is really very passive. We want to be spoon fed, done to, and entertained — perhaps because every day we put so much energy into so many things we don't really believe in that it's almost as if, without making an effort, we want to be repaid. We have an inner sadness, anger even, that our imaginations, our creativity, and above all, our time, are not being spent on the things that just in themselves would brighten our spirits.

✂ *You fill in the blank. He follows your wishes. You both get to play.*

Passion Coupon

ANYTHING GOES!

*The bearer of this coupon is about to stretch out
on the bed, where the recipient will*

_____

for ten minutes.

Special Delivery

Boredom and routine are the two biggest enemies of romance. And they're so *quiet* — they just sneak up on you and slowly start choking the life out of your relationship.

Of course, that's one big reason why I wrote this book. Sure, I talk a lot about communication and understanding — all those things are important. But most of all I want to make sure you don't forget to get out and *just have a good time with your lover,* like you did when you were first courting! Hey, I love a comfy Sunday cuddled up at home as much as anyone, but if it's been too long since you took your guy out and showed him a good time — then get ready to light up his life this week.

High-light up his life, actually!

You'll need a high-lighter, or some other kind of bold marking pen. Get up early Sunday morning, grab the paper, and go through it circling events he might be interested in. Classic cars on display? Auctions? Swap Meets? Men love gadgets at work, like remote control planes. The boat show! The RV show! An Air Show! When was the last time you rode a roller coaster? Is the State Fair coming up?

You're home free if you can find a consumer electronics show; he'll be in hog heaven as he browses through the latest and greatest toys. How about a medieval Renaissance Festival? Concert in the park? Big sale in the Craftsman department at Sears? Check them all off —

Then fold up the paper exactly the way you found it and *put it back outside!*

The smell of coffee will bring him out of the bedroom while you work on his favorite breakfast. He may not be at his sharpest first thing in the morning, but you can bet he'll snap to attention when he sees those big, bold marks all through the paper!

Slip him a note with his bacon and eggs —

"Good morning! Today is your day. Let's have some fun and do something different! Something we haven't done in a while. Pick anything you like from the items I marked off . . . and that's what we'll do.

"Right after you wash the dishes!"

Just kidding about that last part. It is his day, after all! (But once you've spoiled him rotten and made him very happy . . . it'll be *your* night!)

INGREDIENTS

1 Sunday • 1 Sunday paper

1 highlighter • 1 happy tolerance for guy stuff

FOR HER EYES ONLY.

CONVERSATION PIECE

LIGHT HIS FIRE
Ellen Kreidman

Your Hero Forever

For every action there is a reaction. For every trait there is a response to that trait. You must learn to react in a positive way and stop being judgmental. When you concentrate on a man's strengths instead of his weaknesses, you get more positive behavior.

During an appearance on the Johnny Carson show, Mort Sahl once said, "Women always marry a man and hope he'll change. Men always marry a woman and hope she'll never change."

Women seem to go into a relationship saying, "I know there are a lot of things about him that I don't like, but wait until I get through with him. You won't even recognize him."

Men, on the other hand, say, "when I'm with this woman, I feel like a king. It's wonderful. I hope she never changes. I always want to feel like this." That, by the way, is why he wants to marry this woman. He wants to feel like her hero for the rest of her life.

Once you begin to focus on all the things you consider weaknesses and try to change him, the love you had in the beginning starts to die.

1001 WAYS TO BE ROMANTIC
Gregory J.P. Godek

Romantics "work at it"— and "play at it," too!

Being a romantic is not the same as being a starry-eyed, unrealistic dreamer. Romantics often work long and hard to pull off some of their "romantic masterpieces." Romantics plan and scheme, buy gifts ahead-of-time, search for sales, and stock-up on greeting cards.

✂

Passion Coupon

SOMETHING WILD

Bearer is entitled to 1 Motel 6 Quickie!

Starting now!

(They'll leave the light on for you.)

Saturday Surprise

"We're going riding on the Freeway of Love in my pink cadillac."
ARETHA FRANKLIN

More and more Americans are hitting the highways these days. Why? Well, I have a theory. I think a lot of people have discovered what *you're* about to learn — that a road trip can be an exhilarating experience, an instant *mini-vacation* that can recharge your batteries and rev up your relationship. This weekend, you and your sweetie are riding the Road to Romance.

And here's a terrific place to start — right in your own back yard! Figuratively speaking, I mean. I'll bet there's a fun, funky little town not more than a few hours away from you that caters to artists and eccentrics and tourists. The shopping and browsing in these spots are half the fun! Find it on a map, then carefully mark the whole route to it in brightly colored ink. Seal the map in an envelope, write "Saturday Surprise" on the front, and hand it to your sweetie on Wednesday night. *Sorry, you can't open it until I say so. Oh, and honey, would you check out the car for me? All that oil and air stuff? I want you to take me for a ride this weekend. Pretty please?*

Saturday morning, while he's in the shower, grab some of his essentials and throw them in a small bag. When he comes out, tell him to open his surprise. *C'mon, let's go! I even picked out a little restaurant on the way for breakfast. It'll be fun!*

He's the driver — you *know* how men are about their cars! — and you're the Entertainment Captain. That title comes with two responsibilities. First, you supply the fun, in the form of all his favorite tapes and a bag full of road snacks. Second — you are the fun! Flirt with him all the way. Snuggle next to him. When traffic's light, lean over and *nibble on his neck.* A man never feels more like man than when he's with a woman who wants him, and isn't afraid to show it.

And that leads me to the single best reason to hit the highway like this. When you get away from the old neighborhood, it always seems a little easier to hold hands, kiss on street corners, and generally act like teenagers again. Even better —

Teenagers with credit cards. *Teenagers with no curfew.*

Oh, my. This is supposed to be just a day trip. But I have a feeling that nighttime could be the most interesting part of *this* day!

INGREDIENTS

1 map • 1 car • 1 hip little town • Lots of great road tapes

(Romantic hint: this is a terrific opportunity to listen to some relationship-enhancing audiotapes. I recommend:

• Light Her Fire and Light His Fire by Ellen Kriedman 1-800-634-2029 Incredible tapes! Ellen's my idol.

• Men Are From Mars, Women Are From Venus by John Gray 1-800-834-2110 Communication genius!

• And my very own Little Black Book of Answers — This audio cassette contains the most popular and

provocative responses to the questions asked in my best selling book, 237 Questions Every Woman Should Ask

A Man. You will hear over **one hundred men** *reveal their innermost feelings about sex, love and romance.*

Their sensitive and outrageous answers will really surprise you! 1-800-547-2665

FOR HER EYES ONLY.

CONVERSATION PIECE

BORN FOR LOVE
Leo Buscaglia

Love Quiz

Asking yourself questions and answering them honestly is a good path to self-knowledge. In keeping with this idea, I'd like to propose a few end-of-the-day questions for each of us...

- Is anyone a little happier because I came along today?

- Did I leave any concrete evidence of my kindness, any sign of my love?

- Did I try to think of someone I know in a positive light?

- Did I help someone to feel joy, to laugh, or at least, to smile?

- Have I attempted to remove a little of the rust that is corroding my relationships?

- Have I gone through the day without fretting over what I don't have and celebrating the things I do have?

- Have I forgiven others for being less than perfect?

- Have I forgiven myself?

- Have I learned something new about life, living or love?

✂

Passion Coupon

SHE'S IN CHARGE!

*For the next fifteen minutes, recipient will fall under
the bearer's spell and do exactly what she says*

The Do-Me Decimal System

So what do men *really* want?

Besides women, I mean! Well, more than anything else a man wants to know that his mate respects him. He wants to know that she thinks he's special. Nothing will boost his self-esteem faster than the knowledge that *you hold him in high esteem.*

That's why so much of romance consists of nothing more than nice gestures done for your lover. Even small things can mean a lot. Every kind act, every thoughtful gift drives home the message that you think he's just great. I mean *Grrreat!*

And this week you're going to give him that message in a way he's never heard it before! To make it work, you have to get him to go with you to the public library. Early in the week, leave an invitation on his dresser asking him to join you there Saturday. If he asks why, tell him you've got a little project you're working on and you'd just love his company.

Once you're there — lose him! What I mean is that he can't watch you work, or even know what you're up to. So set him down in the magazine department, or send him off to the home-improvement section. (*Ooh!* Power tools! Drawings! Expert advice! I wouldn't be surprised if he flips through those books and decides he just *has* to build you a new patio. Or a new house.) While he's browsing, head for the archives — most of them are kept on computers these days and are really easy to search.

Tucked away in your bag is your masterpiece-in-progress. You've already put together a collection of his favorite pictures, articles, invitations, programs and other special memorabilia. What you're looking for now is the final ingredient, all the newspapers and magazines you can find that were printed on or near the date of his birth. Make copies of the most interesting articles. Now, start cutting and pasting — a glue stick will make it simple to attach the clippings to the empty pages in your album. In half an hour, you'll have put the finishing touches on his *This Is Your Life Scrapbook.* Watch his reaction as you present your handiwork. He'll be thrilled by the montage itself — but he'll be completely knocked out by the fact that *you did it just because you love him.*

You'll probably have to remind him to keep his voice down as he raves about your gift and expresses his appreciation. There are rules about talking in a library, after all!

But I don't think there's any rule that forbids a thank-you *kiss.* Or two. Or ten. And if he gets more passionate than that, well, you can always check out your books. *And check in to a room!*

INGREDIENTS

1 public library • 1 scrapbook • 1 glue stick or roll of tape

FOR HIS EYES ONLY.

$

CONVERSATION PIECE

IT WAS ON FIRE WHEN I LAY DOWN ON IT
Robert Fulghum

Show-and-Tell was the very best part of school for me, both as a student and as a teacher. Not recess or lunch, but that special time set aside each week for students to bring something important of their own to class to share and talk about.

As a kid, I put more into getting ready for my turn to present then I put into the rest of my homework. Show-and-Tell was real in a way that much of what I learned in school was not. It was education that came out of my life experience. And there weren't a lot of rules about Show-and-Tell —— you could do your thing without getting red-penciled or gonged to your seat.

As a teacher, I was always surprised by what I learned from these amateur hours. A kid I was sure I knew well would reach down into the paper bag he carried and fish out some odd-shaped treasure and attach meaning to it beyond my most extravagant expectation. It was me, the teacher, who was being taught at such moments.

Again and again I learned that what I thought was only true for me . . . only valued by me . . . only cared about by me . . . was common property.

Show-and-Tell was a bit disorderly and unpredictable. What the presentations lacked in conventional structure was compensated for by passion for the subject at hand.

Passion Coupon

A QUIET ECSTASY

While you put on the <u>teddy</u> that accompanied this coupon, it's presenter will put on soft music and light candles. While you straddle his bare back and massage his shoulders, he will describe his favorite act of intimacy in detail. While his temperature rises and his breathing grows harder, you will <u>whisper in his ear</u> exactly how you plan to make his steamiest fantasy come true.

Show and Tell

What's romantic? A moonlit ride in a horsedrawn carriage through Paris? Dinner at Four Seasons? Diamond earrings?

Those things are all *expensive*, for sure. And guaranteed to get you a date, at the very least! But are they *romantic?*

Well, maybe. Maybe not. The key to romance isn't in any gift. You can't put it in a package. Romance occurs in that special moment when your sweetheart realizes that you really, truly care about her. That feeling is magical, and it can come from something as simple as a gesture or a kind word. And yes, it can start with a present, but it doesn't have to be a huge one. See for yourself! This week, you're going to create a very romantic scene by giving your lover a whole bunch of gifts, but — with one inexpensive exception — it's all *her own stuff you're giving!!*

Tomorrow, start picking out some of her things and hiding them. Not just any old stuff; you're looking for items that *remind you of her.* Stuff that points out the best parts of your relationship. Put each item in a gift-wrapped package, and as the week goes by, pile them all up on your coffee table. Make a date with her for *Show and Tell* on Friday night, and make sure the living room looks *grrreat* when the moment arrives. Cushions on the floor, music on the stereo. Lots of candles. Fire in the fireplace. And as she opens her "presents," explain what each one means.

Oh, that necklace — do you remember when you wore it on New Year's Eve? Wow . . . you looked so gorgeous I fell in love with you all over again. The casserole dish, well!! It reminds me of that week when my Mom visited and you went <u>so far</u> out of your way to be sweet when she kept poking around in your kitchen. You went beyond the call of duty that night! Oh, and that's the sweater you surprised me with last winter . . . you know, I get compliments on it every time I wear it. Ahh, your garden gloves. Did I ever tell you how much I love to watch you weeding and digging and planting every year? Dunno why . . . . Hey, that's the seashell you picked up in Santa Monica! What a <u>great</u> vacation! Remember that stroll along the pier?? . . . .

And so it goes. Every gift tells a story, and the point of each one is *how much she means to you*, and why. Women love stories; language has the power to move us deeply. And that's why the last present — the new one, the sweet, tiny gift she hasn't seen before — also needs a tale attached. It shouldn't be expensive . . . maybe a little teddy bear, or an angel candle. It's real value is in the *meaning you give it* when you tell her why it made you think of her.

Tonight you're giving her what she wants most of all — your love and adoration, expressed in honest, heartfelt words.

INGREDIENTS

Her own stuff • 1 small gift

Wrapping paper • Some great memories

FOR HIS EYES ONLY.

CONVERSATION PIECE

LIGHT HER FIRE
Ellen Kreidman

There's a saying, "We always want what we don't have." If you are a man who always wears a suit to work, change your image for one night. Be a soldier, an astronaut, a doctor, a fireman, or a policeman. You'd be surprised at how many women get turned on by uniforms. They can be rented for an evening very inexpensively at a costume shop. Imagine her shock if you secretly change into this costume when she leasts expects it. Here's your chance to be a football or baseball player as well. Costumes have a way of transforming people into the characters they're pretending to be. Certainly, Halloween is an example of a holiday where many men allow their creative, imagination sides to come out. The most conservative men become the most outrageous characters one night a year.

Here's the secret of not having a boring relationship. *The best way to avoid a boring relationship is not to be a boring person.* Take responsibility for boredom and don't sit around waiting for her to provide the excitement. Some men keep changing partners because they are so easily bored; they're always looking for a new woman to entertain them. You can provide the excitement and unpredictability that is vital in a committed relationship.

✂ -

Passion Coupon

SOMETHING WET AND WILD

*Bearer is entitled to 1 Bathroom Quickie -
with the shower on.*

Starting now!

Open Me October 25!

Do you still get a kick out of Halloween? Boy, I sure do. Ever since people started throwing fewer and fewer masquerade parties for New Year's Eve, Halloween has become the one time of year when otherwise respectable and mature adults can become *anything they want*. (Unless you live in New Orleans, where Mardi Gras makes Halloween look like a tea party!)

Well, if this book is able to communicate anything at all, I hope it's the idea that romance should be incorporated into every part of your life, so this year— pack a little love into Halloween! For sheer sex appeal and raw sensual power (and also a really easy costume to get together!), you can't do better than the new King of Movie Romance, *Don Juan De Marco*.

Do you remember the scene where Johnny Depp approaches the young woman who's waiting for her date? His come-on is so smooth, his passion so believable, that she is seduced in a moment. Oh sure, you may have laughed it off, but when I saw it in the theaters *every woman in the building broke into cheers and applause*. That scene plucked a few heartstrings!

You can do the same, and all it takes is a mask, a pencil-thin mustache, a rose and a video. Rent the movie and watch it with your sweetie this week. Keep some hankies nearby— I don't know any women who can get all the way through it without a few tears! Then, on Halloween night, sneak outside and put on your Don Juan disguise. When the doorbell rings, she'll expect more kids hunting down their next sugar buzz, but instead she'll find you, black mask in place, with a rose between your teeth.

"I am Don Juan De Marco," you'll say in your best fake accent, *"And I must have you...."* With a dramatic flourish, step through the door and sweep her into your arms. *"You are the most beautiful woman upon which this poor soul has ever laid his eyes. You have captured my heart. Kiss me...."*

Ravish her. Pull her to the sofa and kiss her. Yeah, she'll be laughing— but she'll also be deeply moved by your gesture. Kiss her some more. *Kiss her good and hard...* And then bid her a fond farewell, with the promise that you will return.

Then off you go into the night, leaving a, satisfied and slightly dazed woman behind. Well, maybe. Either that, or she'll put the candy on the porch, turn off the front light, and lock you inside.

Now that's a trick, *and* a treat!

INGREDIENTS

1 Don Juan video • 1 mask • 1 mustache • 1 rose

FOR HER EYES ONLY.

FOR HIS EYES ONLY.

CONVERSATION PIECE

DAVE BARRY'S GUIDE TO MARRIAGE AND OR SEX
Dave Barry

What's the secret of a happy marriage? Call me a romantic if you want, but for me, the answer is the same simple, beautiful idea that has been making relationships work for thousands of years: separate bathrooms. You give two people room to spread out their toiletry articles, and you have the basis of a long-term relationship. But you make them perform their personal hygiene activities in the same small enclosed space, year in and year out, constantly finding the other person's bodily hairs stuck on their deodorant sticks, and I don't care how loving they were when they started out. I don't care if they were Ozzie and Harriet. They'll be slipping strychnine into each other's non-dairy creamer.

Of course even an ideal marriage, even a marriage where the bathrooms are 75 feet apart, is going to have a certain amount of conflict. This is because marriages generally involve males and females, which are not called "opposite sexes" for nothing.

1001 WAYS TO BE ROMANTIC (NEW & EXPANDED)
Gregory J.P. Godek

Do you know the difference between the "urgent" and the "important"?

- The **urgent** is what demands your attention *right now:* Deadlines, details and short-term priorities. It *may* be what's important to you, but more often it reflects the priorities of *others.*

- The **important** is what reflects *your* priorities and values. It is more long-term in nature and *therefore easier to defer.*

Love is **important** – car troubles are **urgent.** Beware of the urgent eclipsing the important in your life!

Sneak Attack

Okay, so you want to completely enchant your baby? Bewitch and beguile her? Overwhelm your lover with your gift for romance?

Well, there's nothing like a new Mercedes convertible to charm the daylights out of a woman. Or a month at Club Med. If you can afford gifts like these, well, more power to you. (And gee, what's your phone number?? For, um a friend of mine, I mean!)

But if you could deliver a present to your sweetheart that had all the impact of those extravagant acts, maybe even more... *and cost you nearly nothing...* wouldn't it be worth getting up a little early on Saturday morning?

Of course it would, especially when you consider what Saturday *night* might bring! So set your internal alarm a little early this weekend— you'll need the time to prepare a morning of *total sensual indulgence* for the woman of your dreams.

She'll be smiling before she even opens her eyes when she awakens to the gentle fragrance of rose petals, strewn all about the bed On her nightstand, a big glass of orange juice waits; just the thing to rouse her tastebuds. Under the glass is a note— *Well, Princess, this is a morning you'll never forget. Your bath is ready, breakfast is cooking, and I've taken care of the kids. All you have to do is enjoy....*

Rose petals mark a path to the bathroom, and still more of them float in a steaming tub full of soft, silky, scented water. Next to it is a *bath pillow*, one of those inflated cushions designed to cradle your neck and head— perfect for reading the morning paper, which is conveniently placed next to the tub. A bottle bobs in the water, sealed and containing another note— *You deserve this treatment every day. You're the best, and I love you.*

Think she'll be knocked out by all this thoughtful luxury? Wait 'til you *bring her breakfast in the bath*— a tray full of all her favorites, including that gourmet coffee or tea she likes so much. Now disappear for a while. Let her unwind. When she's ready to come out, you'll have a huge, fluffy towel waiting, along with an invitation to lie down so you can massage her back with some baby lotion. Can't let your baby get dry skin!

She's relaxed. Pampered. Feeling cherished. Let's face it, the woman is melting like butter. (The kind that has no calories or cholesterol, so you can, uh, eat as much as you want!)

INGREDIENTS

3 roses • bath pillow • bath oil • lotion

1 bottle with note • 1 newspaper • breakfast

CONVERSATION PIECE

ROMANCE 101 LESSONS IN LOVE
Gregory J.P. Godek

Change a Pattern Exercise

Sometime during the next week, when you catch yourself doing the same old thing you do every day at this time-do something different! If you're watching TV . . . Leap out of your chair, grab your partner, and go out dancing! If you're about to have dinner. . . pick up the whole table and move it into your back yard! If you're between crisis at work . . . fake a minor illness, go home and make love with your partner!

FROM THIS DAY FORWARD
Toni Sciarra Poynter

No More "Nice Girl"

"The bow too tensely strung is easily broken."
-Publilius Syrus, Maxim 388

A wise colleague once told me, "Don't get too good at jobs you don't really want to do." The same goes for marriage. It's tempting to be the perfect, willing spouse, doing all sorts of tasks you hate, to show that you're a good sport. This is part of what we were taught as "nice girls" at home and team players at work. But it can run you into trouble. Always being the first to jump up and clear the table after dinner-when what you'd really like is to sit and enjoy the rest of your glass of wine-is a sure path to resentment of the fact that your husband, naturally, will begin to expect this behavior from you. You discover that the job that you pitched in to do just to be helpful ends up defining you, not the other way around. Do you find yourself doing things in your marriage that you wouldn't even have considered doing when you were single!? If so, it's time to break the pattern. Make a conscious effort to refrain from those jobs-and resist the urge to polish your skills at other tasks you don't really care if you ever get good at.

Be careful that your urge to rescue situations doesn't put you at risk.

Gem Dandy to the Rescue

So what's a typical night like for you and your mate? After a while, most couples fall into a pattern that involves dinner, television, and bed. Does that describe your relationship?

Now, I'm a big believer in the value of comfort. If you're going to be together a long time, you'd *better* be able to enjoy simple and ordinary things! That's half of life, after all. But predictability is the enemy of romance, so— *plan something*. Do something. Every so often, break whatever pattern you have and try something new.

Horseback riding, for instance! You may not know an Appaloosa from an apple, but if you check around I'll bet you can find stables not far from you, and I'll bet they offer one of the most incredibly beautiful, amazingly romantic events I know of— evening trail rides when the moon is full.

Me, ride a horse?! Laura Corn, you've lost your mind!

Oh, don't be such a sissy. Every commercial stable keeps horses around just for beginners, horses that are so tame they're practically comatose. Decaf horses! And you're not racing in the Derby— this is a slow, loping walk through nature by night, taking in sights you never see in the city. Some of these moonlight rides end up around a roaring campfire, where you and your lover can snuggle the evening chill away. Trust me, this can be a truly magical moment under stars.

And if I can't quite persuade you to try Cowboy Romance, then pick some other activity. Nighttime tennis, maybe, or golf on a well-lit driving range. When's the last time you went bowling? The whole point is to get up and do *something physical* one night after dinner, even if it's just an evening workout session at your gym. It'll break your routine and remind your sweetie of all the fun you indulged in when you were first dating. It's *gr-reat* for your health, of course.

And a little exercise always seems to have the most amazing effect on men. *So ride 'em, cowgirl!* (And watch out for those saddle sores!)

INGREDIENTS

1 spectacular evening • 2 horses • A lot of horsing around

FOR HIS EYES ONLY.

♥ 🚗 $$

FOR HER EYES ONLY.

CONVERSATION PIECE

EMOTIONAL INTELLIGENCE
Daniel Goleman

Most notably missing in couples who eventually divorce are attempts by either partner in an argument to de-escalate the tension. The presence or absence of ways to repair a rift is a crucial difference between the fights of couples who have a healthy marriage and those of couples who eventually end up divorcing. The repair mechanisms that keep an argument from escalating into a dire explosion are simple moves such as keeping the discussion on track, empathizing, and tension reduction. These basic moves are like an emotional thermostat, preventing the feelings being expressed from boiling over and overwhelming the partners' ability to focus on the issue at hand.

One overall strategy for making a marriage work is not to concentrate on the specific issues-childrearing, sex, money, housework-that couples fight about, but rather to cultivate a couple's shared emotional intelligence, thereby improving the chances of working things out. A handful of emotional competencies-mainly being able to calm down (and calm your partner), empathy, and listening well-can make it more likely a couple will settle their disagreements effectively. These make possible healthy disagreements, the "good fights" that allow a marriage to flourish and which overcome the negativity's that, if left to grow, can destroy a marriage.

Of course, none of these emotional habits changes overnight; it takes persistence and vigilance at the very least. Couples will be able to make the key changes in direct proportion to how motivated they are to try. Many or most emotional responses triggered so easily in marriages have been sculpted since childhood, first learned in our most intimate relationships or molded for us by our parents, and then brought to marriage fully formed. And so we are primed for certain emotional habits-overeating to perceived slights, say, or shutting down at the first sign of a confrontation-even though we may have sworn that we would not act like our parents.

✂ *You fill in the blanks. He follows your wishes. You both get to play.*

The Lovers Lexicon

Love. Commitment. Cherish. Adore. Devotion. Inamorata.

How often do you hear a guy use words like *those??* Not often enough, most women tell me, but here's an idea that'll have him spouting off like a talking romance novel!

It's Scrabble For Sweethearts®, a game that can actually scramble a man's brains. That's because it's a competition, which men thrive on, but the only way to win is to think romance —— and I don't have to tell *you* how most men fare in that department. Of course, your guy has a major advantage over the rest. He's reading this book, too.

The rules are pretty simple. Set out a standard Scrabble™ board, and give each player two tile holders and fourteen tiles. Play the game like always, *but* —— any words that relate to romance or love *automatically get triple points.* And if he manages to spell out the name of an item of clothing you're wearing... you have to show it to him! (Really advanced players may want to check out my other book, *101 Nights Of GRRREAT Sex,* for the rules to Strip Scrabble™!)

Kiss . . . Angel . . . Vow . . . Backrub . . . Teddy . . . Marry . . . Worship . . . Panty! Don't forget the special vocabulary of your own relationship. *Hilton (where you had that wild night!) . . . DaVinci (your favorite restaurant) . . . Kenny G (your last concert) . . . SantaFe (your last vacation).* You get the idea.

Some on-the-fly rulemaking will be required —— for instance, is *lick* a romantic word or not? Depends on how well you know each other. If you like the way the game is going, four-letter words may be exactly what you want. On the board, or off!

The prize? One night of *anything you want,* whether it's sentimental old movies in bed, a night at the opera, or practicing the Kama Sutra. (Hint: Making him vacuum the house and do the laundry all night is *not* likely to get you a re-match! Or especially clean laundry.)

Have fun. Don't be afraid to bend the rules, or make up new ones. And let your imagination go — this is a concept that can be applied to *lots* of games. Like Hide-N-Go-Kiss®. Chocolate Candyland™. Naked Twister©!

INGREDIENTS

1 Scrabble™ game • 2 lovers • sexy lingerie! • 1 full moon

A list of Popular Games (Check your local toy store or game shop)

• Recipes for Romance, Love, Laughter & Romance, Mid-Life Crisis, Mystic Romance & Adult Trivia Pursuit

• Romantic Sensations and Sexsational, produced by Games Partership Inc. (1-800-776-7662) - If you pulled this page before seduction # 75, (An Enchanted Evening), you should know that this company also produces the Enchanted Evening Board Game that you will need later. You might want to pick them both up at the same time.)

• Couples who play together stay together!

98 | *First Class*

FOR HER EYES ONLY.

CONVERSATION PIECE

BORN FOR LOVE
Leo Buscaglia

Love Thrives on Continual Enrichment

To have a long-lasting relationship, we must avoid complacency. More love has been lost in the island of contentment than in any sea of torment.

Love demands that we keep our minds open and stimulated, which is really easier than we think. It can be accomplished in a hundred simple ways.

I know a couple who have been married over forty years and have never stopped growing. She is presently in a water coloring class, while he is attending an income tax preparation seminar. Together they are studying Italian in anticipation of a trip to southern Italy. There is no time in their life for boredom and I have never known them to run out of something to share.

Relationships do not grow or remain stimulating without conscious effort. We must take the time to enrich our lives, and therefore our love, or we are merely coexisting. Complacency kills.

1001 WAYS TO BE ROMANTIC
Gregory J.P. Godek

The highest form of romance is **optional romance**—gestures made that are not required or expected.

The middle form—**obligatory romance**— is that which is required by custom or culture. It's important, but of minor consequence in the larger scheme of keeping relationships functioning at a high level of passion.

The lowest form—**reluctant romance**—is hardly worth mentioning. It's dishonest on the part of the giver, and an insult to the recipient.

Beware of the phenomenon of "Relationship Entropy"—the tendency of relationships to become more diffuse if not cared-for and nurtured; the tendency for once-close lovers to drift apart if both of them don't work at it on a consistent basis. (File under "Better Relationships Through Physics Concepts.")

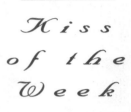

101 NIGHTS
OF GRRREAT
ROMANCE

Kiss of the Week

STEAMING KISSES

Kiss the mirror in your bathroom with Vaseline lips. When the mirror steams up, the lips stand out. This is a nice surprise when your love gets out of the shower. *

Passion Coupon

SOMETHING SENSUOUS

Bearer is entitled to 15 minutes of creative touching on the body parts of her choice.

Starting now!

First Class

There are a lot of ways to nurture a relationship — one hundred one of them right here in this book alone! Use the techniques written into these seductions and, over time, you'll find that they become second nature. You and your mate will find romance everywhere! On the other hand, if you don't do anything at all to maintain your passion, it won't *simply stay the same*. It will shrink and fade and wither. That's because there are a handful of forces constantly working *against* successful relationships, and number one among them... is boredom.

So this week, learn something new! Check out the offerings at your local community colleges or extension universities. Photography, acting, skydiving, stamp collecting, whatever you choose, the basic principle is this— *improve yourself, and you improve your relationship*. Grow together, or you risk growing apart. Pick something fun and exciting, and if it also happens to be romantic, so much the better. My advice? Cooking class.

The kitchen, it seems, is one of the most romantic rooms in the house. While researching my first book, *237 Intimate Questions Every Woman Should Ask A Man*, I heard hundreds of men talk about how turned on they get in the kitchen. All those great aromas, all that touching and squeezing, all that sheer creativity — it stimulates a lot more than just your appetite! When two people work together on a culinary masterpiece, it becomes a ballet, a dance of love that almost always leads from the most romantic room in the house to the most *intimate* one.

Early this week, reserve two spots in a cooking class, but don't tell your sweetie right away — just leave him a note inviting him to join you for a special evening of messy fun. (You might have to wait a couple of weeks for a class to begin so you're on your own this week). He might be a little intimidated when you drive him to the classroom, but believe me, he'll warm right up when he discovers what it's all about. Even though most men can't prepare anything that doesn't involve charcoal, *all* of them think they can be great cooks. Now your guy has a chance to prove it, in a fun atmosphere with professional help and *all the tools he could possibly need*.

You'll both have a blast. You'll be surrounded by other people who are also interested in learning something new. You could strike up whole new friendships. You get a terrific meal at the end of the class. Best of all, if your guy really gets into it, you might find yourself eating a lot better, and working a lot less, at home! Nothing beats having your man cook for you.

And don't worry about all those calories. If my theory about the link between the kitchen and the bedroom is correct, you'll find a way to work them off.

INGREDIENTS

1 special class for both of you. (Check your local Learning Annex or Community College.

Suggestions: Massage, photography, personal growth, languages, art, scuba, sailing, pottery, astronomy, CPR,.)

CONVERSATION PIECE

MEN, WOMEN AND RELATIONSHIPS
John Gray, Ph.D.

A woman needs symbols of love. When a man brings a woman flowers, for example, they validate her beauty and femininity as being of great value. Women need to be given flowers on an ongoing basis. To her, flowers are symbols of a man's love. They make his love concrete. It is unfortunate, then, when a man assumes that she will tire of them and therefore stops giving them to her.

Big presents or very little presents, all serve a very important romantic function. They help a woman know that she is special. She feels special when he treats her in a special way. Giving presents is a way of honoring a woman's need to be reassured.

*   *   *

From time to time, when I'd forget something, she'd come unglued, often telling me she didn't feel that I loved her. How, I wondered, could she interpret my forgetting to pick up a newspaper as a signal that I didn't love her?

Finally, I came to realize that from her point of view, remembering the little things was an expression of my love. Those "little things," being her needs, were related directly to her. When I'd forget them, it was hard for her not to interpret my action as a lack of concern and caring for her. When I'd treat them as unimportant, I was actually making her feel as if she was unimportant.

When a man ignores something a woman considers important, she feels he's ignoring her. I found that being responsive and responsible about the little things was a significant way I could express my love for my wife and give her reassurance. Since she really is the most important person in my life, once I understood the importance of "little things," it became more automatic to pay attention to her wishes. In fact, once I understood that this was a legitimate need of hers, I could bring my masculine focus to bear on solving the problem.

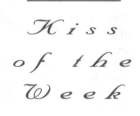

Passion Coupon

WILD CARD

For the next ten minutes, recipient must join the bearer — bare! — in his favorite chair.

Secret Admirer

I admit it — women *are* beyond understanding. You've suspected it for years, and now, I confess. We don't always make sense. You will never figure us out. (Good thing, too. If we were perfectly predictable, it'd be like living, well, with another *guy!*)

Take flowers, for instance. Now, some men — and I don't mean you, you Romance God, but the kind of guys who generally have to spend Saturday night alone — *just don't get it.* "Flowers cost so much, and they just turn brown and die, and what's the point anyway?" Well, here's the answer:

We like 'em.

That's it. We just like 'em, and we especially like 'em when a man gives them to us. So give! Take advantage of our inbred weakness for them. Just seduce us with them, and be grateful it works.

And do you know what we love even more than flowers? *Surprises!* That's why the presentation is as important as the gift itself. Hand a woman flowers and you make an impression, for sure. But give her flowers in a dramatic, fun and totally unexpected way, and you make a *gigantic* splash, the kind she'll be talking about with her girlfriends for weeks to come. (And while flowers may cost money, the surprise part is nearly free! A small investment in imagination can yield a huge return.)

So this week, combine these two elements. Send your lady lots of flowers, but send them *from a secret admirer.* You'll need a handful of cards written by somebody else so she doesn't recognize your hand-writing. The first arrangement is delivered to her office early in the week — *"From a Secret Admirer."*

And when she gets home that evening . . . *Flowers? What flowers?* Play it as nonchalant as you can, and keep up the act the next day when she finds a single carnation tucked under her windshield wiper. *"I think you're just beautiful. S.A . . . ."* She may be perplexed, but she will definitely be thrilled! The next day, the mystery takes an intriguing twist. She finds a small bouquet of wildflowers hiding in the mailbox. *"I worship you from afar. Your Secret Admirer . . . ."* She may be a little apprehensive at this point.

Now, honey, it's nothing to worry about. The poor guy just has a crush on you. Hey, who could blame him? You are beautiful, and funny, and charming, and I'll bet there's a whole fan club out there in love with you. I know I am!

The cat's out of the bag the next day, though. Find a couple of really tall blossoms . . . . sunflowers, maybe . . . and put them in a vase inside her closet. Hide some more wildflowers in the shower stall and the fridge. Every one has an *"I Love You — S.A."* attached. She'll laugh at each discovery, and of course you'll have to admit it. She does have a fan club . . . .

And you're the president! (*Now show her the initiation rites!!*)

INGREDIENTS

Lots of flowers (Pick your own!) • *Several secret messages*

FOR HER EYES ONLY.

🚗 $$

CONVERSATION PIECE

HOT MONOGAMY
Dr. Patricia Love and Jo Robinson

He strokes her "soft, moist petals." She fondles his "throbbing manhood."

An estimated twenty million women pay good money for this form of titillation. Romance novels account for 46 percent of the mass-market paperbacks sold in the United States, an estimated $1 billion worth of sales in 1996.

There are some common misconceptions about the kind of woman who reads these novels. One might assume that the only romance she sees is between the embossed covers of her paperback. Not so. Two researchers recently tried to determine what distinguishes women who read romance novels from those who do not. They found no apparent difference in marital status, education, or income. The only notable difference between the two groups was in sexual activity. Surprisingly, women who read romance novels appear to experience greater sexual satisfaction and have sexual relations *twice as often* as those who do not. The researchers concluded that "erotic romances provide a form of sexual stimulation for their readers similar to that provided by sexual fantasies and that they are a form of 'softcore' pornography that women find socially acceptable and non threatening.... By grafting explicit sexual elements onto the existing Gothic novel form, a kind of erotica is created that has no social or emotional stigma for the reader."

I happen to be an advocate of romance novels. I believe that reading stories about lustful women can give a sexually inhibited woman the permission she needs to be a more passionate lover — especially when she reads the books last things at night.

---

101 NIGHTS OF GRRREAT ROMANCE

Kiss of the Week

THE FINGER MASSAGE KISS

Take his hand in yours and begin to massage his palm. One by one, work your way down the length of his fingers, slowly rubbing and kneading them along the way. Raise each fingertip to your lips and kiss it. Draw it into your mouth and nibble on it; roll your tongue around it. Suck on it exactly as if it were a, well . . . A highly aroused finger.

♥♥

✂

Passion Coupon

SOMETHING SENSUOUS

For the next 10 minutes, bearer is entitled to be kissed and caressed anywhere but there!

Lola

"I'm in the mood for love," your card reads. "And I'll be looking for it tonight at eight in the lobby bar at the Westin. My name is Lola. What's yours?"

This exceptionally provocative note should be left on the seat of your sweetie's car Friday morning. You can bet his usual expression will be changed to a sly grin all day at work! Your change will be even more dramatic, though, as the staff at the beauty salon transforms you into *someone else* — someone just as sweet and sharp as you, but who looks a little different, a bit more exotic. Someone who has never met the charming man she's going to flirt with this evening at the most elegant bar in town.

Why? Well, partly because romance is about the constant renewal of your relationship. Partly to remind yourselves of all the excitement and air of mystery that surrounded your first meeting. But mostly because it's *so much fun!*

Change your hair. A new style or cut at least, new color if you're feeling frisky. And pick an outfit that's *not* you! I don't necessarily mean skimpy and sultry. (But then again, why not?) A tailored business suit with a barely visible bra peeking out can be startlingly seductive, and a short leather skirt with high heels just might steal his breath away. The object, of course, is to meet the man of your dreams for the first time — *again.*

You'll spot him first — remember, he's looking for the *old* you. Send him a drink, and just as the waiter points out the beautiful woman who ordered it, stroll over and introduce yourself. *"Hi, I'm Lola. I'm stuck here all by myself and couldn't help notice that you seem to be in the same boat. I hope you don't mind me being so presumptuous . . . ."*

Mind??! This man is going to be *thrilled* by the game you're playing. You're intriguing, sexy, flirty, playful. *"Well, I'm here for the bar association meeting — did I tell you I'm an attorney? Mergers and acquisitions. And you? Oh, really, that's so interesting . . . ."* He's witty and clever, and so obviously turned on by you. *"Yeah, I did the structural design work for this hotel. Turned out well; the company has me starting a new one in Honolulu next month. You know, I can't believe a woman as lovely as you isn't spoken for yet . . . ."*

Play it up, Lola. You may get to see that hotel in Hawaii yet! (Or at least some more private parts of *this* one!)

INGREDIENTS

1 whole new look • 1 elegant bar • 2 active imaginations

FOR BOTH OF YOU.

CONVERSATION PIECE

IN THE MOOD
Doreen Virtue, Ph.D.

Date Night

Every couple needs to date, regardless of how long they've been together. Just like an exercise program, which takes effort and planning but which yields tremendous benefits, a weekly date ensures that your love will stay healthy and vital.

If you take only one step toward improving your love life, this must be it.

I've discovered, when working with couples like Terry and Wendy, that both partners are anxious to have a fun, happy relationship. Neither partner wants a routine, overly-responsible life that is devoid of great sex or passionate romance. Usually, however, both partners feel that the other person should do something to improve the situation.

Since both partners feel overwhelmed by their day-to-day responsibilities, they resent the "obligation" to create romance in the relationship. "Don't I do enough already?" is the angry thought accompanying this dilemma. So, they wait for their partner to pull a romantic trick out of his or her hat.

As a psychotherapist, I've learned that the best solution to this common impasse is to assign a weekly "Date Night" to couples. This means that they choose a night, say Thursday or Saturday, to be their official "Date night."

Passion Coupon

WILD CARD

For the next hour, anything goes!

Congratulations! You made it! I don't know about you, but I'm so proud I could just *pop*. Here it is, a year or two later, and you're the two newest graduates from the Laura Corn Institute of the Romantic Arts. Your diploma may be slightly tattered — it's that nearly empty book cover, with all the pages torn out — but display it proudly! Like an empty Champagne bottle, it's a symbol of some grrreat memories.

And it's proof that you're now *Masters of Romance*. How many of your friends can say that? After a hundred classes, all the tips and tricks and advice are a part of you now. You know it all. By instinct alone, you can include romance in your everyday life.

That's why you're on your own this week. Your graduation assignment? Put everything you've learned to work and design your own customized Day Of Ultimate Romance.

For inspiration, I suggest you rent *Breakfast at Tiffany's*. What a great old movie. George Peppard and Audrey Hepburn play two people who finally break out of their old habits and learn to be spontaneous. And what fun they have doing it! At the end of the movie they make a pact to *spend one entire day* doing things they've never done before.

They sip Champagne before breakfast. They go to the library and read together. They go to Tiffany's to get a cheap Cracker Jack ring monogrammed! They skip down the street. (But please note, I am not advising you to follow their example by *shoplifting from a dime store!!* Merchants don't seem to have a sense of humor about that anymore. Go figure.)

Your rules are the same. Plan a day full of *completely new things*. You pick something you've never done before, and then your partner picks something. You come up with something else . . . and then your mate tries to top it! You get to choose three each — which ought to fill up an entire day. (And, need I point out, an entire *night!*) Make it fun. Make it silly. Make it deeply moving and emotional, if you like. And don't forget those important basics — mister, remember to *show* her how much you love her. She likes to be reminded. Madame, remember to *demonstrate* your appreciation of his efforts. He wants to hear it.

And above all, remember to *put each other first*. It should be a breeze for you by now. You've sure practiced enough! So go — get out of those graduation gowns and get busy. You've got *another* 101 Nights of Great Romance to plan.

INGREDIENTS

1 VCR • 1 copy of Breakfast At Tiffany's

*1 entire day of **Grrreat** Romance • Everything you've learned!*

Permissions and Copyright Acknowledgements

The author extends grateful acknowledgment and appreciation to the publishers and authors of the following publications for granting permission to use excerpts from their work in this book.

365 Ways To Kiss Your Love by Tomima Edmark, © 1993, reprinted by permission of The Summit Group, Arlington, Texas. All kisses marked with an * come from this grrreat book. Thanks Tomima!

1001 Ways To Be Romantic by Gregory J.P. Godek, © 1993 reprinted by permission of Casablanca Press, Weymouth, MA

Men Are From Mars, Women Are From Venus by John Gray, Ph.D. © 1992, reprinted by permission of HarperCollions Publishers, Inc. New York

Mars and Venus In The Bedroom by John Gray Ph.D., © 1995, reprinted by permission of HarperCollins Publishing, Inc., New York

Born For Love by Leo Buscaglia © 1992, reprinted by permission of Ballantine Books, a division of Random House, Inc., New York

How To Romance The Woman You Love The Way She Wants You To! By Lucy Sanna with Kathy Miller © 1996, Prima Publishing, Rocklin Ca, 800-632-8676

In The Mood by Doreen Virtue, Ph. D. © 1994, reprinted by permission of National Press Books, Inc., Bethesda, Md

Hot Monogamy by Dr. Patricia Love and Jo Robinson, © 1994, reprinted by permission of The Penguin Group, USA, Inc., New York

Light Her Fire by Ellen Kreidman © 1991, reprinted by permission of Dell Publishing A Division Of Bantam Doubleday Dell Publishing Group, Inc. New York

What Your Mother Couldn't Tell You & Your Father Didn't Know by John Gray Ph.D. © 1994, reprinted by permission of HarperCollins Publishers, Inc., New York

Chicken Soup For The Soul by Jack Canfield & Mark Victor Hansen © 1993, reprinted by permission of Health Communications, Inc.,Deefield Beach, Fl

Light His Fire by Ellen Kreidman © 1989, reprinted by permission of Dell Publishing a division of Bantam Doubleday Dell Publishing Group, Inc., New York

Romance 101 Lessons In Love by Gregory J.P. Godek, © 1993, reprinted by permission of Casablanca Press, Weymouth, MA

Care Of The Soul by Thomas Moore © 1992, reprinted by permission of HarperCollions Publishers, Inc., New York

Dave Barry's Guide To Marriage And Or Sex by Dave Barry © 1987 reprinted by permission Rodale Press, Emmaus, PA and St. Martin's Press. Inc., New York

Heart & Soul by Daphne Rose Kingma © 1995, reprinted by permission of Conari Press, Emeryville, CA.

The Lovers' Bedside Companion by Gregory J.P. Godek, © 1994, reprinted by permission of Casablanca Press, Weymouth, MA

Love Notes For Lovers by Larry James © MCMXCV. reprinted by permission of Career Assurance Press and Larry James Relationship Enrichment LoveShops (TM), PO Box 12695, Scottsdale, AZ 85267, 800-725-9223

Men, Women, And Relationships by John Gray, Ph.D. © 1992, reprinted by permission of HarperCollions Publishers, Inc., New York

Specialty Shops

For romantic products, ideas, catalogs, flowers, and unusual items, including many of the products mentioned in this book, call the following companies.

THE LOVELETTER NEWSLETTER
The newsletter of incredible romantic ideas! Call now for a free one year subscription (it's a $25 dollar value!) Produced by Gregory J.P. Godek, "America's Romance Coach." Greg is the best selling author of six bestselling books and creator of the acclaimed Romance Seminars. He's my idol!
1-800-LOVE-026

CELEBRATE ROMANCE
A romantic hotline, dedicated to helping couples keep their love life sizzling. Romance consultants offer personalized suggestions and free romance "tip sheets".
1-800-36-TRYST

CELEBRATION FANTASTIC
A catalogue of wit and whimsy, nonsense and necessities. Neat cool, one-of-a-kind romantic gifts! Call now for your free catalogue!
1-800-235-3272

1-800-FLOWERS - *A very unique flower company*
• The calender club allows you to pre-register for as many flower dates as you desire . . . And on those dates, they'll send flowers to your honey automatically.
• With the flora minder program, the 800 flower folks will call or write to remind you of important uncoming dates.

FTD FLORIST
1-800-SEND-FTD

GIANT BANNERS
1-800-3-BANNER

VICTORIA SECRET CATOLOGUE
1-800-888-8200

GOOD VIBRATIONS
A grrreat catalogue of adult joys and toys
1-800-289-8423

SWAN PUBLISHING
A personalized romance novel
1-800-535-SWAN